THE COLOSSUS OF MAROUSSI

BOOKS BY HENRY MILLER
AVAILABLE FROM NEW DIRECTIONS

———

The Air-Conditioned Nightmare
Aller Retour New York
Big Sur and the Oranges of Hieronymus Bosch
The Books in My Life
The Colossus of Maroussi
The Cosmological Eye
A Devil in Paradise
From Your Capricorn Friend
Henry Miller on Writing
The Henry Miller Reader
Into the Heart of Life
Just Wild About Henry
Letters to Emil
The Nightmare Notebook
Sextet
The Smile at the Foot of the Ladder
Stand Still Like the Hummingbird
The Time of the Assassins
The Wisdom of the Heart

HENRY MILLER

THE COLOSSUS
OF MAROUSSI

Introduction by Will Self
Afterword by Ian S. MacNiven

A NEW DIRECTIONS BOOK

Manufactured in the United States of America
Design by Erik Rieselbach
New Directions Books are printed on acid-free paper.
Published as a New Directions Paperbook (NDP1169) in 2010

Library of Congress Cataloging-in-Publication data

Miller, Henry, 1891-1980.
The colossus of Maroussi / Henry Miller ; introduction by Will Self ; afterword by Ian S. MacNiven.
p. cm.
ISBN-13: 978-0-8112-1857-3 (pbk. : alk. paper)
ISBN-10: 0-8112-1857-0 (pbk. : alk. paper)
1. Greece--Description and travel. I. Title.
DF726.M63 2010
914.9504'74—dc22

2009050057

10 9 8 7 6 5 4 3

New Directions Books are published for James Laughlin
by New Directions Publishing Corporation
80 Eighth Avenue, New York, NY 10011

CONTENTS

INTRODUCTION
by Will Self

I FIRST WENT TO GREECE IN THE SUMMER OF MY SEVEN-teenth year. In the 1970s flying was an expensive option, so we took the bus from London to Athens. It cost £40 round-trip, and took four days each way. *In The Colossus of Maroussi,* Henry Miller writes of his first-ever experience of flight: "I felt fool-ish sitting in the sky with my hands folded ... We were probably making a hundred miles an hour, but since we passed nothing but clouds I had the impression of not moving. In short, it was unrelievedly dull and pointless."

I can't imagine that Miller would've found the four-day grind across England, Belgium, Germany, Switzerland, Italy and Yugo-slavia (as it was then) any less unrelievedly dull; as I recall it, the national distinctions were meted out in lavatorial styles—from Helvetian spotlessness to Italian maculate to the active middens of the Balkans—until we ground down through Macedonia and reached the Greek peninsula. Miller, who had a pithy line in aph-orisms when he wanted to, subsumes air travel to his aggressive primitivism: "Mechanical devices have nothing to do with man's real nature—they are merely traps which nature has baited for him."

Not that the writer flew to Greece—his plane trip was from Athens to Crete—but while water was his preferred traveling element, and *Colossus* contains memorable descriptions of his wave-tossed crossing of the Aegean and small boats near foundering in the Adriatic, Miller is no snob—inverted or otherwise—when it comes to getting around. He'll take the fancy Packard if it's on offer, and if not make do with bus or train; he has an omnivorous attitude, seeking—like some monstrous bivalve—to suck up *everything*. Besides: "The *wheel* was the great discovery; men have since lost themselves in a maze of petty inventions which are merely accessory to the great pristine fact of revolution itself."

No, the year in which I first went to Greece was almost midway between Miller's voyage and the present day; and with the benefit of so much hindsight—and so many plane flights—it seems an appropriate homage to acknowledge that Miller was right, by 1977 we were gorging on the bait: massed phalanxes of European youth sleeping on the rooftops of Athens, cluttering up Syntagma Square, tramping down the Acropolis, then shipping out to fart around the Cyclades on rented motorcycles or to get drunk in open air discotheques. I remember coming back from Paros on a rusty ferry—the sparkling wine light flickering across red vinyl banquettes in the saloon; the Dutch girls in a lesbian phase, wearing denim overalls and sporting pendants in the shape of double-headed battleaxes, who sat on the deck rolling cigarettes. I scampered up and down, wired on amphetamines, and when we reached the Piraeus the crowds thronging the quayside were all reading newspapers blazoned with the face of the King Rat. It was August the 17th and Elvis was dead.

Now, of course, in 2009, the trap has been sprung.

Although he was in his late forties in 1939, the Miller of *Colossus* is the companion I would've wished for my own fiery baptism in the crucible of Western European culture—sort of. Here, as in the pre-war phantasmagoria, he is a relentless fabulist who advances murderous solipsism to the status of one of the fine arts. But to this he adds other talents, becoming a compulsive expositor and a deranged didact, the alpha and omega of whose teaching is: "The Gods humanized the Greeks." A decade before the Denver days of Allen Ginsberg and Neal Cassady, when gay

poet and car thief, fueled by Benzedrine, sat cross-legged opposite one another to indulge in marathon rap sessions, spinning
the word web from which the hairy spider of "the beats" would
crawl forth, Henry Miller went in search of his own beatitude.
Back in those Parisian days as grey as slops slung against stone
steps, he had wished for this breakthrough as he wrote in *Tropic
of Cancer*, "... all my life I had been looking forward to something happening, some intrinsic event that would alter my life."
And so, ground down by typing and poverty and the failure of
the world to see his incandescent genius, Miller was drawn towards Greece as a moth might be drawn to a votive statue of a
moth god, were it a creature subject to the deceptive bends of
self-consciousness.

For that's Henry Miller: he may present *Colossus* as a portrait
of the Athenian *homme de lettres* George Katsimbalis, but his description of magniloquence is surely a self portrait; to read this
book is to feel yourself trapped in a confined place—a plane
flight, perhaps, or a four-day bus ride—and simultaneously as-
saulted and enthralled by a brilliant monologist, incapable of
leaving anything out. Miller is confident you will be as interested
in his bowel movements as you are in the state of his clothes,
or the emptiness of his wallet; he mixes then matches the sublime and the ridiculous. He is cocksure: no matter that he is ignorant of Greek history, nor that he has never read "a word" of
Homer, his opinions have a validity by virtue of the fact that he
is a man—a *mensch* one might even say.

Reading *Colossus*, I was insistently reminded of Julian Jaynes's
masterfully wacky *The Origin of Consciousness in the Breakdown
of the Bicameral Mind.* Jaynes theorized that the Homeric Greeks
who composed the earliest verses of the *Iliad* were functioning
schizoids, not yet possessed of a unitary mind, so that when
their right lobe spake unto their left, they experienced this as the
voices of the gods. By the time the *Odyssey* was being declaimed,
the first inklings of the thinking "I" were glimmering, and so
the corpus callosum fused the brain, while the gods disappeared
in a puff of evolutionary psychology. Miller remains rived: his

ego cloven in two by Elysian ecstasy and corybantic abandon. Left lobe Miller closely observes the crazy antics of right lobe Miller—then writes it all down, convinced of its divinity.

The declarative essentialism you would expect such a throwback to produce is everywhere in *Colossus*: "Every single thing that exists, whether made by God or man, whether fortuitous or planned, stands out like a nut in an aureole of light, of time and of space." Miller is the tourist in a drip-dry hat that thrusts his camera into your hand and demands you take his picture while he poses with quiddity. There's an odd selflessness about such self-absorption—and we are carried forward by *the great discovery,* that just as history repeats itself—for without, presumably, having read a word of any of them, Miller is a disciple of Spengler and Vico—so the successive revolutions of his frenzied subclauses, ranking up until they form sentences fifty, a hundred, two hundred words long—become an incantation, an *om mani padme hum.* "Imagine what it would be like to find two businessmen and a stenographer on Easter Island! Imagine how a typewriter would sound in that Oceanic silence!"

Sad to relate, I have found two businessmen and a stenographer on Easter Island—or, at any rate, their third-millennial equivalents.

Miller, scuttling along the Mediterranean littoral under the scudding cloud of the coming world war, sees the landscape about him lit up by divine light then plunged into the darkness of the American century. For him, there is no phenotype that cannot be stereotyped: "The French ... know neither how to give nor to ask for favors ... It's the wall again. A Greek has no walls around him; he gives and takes without stint." Whereas: "The Englishman in Greece is a farce and an eyesore: he isn't worth the dirt between a poor Greek's toes." And again: 'For centuries the Greeks have had the cruelest enemy a people could have—the Turks."

This is no mere braggadocio—Miller has seen the future, and it is Dubya, Dick Cheney and the Neocons. "The present way of life, which is America's, is doomed as surely as that of Europe.

No nation on earth can possibly give birth to a new order of life until a world view is established." Naturally, the establishment of any such "world view" is, for Miller, as impossible as going back to the future. For students of the writer's development, you can see here in *Colossus,* with its furious denunciations of the "go-getting" American century (*I can't stand this idea, which is rooted in the minds of little peoples, that America is the hope of the world*— and even more fierce condemnations of the pernicious and corrupting influence of the USA on returning Greek economic migrants), the shape of Miller's coming anti-American jeremiad *The Air-Conditioned Nightmare,* for an essentialist can never be beaten to the punch; given that he seeks esoteric knowledge that lies outside of space and time, he must already know the given shape of any bruise.

But if *Colossus* is politically prescient, it is culturally as well. In shaping the contours of what has come to be known as multiculturalism (even if this entails riffs of a fruity primitivism such that would make a Henry Moore bronze blush), Miller is *sans pareil.* He loves peoples in so far as they exemplify themselves—loathes them in as much as they betray that essentialism. In Greece, and in particular at her ancient sites, he finds the long golden thread of cultural transmission lying in the dust; so, Minotaur that he is, he doesn't simply follow it—but yanks hard. Like I said, I could have done with him for a companion when I was first smitten by the aching cerulean of the Attic sky, when I first glugged the wood-smoky retsina and lugged on a Karelia cigarette.

I could've done with Miller by my side when my tour bus jolted into Delphi, and the polyglot cultural sheep were herded off to be deracinated. I tried my best, and when the site closed for the night, hid among the jumble of temples, waiting to have the place to myself so I could run races in the gymnasium, drink from the Castalian spring and consult the sibyl. No dice. Forty years of rising disposable income and a concomitant Malthusian population explosion had done their work: scores of guards with flashlights fanned out among the ruins, so I took to the scrubby mountainside and spent the night, shivering and mosquito plagued, stuck on a ledge. The following day my eyes were so swollen I could barely *see* Antinous, let alone conceive of him — as Miller had — as the last of the gods.

"Greece is the home of the gods; they may have died but their presence still makes itself felt. The gods were of human proportion: they were created out of the human spirit." Nowadays, alas, while the presence of the gods may still be felt in Greece, I wonder if there's anyone much who can feel it. That may be, but if you believe in the brand of sympathetic literary magic that Henry Miller purveys, perhaps you will take his existential leap, go there yourself — and feel it anew. That's what he would have wanted.

True avant-garde — still had torsion. Delphi. The rest is noise.

LONDON, 2009

THE COLOSSUS OF MAROUSSI

PART ONE

I WOULD NEVER HAVE GONE TO GREECE HAD IT NOT been for a girl named Betty Ryan who lived in the same house with me in Paris. One evening, over a glass of white wine, she began to talk of her experiences in roaming about the world. I always listened to her with great attention, not only because her experiences were strange but because when she talked about her wanderings she seemed to paint them: everything she described remained in my head like finished canvases by a master. It was a peculiar conversation that evening: we began by talking about China and the Chinese language which she had begun to study. Soon we were in North Africa, in the desert, among peoples I had never heard of before. And then suddenly she was all alone, walking beside a river, and the light was intense and I was following her as best I could in the blinding sun but she got lost and I found myself wandering about in a strange land listening to a language I had never heard before. She is not exactly a story-teller, this girl, but she is an artist of some sort because nobody has ever given me the ambiance of a place so thoroughly as she did Greece. Long afterwards I discovered that it was near Olympia that she had gone astray and I with her, but at the time it was just Greece to me, a world of light such as I had never dreamed of and never hoped to see.

For months prior to this conversation I had been receiving letters from Greece from my friend Lawrence Durrell who had practically made Corfu his home. His letters were marvelous too, and yet a bit unreal to me. Durrell is a poet and his letters were poetic: they caused a certain confusion in me owing to the fact that the dream and the reality, the historical and the mythological, were so artfully blended. Later I was to discover for myself that this confusion is real and not due entirely to the poetic faculty. But at the time I thought he was laying it on, that it was his way of coaxing me to accept his repeated invitations to come and stay with him.

A few months before the war broke out I decided to take a long vacation. I had long wanted to visit the valley of the Dordogne, for one thing. So I packed my valise and took the train for Rocamadour where I arrived early one morning about sunup, the moon still gleaming brightly. It was a stroke of genius on my part to make the tour of the Dordogne region before plunging into the bright and hoary world of Greece. Just to glimpse the black, mysterious river at Dômme from the beautiful bluff at the edge of the town is something to be grateful for all one's life. To me this river, this country, belong to the poet, Rainer Maria Rilke. It is not French, not Austrian, not European even: it is the country of enchantment which the poets have staked out and which they alone may lay claim to. It is the nearest thing to Paradise this side of Greece. Let us call it the Frenchman's paradise, by way of making a concession. Actually it must have been a paradise for many thousands of years. I believe it must have been so for the Cro-Magnon man, despite the fossilized evidences of the great caves which point to a condition of life rather bewildering and terrifying. I believe that the Cro-Magnon man settled here because he was extremely intelligent and had a highly developed sense of beauty. I believe that in him the religious sense was already highly developed and that it flourished here even if he lived like an animal in the depths of the caves. I believe that this great peaceful region of France will always be a sacred spot for man and that when the cities have killed off the poets this will be the refuge and the cradle of the poets to come. I repeat, it was most important for me to have seen the Dordogne: it gives me hope for the future of the race, for the future of the earth itself. France may one day exist no more, but the Dordogne will live on just as dreams live on and nourish the souls of men.

At Marseilles I took the boat for Piraeus. My friend Durrell was to meet me in Athens and take me to Corfu. On the boat there were many people from the Levant. I singled them out immediately, in preference to the Americans, the French, the English. I had a strong desire to talk to Arabs and Turks and Syrians and such like. I was curious to know how they looked at the world. The voyage lasted four or five days, giving me ample time to make acquaintance with those whom I was eager to know more about. Quite by accident the first friend I made was a Greek medical student returning from Paris. We spoke French together. The first evening we talked until three or four in the morning, mostly about Knut Hamsun, whom I discovered the Greeks were passionate about. It seemed strange at first to be talking about this genius of the North whilst sailing into warm waters. But that conversation taught me immediately that the Greeks are an enthusiastic, curious-minded, passionate people. *Passion*—it was something I had long missed in France. Not only passion, but contradictoriness, confusion, chaos—all these sterling human qualities I rediscovered and cherished again in the person of my new-found friend. And generosity. I had almost thought it had perished from the earth. There we were, a Greek and an American, with something in common, yet two vastly different beings. It was a splendid introduction to that world which was about to open before my eyes. I was already enamored of Greece, and the Greeks, before catching sight of the country. I could see in advance that they were a friendly, hospitable people, easy to reach, easy to deal with.

The next day I opened conversation with the others—a Turk, a Syrian, some students from Lebanon, an Argentine man of

Italian extraction. The Turk aroused my antipathies almost at once. He had a mania for logic which infuriated me. It was bad logic too. And like the others, all of whom I violently disagreed with, I found in him an expression of the American spirit at its worst. Progress was their obsession. More machines, more efficiency, more capital, more comforts—that was their whole talk. I asked them if they had heard of the millions who were unemployed in America. They ignored the question. I asked them if they realized how empty, restless and miserable the American people were with all their machine-made luxuries and comforts. They were impervious to my sarcasm. What they wanted was success—money, power, a place in the sun. None of them wanted to return to their own country; for some reason they had all of them been obliged to return against their will. They said there was no life for them in their own country. When would life begin? I wanted to know. When they had all the things which America had, or Germany, or France. Life was made up of things, of machines mainly, from what I could gather. Life without money was an impossibility: one had to have clothes, a good home, a radio, a car, a tennis racquet, and so on. I told them I had none of those things and that I was happy without them, that I had turned my back on America precisely because these things meant nothing to me. They said I was the strangest American they had ever met. But they liked me. They stuck to me throughout the voyage, plying me with all sorts of questions which I answered in vain. Evenings I would get together with the Greek. We understood one another better, much better, despite his adoration for Germany and the German régime. He too, of course, wanted to go to America some day. Every Greek dreams of going to America and making a nest egg. I didn't try to dissuade him; I gave him a picture of America as I knew it, as I had seen it and experienced it. That seemed to frighten him a little: he admitted he had never heard anything like that about America before. "You go," I said, "and see for yourself. I may be wrong. I am only telling you what I know from my own experience." "Remember," I added, "Knut Hamsun didn't have such a wonderful time of it there, nor your beloved Edgar Allan Poe...."

There was a French archaeologist returning to Greece who sat opposite me at the table; he could have told me a lot of things about Greece but I never gave him a chance; I disliked him from the time I first laid eyes on him. The chap I really liked most during the voyage was the Italian from the Argentine. He was about the most ignorant fellow I have ever met and charming at the same time. At Naples we went ashore together to have a good meal and to visit Pompeii which he had never even heard of. Despite the overpowering heat I enjoyed the trip to Pompeii; if I had gone with an archaeologist I would have been bored stiff. At Piraeus he came ashore with me to visit the Acropolis. The heat was even worse than at Pompeii, which was pretty bad. At nine in the morning it must have been 120 degrees in the sun. We had hardly gotten through the gate at the dock when we fell into the hands of a wily Greek guide who spoke a little English and French and who promised to show us everything of interest for a modest sum. We tried to find out what he wanted for his services but in vain. It was too hot to discuss prices; we fell into a taxi and told him to steer us straight to the Acropolis. I had changed my francs into drachmas on the boat; it seemed like a tremendous wad that I had stuffed into my pocket and I felt that I could meet the bill no matter how exorbitant it might be. I knew we were going to be gypped and I looked forward to it with relish. The only thing that was solidly fixed in my mind about the Greeks was that you couldn't trust them; I would have been disappointed if our guide had turned out to be magnanimous and chivalrous. My companion on the other hand was somewhat worried about the situation. He was going on to Beirut. I could actually hear him making mental calculations as we rode along in the suffocating dust and heat.

The ride from Piraeus to Athens is a good introduction to Greece. There is nothing inviting about it. It makes you wonder why you decided to come to Greece. There is something not only arid and desolate about the scene, but something terrifying too. You feel stripped and plundered, almost annihilated.

The driver was like an animal who had been miraculously taught to operate a crazy machine: our guide was constantly directing him to go to the right or the left, as though they had never made the journey before. I felt an enormous sympathy for the driver whom I knew would be gypped also. I had the feeling that he could not count beyond a hundred; I had also the feeling that he would drive into a ditch if he were directed to. When we got to the Acropolis—it was an insane idea to go there immediately—there were several hundred people ahead of us storming the gate. By this time the heat was so terrific that all I thought of was where to sit down and enjoy a bit of shade. I found myself a fairly cool spot and I waited there while the Argentine chap got his money's worth. Our guide had remained at the entrance with the taxi driver after turning us over to one of the official guides. He was going to escort us to the Temple of Jupiter and the Thesion and other places as soon as we had had our fill of the Acropolis. We never went to these places, of course. We told him to drive into town, find a cool spot and order some ice cream. It was about ten thirty when we parked ourselves on the terrace of a café. Everybody looked fagged out from the heat, even the Greeks. We ate the ice cream, drank the iced water, then more ice cream and more iced water. After that I called for some hot tea, because I suddenly remembered somebody telling me once that hot tea cools you off.

The taxi was standing at the curb with the motor running. Our guide seemed to be the only one who didn't mind the heat. I suppose he thought we would cool off a bit and then start trotting around again in the sun looking at ruins and monuments. We told him finally that we wanted to dispense with his services. He said there was no hurry, he had nothing special to do, and was happy to keep us company. We told him we had had enough for the day and would like to settle up. He called the waiter and paid the check out of his own pocket. We kept prodding him to tell us how much. He seemed reluctant as hell to tell us. He wanted to know how much we thought his services were worth. We said we didn't know—we would leave it to him to decide. Whereupon, after a long pause, after looking us over from head to foot, scratching himself, tilting his hat back, mopping his brow, and so on, he blandly announced that he thought 2500 drachmas would square the account. I gave my companion a look and told him to open fire. The Greek of course was thoroughly prepared for our reaction. And it's this, I must confess, that I really like about the Greeks, when they are wily and cunning. Almost at once he said, "Well, all right, if you don't think my price is fair then you make me a price." So we did. We made him one as ridiculously low as his was high. It seemed to make him feel good, this crude bargaining. As a matter of fact, we all felt good about it. It was making service into something tangible and real like a commodity. We weighed it and appraised it, we juggled it like a ripe tomato or an ear of corn. And finally we agreed, not on a fair price, because that would have been an insult to our guide's ability, but we agreed that for this unique occasion, because of the heat, because we had not seen everything, and so on and so forth, that we would fix on thus and such a sum and part good friends. One of the little items we haggled about a long time was the amount paid by our guide to the official guide at the Acropolis. He swore he had given the man 150 drachmas. I had seen the transaction with my own eyes, and I knew he had given only fifty drachmas. He maintained that I had not seen well. We smoothed it out by pretending that he had inadvertently handed the man a hundred drachmas more than he intended to, a piece of casuistry so thoroughly un-Greek that had he then and there decided to rob us of all we possessed he would have been justified and the courts of Greece would have upheld him.

An hour later I said good-bye to my companion, found myself a room in a small hotel at double the usual price, stripped down and lay on the bed naked in a pool of sweat until nine that evening. I looked for a restaurant, tried to eat, but after taking a few mouthfuls gave it up. I have never been so hot in all my life. To sit near an electric light was torture. After a few cold drinks I got up from the terrace where I was sitting and headed for the park. I should say it was about eleven o'clock. People were swarming in all directions to the park. It reminded me of New York on a sweltering night in August. It was the herd again, something I had never felt in Paris, except during the aborted revolution. I sauntered slowly through the park towards the Temple of Jupiter. There were little tables along the dusty paths set out in an absent-minded way: couples were sitting there quietly in the dark, talking in low voices, over glasses of water. *The glass of water ...* everywhere I saw the glass of water. It became obsessional. I began to think of water as a new thing, a new vital element of life. Earth, air, fire, water. Right now water had become the cardinal element. Seeing lovers sitting there in the dark drinking water, sitting there in peace and quiet and talking in low tones, gave me a wonderful feeling about the Greek character. The dust, the heat, the poverty, the bareness, the containedness of the people, and the water everywhere in little tumblers standing between the quiet, peaceful couples, gave me the feeling that there was something holy about the place, something nourishing and sustaining. I walked about enchanted on this first night in the Zapion. It remains in my memory like no other park I have known. It is the quintessence of park, the thing one feels sometimes in looking at a canvas or dreaming of a place you'd like to be in and never find. It is lovely in the morning, too, as I was to discover. But at night, coming upon it from nowhere, feeling the hard dirt under your feet and hearing a buzz of language which is altogether unfamiliar to you, it is magical—and it is more magical to me perhaps because I think of it as filled with the poorest people in the world, and the gentlest. I am glad I arrived in Athens during that incredible heat wave, glad I saw it under the worst conditions. I felt the naked strength of the people, their purity, their nobility, their resignation. I saw their children, a sight which warmed me, because coming from France it was as if children were missing from the world, as if they were not being born any more. I saw people in rags, and that was cleansing too. The Greek knows how to live with his rags: they don't utterly degrade and befoul him as in other countries I have visited.

•

The following day I decided to take the boat to Corfu where my friend Durrell was waiting for me. We pulled out of Piraeus about five in the afternoon, the sun still burning like a furnace. I had made the mistake of buying a second class ticket. When I saw the animals coming aboard, the bedding, all the crazy paraphernalia which the Greeks drag with them on their voyages, I promptly changed to first class, which was only a trifle more expensive than second. I had never traveled first class before on anything, except the Metro in Paris—it seemed like a genuine luxury to me. The waiter was continuously circulating about with a tray filled with glasses of water. It was the first Greek word I learned: *nero* (water) and a beautiful word it is. Night was coming on and the islands were looming up in the distance, always floating above the water, not resting on it. The stars came out with magnificent brilliance and the wind was soft and cooling. I began to get the feel of it at once, what Greece was, what it had been, what it will always be even should it meet with the misfortune of being overrun by American tourists. When the steward asked me what I would like for dinner, when I gathered what it was we were going to have for dinner, I almost broke down and wept. The meals on a Greek boat are staggering. I like a good Greek meal better than a good French meal, even though it be heresy to admit it. There was lots to eat and lots to drink: there was the air outside and the sky full of stars. I had promised myself on leaving Paris not to do a stroke of work for a year. It was my first real vacation in twenty years and I was ready for it. Everything seemed right to me. There was no time any more, just me drifting along in a slow boat ready to meet all corners and take whatever came along. Out of the sea, as if Homer himself had arranged it for me, the islands bobbed up, lonely, deserted, mysterious in the fading light. I couldn't ask for more, nor did I want anything more. I had everything a man could desire, and I knew it. I knew too that I might never have it again. I felt the war coming on—it was getting closer and closer every day. For a little while yet there would be peace and men might still behave like human beings.

We didn't go through the Corinth canal because there had been a landslide: we practically circumnavigated the Peloponnesus. The second night out we pulled into Patras opposite Missolonghi. I have come into this port several times since, always about the same hour, and always I experienced the same fascination. You ride straight into a big headland, like an arrow burying itself in the side of a mountain. The electric lights strung along the waterfront create a Japanese effect; there is something impromptu about the lighting in all Greek ports, something which gives the impression of an impending festival. As you pull into port the little boats come out to meet you: they are filled with passengers and luggage and livestock and bedding and furniture. The men row standing up, pushing instead of pulling. They seem absolutely tireless, moving their heavy burdens about at will with deft and almost imperceptible movements of the wrist. As they draw alongside a pandemonium sets in. Everybody goes the wrong way, everything is confused, chaotic, disorderly. But nobody is ever lost or hurt, nothing is stolen, no blows are exchanged. It is a kind of ferment which is created by reason of the fact that for a Greek every event, no matter how stale, is always unique. He is always doing the same thing for the first time: he is curious, avidly curious, and experimental. He experiments for the sake of experimenting, not to establish a better or more efficient way of doing things. He likes to do things with his hands, with his whole body, with his soul, I might as well say. Thus Homer lives on. Though I've never read a line of Homer I believe the Greek of to-day is essentially unchanged. If anything he is more Greek than he ever was. And here I must make a parenthesis to say a word about my friend Mayo, the painter, whom I knew in Paris. Malliarakis was his real name and I think he came originally from Crete. Anyway, pulling into Patras I got to thinking about him violently. I remembered asking him in Paris to tell me something about Greece and suddenly, as we were coming into the port of Patras, I understood everything he had been trying to tell me that night and I felt bad that he was not alongside me to share my enjoyment. I remembered how he had said with quiet, steady conviction, after describing the country for me as best he could—"Miller, you will like Greece, I am sure of it." Somehow those words impressed me more than anything he had said about Greece. *You will like it* ... that stuck in my crop. "By God, yes, I like it," I was saying to myself over and over as I stood at the rail taking in the movement and the hubbub. I leaned back and looked up at the sky. I had never seen a sky like this before. It was magnificent. I felt completely detached from Europe. I had entered a new realm as a free man— everything had conjoined to make the experience unique and fructifying. Christ, I was happy. But for the first time in my life I was happy with the full consciousness of being happy. It's good to be just plain happy; it's a little better to know that you're happy; but to understand that you're happy and to know why and how, in what way, because of what concatenation of events or circumstances, and still be happy, be happy in the being and the knowing, well that is beyond happiness, that is bliss, and if you have any sense you ought to kill yourself on the spot and be done with it. And that's how I was—except that I didn't have the power or the courage to kill myself then and there. It was good, too, that I didn't do myself in because there were even greater moments to come, something beyond bliss even, something which if anyone had tried to describe to me I would probably not have believed. I didn't know then that I would one day stand at Mycenae, or at Phaestos, or that I would wake up one morning and looking through a port hole see with my own eyes the place I had written about in a book but which I never knew existed nor that it bore the same name as the one I had given it in my imagination. Marvelous things happen to one in Greece—marvelous good things which can happen to one nowhere else on earth. Somehow, almost as if He were nodding, Greece still remains under the protection of the Creator. Men may go about their puny, ineffectual bedevilment, even in Greece, but God's magic is still at work and, no matter what the race of man may do or try to do, Greece is still a sacred precinct—and my belief is it will remain so until the end of time.

It was almost high noon when the boat pulled in at Corfu. Durrell was waiting at the dock with Spiro Americanus, his factotum. It was about an hour's drive to Kalami, the little village towards the north end of the island where Durrell had his home. Before sitting down to lunch we had a swim in front of the house. I hadn't been in the water for almost twenty years. Durrell and Nancy, his wife, were like a couple of dolphins; they practically lived in the water. We took a siesta after lunch and then we rowed to another little cove about a mile away where there was a tiny white shrine. Here we baptized ourselves anew in the raw. In the evening I was presented to Kyrios Karamenaios, the local gendarme, and to Nicola, the village schoolmaster. We immediately became firm friends. With Nicola I spoke a broken-down French; with Karamenaios a sort of cluck-cluck language made up largely of good will and a desire to understand one another.

About once a week we went to town in the caique. I never got to like the town of Corfu. It has a desultory air which by evening becomes a quiet, irritating sort of dementia. You are constantly sitting down drinking something you don't want to drink or else walking up and down aimlessly feeling desperately like a prisoner. Usually I treated myself to a shave and haircut whenever I went to town: I did it to while away the time and because it was so ridiculously cheap. It was the King's barber, I was informed, who attended me, and the whole job came to about three and a half cents, including the tip. Corfu is a typical place of exile. The Kaiser used to make his residence here before he lost his crown. I went through the palace once to see what it was like. All palaces strike me as dreary and lugubrious places, but the Kaiser's madhouse is about the worst piece of gimcrackery I have ever laid eyes on. It would make an excellent museum for Surrealistic art. At one end of the island, however, facing the abandoned palace, is the little spot called Kanoni, whence you look down upon the magical Toten Insel. In the evening Spiro sits here dreaming of his life in Rhode Island when the boot-legging traffic was in full swing. It is a spot which rightfully belongs to my friend Hans Reichel, the water colorist. The associations are Homeric,

I know, but for me it partakes more of Stuttgart than of ancient Greece. When the moon is out and there is no sound save the breathing of the earth it is exactly the atmosphere which Reichel creates when he sits in a petrified dream and becomes *limitrophe* to birds and snails and gargoyles, to smoky moons and sweating stones, or to the sorrow-laden music which is constantly playing in his heart even when he rears like a crazed kangaroo and begins smashing everything in sight with his prehensile tail. If he should ever read these lines and know that I thought of him while looking at the Toten Insel, know that I was never the enemy he imagined me to be, it would make me very happy. Perhaps it was on one of these very evenings when I sat at Kanoni with Spiro looking down upon this place of enchantment that Reichel, who had nothing but love for the French, was dragged from his lair in the Impasse Rouet and placed in a sordid concentration camp.

One day Theodore turned up—Dr. Theodore Stephanides. He knew all about plants, flowers, trees, rocks, minerals, low forms of animal life, microbes, diseases, stars, planets, comets and so on. Theodore is the most learned man I have ever met, and a saint to boot. Theodore has also translated a number of Greek poems into English. It was in this way that I heard for the first time the name Seferis, which is George Seferiades' pen name. And then with a mixture of love, admiration and sly humor he pronounced for me the name Katsimbalis which, for some strange reason, immediately made an impression upon me. That evening Theodore gave us hallucinating descriptions of his life in the trenches with Katsimbalis on the Balkan front during the World War. The next day Durrell and I wrote an enthusiastic letter to Katsimbalis, who was in Athens, expressing the hope that we would all meet there shortly. *Katsimbalis* ... we employed his name familiarly, as if we had known him all our lives. Soon thereafter Theodore left and then came the Countess X. with Niki and a family of young acrobats. They came upon us unexpectedly in a little boat laden with marvelous victuals and bottles of rare wine from the Countess's estate. With this troupe of linguists, jugglers, acrobats and water nymphs things went whacky right from the start. Niki had Nile green eyes and her hair seemed to be entwined with serpents. Between the first and second visits of this extraordinary troupe, who always came by water in a boat heavily laden with good things, the Durrells and myself went camping for a stretch on a sandy beach facing the sea. Here time was completely blotted out. Mornings we were awakened by a crazy shepherd who insisted on leading his flock of sheep over our prone bodies. On a cliff directly behind us a demented witch would suddenly appear to curse him out. Each morning it was a surprise; we would awake with groans and curses followed by peals of laughter. Then a quick plunge into the sea where we would watch the goats clambering up the precipitous slopes of the cliff: the scene was an almost faithful replica of the Rhodesian rock drawings which one can see at the Musée de l'Homme in Paris. Sometimes in high fettle we would clamber up after the goats, only to descend covered with cuts and bruises. A week passed in which we saw no one except the mayor of a mountain village some miles away who came to look us over. He came on a day when I was dozing alone in the shade of a huge rock. I knew about ten words of Greek and he knew about three words of English. We had a remarkable colloquy, considering the limitations of language. Seeing that he was half-cracked I felt at ease and, since the Durrells were not there to warn me against such antics, I began to do my own cracked song and dance for him, which was to imitate male and female movie stars, a Chinese mandarin, a bronco, a high diver and such like. He seemed to be vastly amused and for some reason was particularly interested in my Chinese performance. I began to talk Chinese to him, not knowing a word of the language, whereupon to my astonishment he answered me in Chinese, his own Chinese, which was just as good as mine. The next day he brought an interpreter with him for the express purpose of telling me a whopping lie, to wit, that some years ago a Chinese junk had been stranded on this very beach and that some four hundred Chinamen had put up on the beach until their boat was repaired. He said he liked the Chinese very much, that they were a fine people, and that their language was very musical, very intelligent. I asked did he mean *intelligible*, but no, he meant intelligent. The Greek language was intelligent too. And the German language. Then I told him I had been in China, which was another lie, and after describing that country I drifted to Africa and told him about the Pygmies with whom I had also lived for a while. He said they had some Pygmies in a neighboring village. It went on like this from one lie to another for several hours, during which we consumed some wine and olives. Then someone produced a flute and we began to dance, a veritable St. Vitus' dance which went on interminably to finish in the sea where we bit one another like crabs and screamed and bellowed in all the tongues of the earth.

We broke up camp early one morning to return to Kalami. It was a strange sultry day and we had a two hour climb ahead of us to reach the mountain village where Spiro awaited us with the car. There was first of all a stretch of sand to be traversed at a gallop, because even with sandals on the sand scorched one's feet. Then came a long trek through a dried-up river bed which, because of the boulders, was a test for even the stoutest ankles. Finally we came to the path that led up the mountainside, a sort of gully rather than path, which taxed even the mountain ponies on which we had loaded our things. As we climbed a weird melody greeted us from above. Like the heavy mist sweeping up from the sea, it enveloped us in its nostalgic folds and then as suddenly died away. When we had risen another few hundred feet we came upon a clearing in the midst of which was a huge vat filled with a poisonous liquid, an insecticide for the olive trees, which the young women were stirring as they sang. It was a song of death which blended singularly with the mist-laden landscape. Here and there, where the vaporish clouds had rolled apart to reveal a clump of trees or a bare, jagged fang-like snag of rocks, the reverberations of their haunting melody sang out like a choir of brass in an orchestra. Now and then a great blue area of sea rose out of the fog, not at the level of the earth but in some middle realm between heaven and earth, as though after a typhoon. The houses too, when their solidity burst through the mirage, seemed to be suspended in space. The whole atmosphere was ridden with a shuddering Biblical splendor punctuated with the tinkling bells of the ponies, the reverberations of the poison song, the faint boom of the surf far below and an undefinable mountain murmuring which was probably nothing more than the hammering of the temples in the high and sultry haze of an Ionian morning. We took spells of resting at the edge of the precipice, too fascinated by the spectacle to continue on through the pass into the clear, bright work-a-day world of the little mountain village beyond. In that operatic realm, where the Tao Teh King and the ancient Vedas fused dramatically in contrapuntal confusion, the taste of the light Greek cigarette was even more like straw. Here the palate itself became metaphysically attuned: the drama was of the airs, of the upper regions, of the eternal conflict between the soul and the spirit.

Then the pass, which I shall always think of as the carrefour of meaningless butcheries. Here the most frightful, vengeful massacres must have been perpetrated again and again throughout the endless bloody past of man. It is a trap devised by Nature herself for man's undoing. Greece is full of such death traps. It is like a strong cosmic note which gives the diapason to the intoxicating light world wherein the heroic and mythological figures of the resplendent past threaten continually to dominate the consciousness. The ancient Greek was a murderer: he lived amidst brutal clarities which tormented and maddened the spirit. He was at war with everyone, including himself. Out of this fiery anarchy came the lucid, healing metaphysical speculations which even to-day enthrall the world. Going through the pass, which demands a sort of swastika maneuvering in order to debouch free and clear on the high plateau, I had the impression of wading through phantom seas of blood; the earth was not parched and convulsed in the usual Greek way but bleached and twisted as must have been the mangled, death-stilled limbs of the slain who were left to rot and give their blood here in the merciless sun to the roots of the wild olives which cling to the steep mountain slope with vulturous claws. In this mountain pass there must also have been moments of clear vision when men of distant races stood holding hands and looking into one another's eyes with sympathy and understanding. Here too men of the Pythagorean stripe must have stopped to meditate in silence and solitude, gaining fresh clarity, fresh vision, from the dust-strewn place of carnage. All Greece is diademed with such antinomian spots; it is perhaps the explanation for the fact that Greece has emancipated itself as a country, a nation, a people, in order to continue as the luminous carrefour of a changing humanity.

At Kalami the days rolled by like a song. Now and then I wrote a letter or tried to paint a water color. There was plenty to read in the house but I had no desire to look at a book. Durrell tried to get me to read Shakespeare's Sonnets and, after he had laid siege to me for about a week, I did read one, perhaps the most mysterious sonnet that Shakespeare ever wrote. (I believe it was "The Phoenix and the Turtle.") Soon thereafter I received a copy in the mail of *The Secret Doctrine* and this I fell on with a will. I also reread Nijinsky's Diary. I know I shall read it again and again. There are only a few books which I can read over and over—one is *Mysteries* and another is *The Eternal Husband*. Perhaps I should also add *Alice in Wonderland*. At any rate, it was far better to spend the evening talking and singing, or standing on the rocks at the edge of the water with a telescope studying the stars.

When the Countess again appeared on the scene she persuaded us to spend a few days on her estate in another part of the island. We had three wonderful days together and then in the middle of the night the Greek army was mobilized. War had not yet been declared, but the King's hasty return to Athens was interpreted by everyone as an ominous sign. Everyone who had the means seemed determined to follow the King's example. The town of Corfu was in a veritable panic. Durrell wanted to enlist in the Greek army for service on the Albanian frontier; Spiro, who was past the age limit, also wanted to offer his services. A

few days passed this way in hysterical gesturings and then, quite
as if it had been arranged by an impresario, we all found ourselves waiting for the boat to take us to Athens. The boat was
to arrive at nine in the morning; we didn't get aboard her until
four the next morning. By that time the quay was filled with an
indescribable litter of baggage on which the feverish owners sat
or sprawled themselves out, pretending to look unconcerned
but actually quaking with fear. The most disgraceful scene ensued when the tenders finally hove to. As usual, the rich insisted
on going aboard first. Having a first-class passage I found myself
among the rich. I was thoroughly disgusted and half minded not
to take the boat at all but return quietly to Durrell's house and
let things take their course. Then, by some miraculous quirk, I
discovered that we weren't to go aboard first, that we were to go
last. All the fine luggage was being taken out of the tenders and
thrown back on the quay. Bravo! My heart went up. The Countess, who had more luggage than anyone, was the very last to go
aboard. Later I discovered to my surprise that it was she who
had arranged matters thus. It was the inefficiency that had annoyed her, not the question of class or privilege. She hadn't the
least fear of the Italians apparently—what she minded was the
disorder, the shameful scramble. It was four in the morning, as I
say, with a bright moon gleaming on a swollen, angry sea, when
we pushed off from the quay in the little caiques. I had never expected to leave Corfu under such conditions. I was a bit angry
with myself for having consented to go to Athens. I was more
concerned about the interruption of my blissful vacation than
about the dangers of the impending war. It was still Summer
and I had by no means had enough of sun and sea. I thought of
the peasant women and the ragged children who would soon be
without food, and the look in their eyes as they waved good-bye
to us. It seemed cowardly to be running away like this, leaving
the weak and innocent to their doom. Money again. Those who
have escape; those who have not are massacred. I found myself
praying that the Italians would intercept us, that we would not
get off scot free in this shameless way.

When I awoke and went up on deck the boat was gliding through a narrow strait; on either side of us were low barren hills, soft, violet-studded hummocks of earth of such intimate human proportions as to make one weep with joy. The sun was almost at zenith and the glare was dazzlingly intense. I was in precisely that little Greek world whose frontiers I had described in my book a few months before leaving Paris. It was like awakening to find oneself alive in a dream. There was something phenomenal about the luminous immediacy of these two violet-colored shores. We were gliding along in precisely the way that Rousseau *le douanier* has described it in his painting. It was more than a Greek atmosphere—it was poetic and of no time or place actually known to man. The boat itself was the only link with reality. The boat was filled to the gunwales with lost souls desperately clinging to their few earthly possessions. Women in rags, their breasts bared, were vainly trying to nurse their howling brats; they sat on the deck floor in a mess of vomit and blood and the dream through which they were passing never brushed their eyelids. If we had been torpedoed then and there we would have passed like that, in vomit and blood and confusion, to the dark underworld. At that moment I rejoiced that I was free of possessions, free of all ties, free of fear and envy and malice. I could have passed quietly from one dream to another, owning nothing, regretting nothing, wishing nothing. I was never more certain that life and death are one and that neither can be enjoyed or embraced if the other be absent.

At Patras we decided to go ashore and take the train to Athens. The Hotel Cecil, which we stopped at, is the best hotel I've ever been in, and I've been in a good many. It cost about 23 cents a day for a room the likes of which could not be duplicated in America for less than five dollars. I hope everybody who is passing through Greece will stop off at the Hotel Cecil and see for themselves. It is an event in one's life.... We breakfasted towards noon on the terrace of the solarium overlooking the sea. Here a terrible wrangle ensued between Durrell and his wife. I felt quite helpless and could only pity them both from the depths of my heart. It was really a private quarrel in which the war was used as a camouflage. The thought of war drives people frantic, makes them quite cuckoo, even when they are intelligent and far-seeing, as both Durrell and Nancy are. War has another bad effect—it makes young people feel guilty and conscience-stricken. In Corfu I had been studying the antics of a superbly healthy young Englishman, a lad of twenty or so, who had intended to be a Greek scholar. He was running around like a chicken with its head off begging someone to put him in the front line where he could have himself blown to smithereens. Now Durrell was talking the same way, the only difference being that he was not so crazy to be killed as to be with the Greek forces in Albania—because he thought more of the Greeks than he did of his own countrymen. I said as little as possible because if I had attempted to dissuade him I would only have succeeded in abetting his suicidal impulse. I didn't want to see him killed; it seemed to me that the war could very well be fought to its fruitless end without the sacrifice of one destined to give so much to the world. He knew what I thought about war and I think in his heart he agrees with me, but being young, being serviceable, being English despite himself, he was in a quandary. It was a bad place in which to discuss a subject of this sort. The atmosphere was charged with memories of Byron. Sitting there, with Missolonghi so near, it was almost impossible to think sanely about war. The British Consul at Patras was far more clear-headed. After a brief talk with him I felt a renewed respect for the British Empire. I also reminded myself that war hadn't actually been declared yet. It had threatened to break out so often—possibly it wouldn't happen after all.

We had a good meal at the public square and towards the late afternoon we took the automotrice for Athens. During the course of a conversation with some fellow travelers a Greek returning from America hailed me in jovial fashion as a brother American and began a long, irritatingly stupid monologue about the glories of Chicago which I doubt he had ever lived in more than a month. The gist of it was that he was eager to get back home—meaning *America*; he found his countrymen ignorant, dirty, backward, inefficient and so on and so forth. Durrell interrupted once to inquire what language the man was speaking—he had never heard a Greek speaking that kind of American. The men I had been talking with were eager to know what this strange countryman of theirs was so excited about. We had been talking in French until this Yahoo came along. I told them in French that the man was an ignoramus. At this the Greek asked me what language I was speaking and when I said French he answered—"I don't know those languages; American's good enough for me... I'm from Chicago." Though I showed him plainly that I wasn't interested in listening to his stories he insisted on telling me all about himself. He said he was now on his way to a little mountain village where his mother lived; he wanted to say good-bye to her before leaving. "Show you how ignorant these people are," he added, "I brought a bathtub for my mother all the way from Chicago; I set it up with my own hands too. Think they appreciated it? They laughed at me, said I was crazy. They don't want to keep themselves clean. Now in Chicago ..." I apologized to my fellow passengers for the presence of this idiot; I explained to them that that's what America does to its adopted sons. At this they all laughed heartily, including the benighted Greek at my side who hadn't understood a word I had said since it was in French I made the remark. To cap it all the dolt asked me where I had learned my English. When I told him I was born in America he replied that he had never heard anyone speak English like me; he said it in a way to imply that the only decent English worth speaking was his own slaughterhouse variety.

In Athens it was actually chilly enough to wear an overcoat when we arrived. Athens has a temperamental climate, like New York. It has plenty of dust, too, if you start walking towards the outskirts. Even in the heart of the city sometimes, where the most fashionable, ultra-modern apartment houses are to be seen, the street is nothing but a dirt road. One can walk to the edge of the city in a half hour. It is really an enormous city containing almost a million inhabitants; it has grown a hundred times over since Byron's day. The color scheme is blue and white, as it is throughout Greece. Even the newspapers use blue ink, a bright sky-blue, which makes the papers seem innocent and juvenile. The Athenians practically devour the newspapers; they have a perpetual hunger for news. From the balcony of my room at the Grand Hotel I could look down on Constitution Square which in the evening is black with people, thousands of them, seated at little tables loaded with drinks and ices, the waiters scurrying back and forth with trays to the cafés adjoining the square.

Here one evening on his way back to Amaroussion I met Katsimbalis. It was definitely a meeting. As far as encounters with men go I have only known two others to compare with it in my whole life—when I met Blaise Cendrars and when I met Lawrence Durrell. I didn't have very much to say that first evening; I listened spellbound, enchanted by every phrase he let drop. I saw that he was made for the monologue, like Cendrars, like Moricand the astrologer. I like the monologue even more than the duet, when it is good. It's like watching a man write a book expressly for you: he writes it, reads it aloud, acts it, revises it, savors it, enjoys it, enjoys your enjoyment of it, and then tears it up and throws it to the winds. It's a sublime performance, because while he's going through with it you are God for him—unless you happen to be an insensitive and impatient dolt. But in that case the kind of monologue I refer to never happens.

He was a curious mixture of things to me on that first occasion; he had the general physique of a bull, the tenacity of a vulture, the agility of a leopard, the tenderness of a lamb, and the coyness of a dove. He had a curious overgrown head which fascinated me and which, for some reason, I took to be singularly Athenian. His hands were rather small for his body, and overly delicate. He was a vital, powerful man, capable of brutal gestures and rough words, yet somehow conveying a sense of warmth which was soft and feminine. There was also a great element of the tragic in him which his adroit mimicry only enhanced. He was extremely sympathetic and at the same time ruthless as a boor. He seemed to be talking about himself all the time, but never egotistically. He talked about himself because he himself was the most interesting person he knew. I liked that quality very much—I have a little of it myself.

We met a few days later to have dinner together—he, his wife Aspasia and the Durrells. After dinner we were to meet some friends of his. From the time he met us he was bubbling over. He was always that way, even on bad days when he complained of headache or dizziness or any of the hundred and one ailments which pestered him. He was taking us to a *taverna* in Piraeus, he said, because he wanted us to enjoy Greek cooking in the Greek way. It was one of his favorite hang-outs in the old days. "I made a mistake to get married," he said—his wife listening and smiling indulgently—"I wasn't cut out for marriage—it's ruining me. I can't sleep, I can't smoke, I can't drink any more.... I'm finished." He was always talking about himself as of someone who was done for: it was a little motif which he wove into the monologue by way of warming up to a subject. Things which happened only yesterday fell into this same nostalgic done-for past. Sometimes, when he talked this way, he gave me the impression of being an enormous tortoise which had slipped out of its shell, a creature which was spending itself in a desperate struggle to get back into the shell which it had outgrown. In this struggle he always made himself look grotesque and ridiculous—he did it deliberately. He would laugh at himself, in the tragic way of the buffoon. We would all laugh, his wife too. No matter how sad or morbid or pathetic the story might be he would have us laughing continuously. He saw the humorous aspect of everything, which is the real test of the tragic sense.

The food ... food was something he was passionate about. He had been enjoying good food since childhood and I guess he will go on enjoying it until he dies. His father had been a great gourmet and Katsimbalis, though perhaps lacking some of his father's sensual refinements and accomplishments, was following the family tradition. Between great carnivorous gulps of food he would pound his chest like a gorilla before washing it down with a hogshead of *rezina*. He had drunk a lot of *rezina* in his time: he said it was good for one, good for the kidneys, good for the liver, good for the lungs, good for the bowels and for the mind, good for everything. Everything he took into his system was good, whether it was poison or ambrosia. He didn't believe in moderation nor good sense nor anything that was inhibitory. He believed in going the whole hog and then taking your punishment. There were a lot of things he couldn't do any more—the war had bunged him up a bit. But despite the bad arm, the dislocated knee, the damaged eye, the disorganized liver, the rheumatic twinges, the arthritic disturbances, the migraine, the dizziness and God knows what, what was left of the catastrophe was alive and flourishing like a smoking dung-heap. He could galvanize the dead with his talk. It was a sort of devouring process: when he described a place he ate into it, like a goat attacking a carpet. If he described a person he ate him alive from head to toe. If it were an event he would devour every detail, like an army of white ants descending upon a forest. He was everywhere at once, in his talk. He attacked from above and below, from the front, rear and flanks. If he couldn't dispose of a thing at once, for lack of a phrase or an image, he would spike it temporarily and move on, coming back to it later and devouring it piecemeal. Or like a juggler, he would loss it in the air and, just when you thought he had forgotten it, that it would fall and break, he would deftly put an arm behind his back and catch it in his palm without even turning his eye. It wasn't just talk he handed out, but *language*—food and beast language. He always talked against a landscape, like the protagonist of a lost world. The Attic landscape was best of all for his purpose: it contains the necessary ingredients for the dramatic monologue. One has only to see the open air theatres buried in the hillsides to understand the importance of this setting. Even if his talk carried him to Paris, for example, to a place like the Faubourg Montmartre, he spiced and flavored it with his Attic ingredients, with thyme, sage, tufa, asphodel, honey, red clay, blue roofs, acanthus trimmings, violet light, hot rocks, dry winds, dust, *rezina*, arthritis and the electrical crackle that plays over the low hills like a swift serpent with a broken spine. He was a strange contradiction, even in his talk. With his snake-like tongue which struck like lightning, with fingers moving nervously, as though wandering over an imaginary spinet, with pounding, brutal gestures which somehow never smashed anything but simply raised a din, with all the boom of surf and the roar and sizzle and razzle-dazzle, if you suddenly observed him closely you got the impression that he was sitting there immobile, that only the round falcon's eye was alert, that he was a bird which had been hypnotized, or had hypnotized itself, and that his claws were fastened to the wrist of an invisible giant, a giant like the earth. All this flurry and din, all these kaleidoscopic prestidigitations of his, was only a sort of wizardry which he employed to conceal the fact that he was a prisoner—that was the impression he gave me when I studied him, when I could break the spell for a moment and observe him attentively. But to break the spell required a power and a magic almost equal to his own; it made one feel foolish and impotent, as one always does when one succeeds in destroying the power of illusion. Magic is never destroyed—the most we can do is to cut ourselves off, amputate the mysterious antennae which serve to connect us with forces beyond our power of understanding. Many a time, as Katsimbalis talked, I caught that look on the face of a listener which told me that the invisible wires had been connected, that something was being communicated which was over and above language, over and above personality, something magical which we recognize in dream and which makes the face of the sleeper relax and expand with a bloom such as we rarely see in waking life. Often when meditating on this quality of his I thought of his frequent allusions to the incomparable honey which is stored by the bees on the slopes of his beloved Hymettos. Over and over he would try to explain the reasons why this honey from Mount Hymettos was unique. Nobody can explain it satisfactorily. Nobody can explain anything which is unique. One can describe, worship and adore. And that is all I can do with Katsimbalis' talk.

•

It was later, after I had returned to Corfu and had had a good taste of solitude, that I appreciated the Katsimbalistic monologue even more. Lying nude in the sun on a ledge of rock by the sea I would often close my eyes and try to re-weave the pattern of his talks. It was then that I made the discovery that his talk created reverberations, that the echo took a long time to reach one's ears. I began to compare it with French talk in which I had been enveloped for so long. The latter seemed more like the play of light on an alabaster vase, something reflective, nimble, dancing, liquid, evanescent, whereas the other, the Katsimbalistic language, was opaque, cloudy, pregnant with resonances which could only be understood long afterwards when the reverberations announced the collision with thoughts, people, objects located in distant parts of the earth. The Frenchman puts walls about his talk, as he does about his garden: he puts limits about everything in order to feel at home. At bottom he lacks confidence in his fellow man; he is skeptical because he doesn't believe in the innate goodness of human beings. He has become a realist because it is safe and practical. The Greek, on the other hand, is an adventurer: he is reckless and adaptable, he makes friends easily. The walls which you see in Greece, when they are not of Turkish or Venetian origin, go back to the Cyclopean age. Of my own experience I would say that there is no more direct, approachable, easy man to deal with than the Greek. He becomes a friend immediately: he goes out to you. With the Frenchman friendship is a long and laborious process: it may take a lifetime to make a friend of him. He is best in acquaintanceship where there is little to risk and where there are no aftermaths. The very word *ami* contains almost nothing of the flavor of friend, as we feel it in English. *C'est mon ami* cannot be translated by "this is my friend." There is no counterpart to this English phrase in the French language. It is a gap which has never been filled, like the word "home." These things affect conversation. One can converse all right, but it is difficult to have a heart to heart talk. All France, it has often been said, is a garden, and if you love France, as I do, it can be a very beautiful garden.

For myself I found it healing and soothing to the spirit; I recovered from the shocks and bruises which I had received in my own country. But there comes a day, when you are well again and strong, when this atmosphere ceases to be nourishing. You long to break out and test your powers. Then the French spirit seems inadequate. You long to make friends, to create enemies, to look beyond walls and cultivated patches of earth. You want to cease thinking in terms of life insurance, sick benefits, old age pensions and so on.

After the succulent repast at the *taverna* in Piraeus, all of us a bit stinko from the *rezina*, we moved back to the big square in Athens. It was midnight or a little after and the square still crowded with people. Katsimbalis seemed to divine the spot where his friends were seated. We were introduced to his bosom comrades, George Seferiades and Captain Antoniou of the good ship "Acropolis." They soon began plying me with questions about America and American writers. Like most educated Europeans they knew more about American literature than I ever will. Antoniou had been to America several times, had walked about the streets of New York, Boston, New Orleans, San Francisco and other ports. The thought of him walking about the streets of our big cities in bewilderment led me to broach the name of Sherwood Anderson whom I always think of as the one American writer of our time who has walked the streets of our American cities as a genuine poet. Since they scarcely knew his name, and since the conversation was already veering towards more familiar ground, namely Edgar Allan Poe, a subject I am weary of listening to, I suddenly became obsessed with the idea of selling them Sherwood Anderson. I began a monologue myself for a change — about writers who walk the streets in America and are not recognized until they are ready for the grave. I was so enthusiastic about the subject that I actually identified myself with Sherwood Anderson. He would probably have been astounded had he heard of the exploits I was crediting him with. I've always had a particular weakness for the author of "Many Marriages." In my worst days in America he was the man who comforted me, by his writings. It was only the other day that I met him for the first time. I found no discrepancy between the man and the writer. I saw in him the born storyteller, the man who can make even the egg triumphant.

As I say, I went on talking about Sherwood Anderson like a blue streak. It was to Captain Antoniou that I chiefly addressed myself. I remember the look he gave me when I had finished, the look which said: "Sold. Wrap them up, I'll take the whole set." Many times since I've enjoyed the pleasure of rereading Sherwood Anderson through Antoniou's eyes. Antoniou is constantly sailing from one island to another, writing his poems as he walks about strange cities at night. Once, a few months later, I met him for a few minutes one evening in the strange port of Herakleion in Crete. He was still thinking about Sherwood Anderson, though his talk was of cargoes and weather reports and water supplies. Once out to sea I could picture him going up to his cabin and, taking a little book from the rack, burying himself in the mysterious night of a nameless Ohio town. The night always made me a little envious of him, envious of his peace and solitude at sea. I envied him the islands he was always stopping off at and the lonely walks through silent villages whose names mean nothing to us. To be a pilot was the first ambition I had ever voiced. I liked the idea of being alone in the little house above the deck, steering the ship over its perilous course. To be aware of the weather, to be in it, battling with it, meant everything to me. In Antoniou's countenance there were always traces of the weather. And in Sherwood Anderson's writing there are always traces of the weather. I like men who have the weather in their blood....

We separated in the early hours of the morning. I went back to the hotel, opened the window and stood for a while on the balcony looking down on the square which was now deserted. I had made two more stalwart Greek friends and I was happy about it. I began to think of all the friends I had made in the short time that I was there. I thought of Spiro, the taxi-driver, and of Kare-menaios, the gendarme. There was also Max, the refugee, living like a duke at the King George Hotel; he seemed to have nothing on his mind but how to make his friends happy with the drachmas which he couldn't take out of the country. There was also the proprietor of my hotel who, unlike any French hotelkeeper I have ever met, used to say to me at intervals—"Do you need any money?" If I told him I was taking a little trip he would say: "Be sure to wire me if you need any money." Spiro was the same way. When we said good-bye at the dock the night of the general panic, his last words were—"Mr. Henry, if you come back to Corfu I want you to stay with me. I don't want any money, Mr. Henry—I want you to come and live with us as long as you like." Everywhere I went in Greece it was the same tune. Even at the prefecture, while waiting to have my papers put in order, the gendarme would send out for a coffee and cigarettes to put me at ease. I liked the way they begged too. They weren't shamefaced about it. They would hold you up openly and ask for money or cigarettes as if they were entitled to it. It's a good sign when people beg that way: it means that they know how to give. The French, for example, know neither how to give nor how to ask for favors—either way they feel uneasy. They make a virtue of not molesting you. It's the wall again. A Greek has no walls around him: he gives and takes without stint.

The English in Greece—a sorry lot, by the way—seem to have a poor opinion of the Greek character. The English are torpid, unimaginative, lacking in resiliency. They seem to think that the Greeks should be eternally grateful to them because they have a powerful fleet. The Englishman in Greece is a farce and an eye-sore: he isn't worth the dirt between a poor Greek's toes. For centuries the Greeks have had the cruelest enemy a people could have—the Turks. After centuries of enslavement they threw off the yoke and, had the big Powers not interfered, they would probably have driven the Turks into the ground and annihilated them. To-day the two peoples, after an exchange of populations which is nothing if not extraordinary, are friends. They respect one another. And yet the English, who would have disappeared from the face of the earth had they been subjected to the same treatment, pretend to look down on the Greeks.

Everywhere you go in Greece the atmosphere is pregnant with heroic deeds. I am speaking of modern Greece, not ancient Greece. And the women, when you look into the history of this little country, were just as heroic as the men. In fact, I have even a greater respect for the Greek woman than for the Greek man. The Greek woman and the Greek Orthodox priest—*they* sustained the fighting spirit. For stubbornness, courage, recklessness, daring, there are no greater examples anywhere. No wonder Durrell wanted to fight with the Greeks. Who wouldn't prefer to fight beside a Bouboulina, for example, than with a gang of sickly, effeminate recruits from Oxford or Cambridge?

I made no English friends in Greece. I felt apologetic towards the Greeks whenever I was found in their company. The friends I made in Greece were Greek and I am proud of them, honored that they consider me a friend. I hope that the few Englishmen I knew in Greece will realize, when they read these lines, what I thought of their behavior. I hope they will consider me an enemy of their kind.

I'd rather talk about something more interesting—about Katsimbalis, for instance, about the visit to his home in Amaroussion one day towards twilight. Another marvelous day, another red letter day in my life! We had been asked to come early in order to watch the sunset. Stephanides had made a translation of some Greek poems—we were going to hear them in English. When we arrived Katsimbalis hadn't quite finished his nap. He was rather ashamed of being caught napping because he was always bragging about how little sleep he required. He came downstairs looking a bit foggy and pasty. He was talking as if to himself, making little futile gestures with his hands as if to get the damned spinet working. He was mumbling something about a word which he had remembered in his dream a few moments ago. He was always rummaging about in his brain for adequate English words and phrases to express some remarkable Greek image which he had just stumbled on in a book. Anyway, as I say, we had roused him from a sound sleep and he was moving about in a drugged way, muttering and gesturing like a man trying to

shake off the cob-webs which still enveloped him. His talk began on the fringe of this dream which he had not wholly shaken
clear of. To begin you begin anywhere, and since he had just
been dreaming he talked dream. The dream was unimportant,
forgotten in a moment, but the remembrance of the dream led
him back to the word which had been bothering him, which he
had been tracking down for days, so he said, and which was now
becoming clearer as he himself became clearer, as the cobwebs
fell away. The word, whatever it was, led to language and language led to honey and honey was good for one, as were other
things, *rezina* for example, especially *rezina*, good for the lungs,
good for the liver, good for anything that ailed you, especially
too much of it, which one should not do, not take too much of
it, but which he did anyway regardless of the doctor's orders,
particularly if it were a good *rezina* such as the one we had the
other night at the *taverna* in Piraeus. The young lamb was good
too, had we noticed? He made the gesture of licking his fingers,
wiped his mouth with the back of his hand, sniffed the air as
though to breathe again the aromatic smoke from the oven.
He paused a moment and looked about him, as if searching for
something with which to wet his tongue before going into the
monologue full tilt. Nobody said anything. Nobody dared to
interrupt now just as he was getting into his stride. The poems
were lying on the table; Seferiades was expected any moment
and the captain with him. I could feel that he was growing a bit
frantic inwardly, that he was making a rapid calculation to see if
there were time enough to get it off his chest before his friends
arrived. He was fluttering a bit, like a bird whose wing is caught.
He kept on mumbling and muttering, just to keep the engine going until he had decided on his direction. And then somehow,
without being aware of the transition, we were standing on the
aerial verandah overlooking the low hills, on one of which there
was a lone windmill, and Katsimbalis was in full flight, a spread
eagle performance about the clear atmosphere and the blue-
violet hues that descend with the twilight, about ascending and
descending varieties of monotony, about individualistic herbs

and trees, about exotic fruits and inland voyages, about thyme
and honey and the sap of the arbutus which makes one drunk,
about islanders and highlanders, about the men of the Peloponnesus, about the crazy Russian woman who got moonstruck one
night and threw off her clothes, how she danced about in the
moonlight without a stitch on while her lover ran to get a strait-
jacket. As he talked I was taking in for the first time with my
own eyes the true splendor of the Attic landscape, observing
with a growing exhilaration that here and there over the bare
brown sward, amidst anomalous and eccentric growths, men
and women, single, solitary figures, were strolling about in the
clear fading light, and for some reason they appeared to me as being very Greek, walking as no other people walk, making clear-
cut patterns in their ethereal meandering, patterns such as I had
seen earlier in the day on the vases in the museum. There are so
many ways of walking about and the best, in my opinion, is the
Greek way, because it is aimless, anarchic, thoroughly and dis-
cordantly human. And this walking about on the brown sward
amidst the eccentric, inelegant trees, the thick foliage flying like
hair stiff-brushed in the well of the distant mountains, blended
strangely with the Katsimbalistic monologue which I heard, di-
gested and silently communicated to the Asiatic loungers below who were fading softly now in the dimming light.... On the
high verandah in Amaroussion, just as the light from the other
worlds began to shed its brilliance, I caught the old and the new
Greece in their soft translucence and thus they remain in my
memory. I realized at that moment that there is no old or new,
only Greece, a world conceived and created in perpetuity. The
man who was talking had ceased to be of human size or proportions but had become a Colossus whose silhouette swooned
backwards and forwards with the deep droning rhythm of his
drug-laden phrases. He went on and on and on, unhurried, un-
ruffled, inexhaustible, inextinguishable, a voice that had taken
form and shape and substance, a figure that had outgrown its
human frame, a silhouette whose reverberations rumbled in the
depths of the distant mountainsides.

After about ten days of it in Athens I had a longing to return to Corfu. The war had begun, but since the Italians had announced their intention of remaining neutral I saw no reason why I should not return and make the most of the remaining days of Summer. When I arrived I found the Greeks still mobilized on the Albanian frontier, I had to get a pass from the police every time I went in or out of the town. Karamenaios was still patrolling the beach from his little reed hut at the edge of the water. Nicola would soon be returning to the village up in the mountains to open school. A wonderful period of solitude set in. I had nothing but time on my hands. Spiro sent his son Lillis out to give me some Greek lessons. Then Lillis went back to town and I was left alone. It was the first time in my life that I was truly alone. It was an experience which I enjoyed deeply. Towards evening I would stop by Nicola's house to chat with him a few minutes and hear about the war. After dinner Karamenaios would drop in. We had about fifty words with which to make lingual currency. We didn't even need that many, as I soon discovered. There are a thousand ways of talking and words don't help if the spirit is absent. Karamenaios and I were eager to talk. It made little difference to me whether we talked about the war or about knives and forks. Sometimes we discovered that a word or phrase which we had been using for days, he in English or I in Greek, meant something entirely different than we had thought it to mean. It made no difference. We understood one another even with the wrong words. I could learn five new words in an evening and forget six or eight during my sleep. The important thing was the warm handclasp, the light in the eyes, the grapes which we devoured in common, the glass we raised to our lips in sign of friendship. Now and then I would get excited and, using a melange of English, Greek, German, French, Choctaw, Eskimo, Swahili or any other tongue I felt would serve the purpose, using the chair, the table, the spoon, the lamp, the bread knife, I would enact for him a fragment of my life in New York, Paris, London, Chula Vista, Canarsie, Hackensack or in some place I had never been or some place I had been in a dream or when lying asleep on the operating table. Sometimes I felt so good, so versatile and acrobatic, that I would stand on the table and sing in some unknown language or hop from the table to the commode and from the commode to the staircase or swing from the rafters, anything to entertain him, keep him amused, make him roll from side to side with laughter. I was considered an old man in the village because of my bald pate and fringe of white hair. Nobody had ever seen an old man cut up the way I did. "The old man is going for a swim," they would say. "The old man is taking the boat out." Always "the old man." If a storm came up and they knew I was out in the middle of the pond they would send someone out to see that "the old man" got in safely. If I decided to take a jaunt through the hills Karamenaios would offer to accompany me so that no harm would come to me. If I got stranded somewhere I had only to announce that I was an American and at once a dozen hands were ready to help me. I would set out in the morning and look for new coves and inlets in which to swim. There was never a soul about. I was like Robinson Crusoe on the island of Tobago. For hours at a stretch I would lie in the sun doing nothing, thinking of nothing. To keep the mind empty is a feat, a very healthful feat too. To be silent the whole day long, see no newspaper, hear no radio, listen to no gossip, be thoroughly and completely lazy, thoroughly and completely indifferent to the fate of the world is the finest medicine a man can give himself. The book-learning gradually dribbles away; problems melt and dissolve; ties are gently severed; thinking, when you deign to indulge in it, becomes very primitive; the body becomes a new and wonderful instrument; you look at plants or stones or fish with different eyes; you wonder what people are struggling to accomplish by their frenzied activities; you know there is a war on but you haven't the faintest idea what it's about or why people should enjoy killing one another; you look at a place like Albania—it was constantly staring me in the eyes—and you say to yourself, yesterday it was Greek, to-day it's Italian, to-morrow it may be German or Japanese, and you let it be anything it chooses to be. When you're right with yourself it doesn't matter what flag is flying over your head or who owns what or whether you speak

English or Monongahela. The absence of newspapers, the absence of news about what men are doing in different parts of the world to make life more livable or unlivable is the greatest single boon. If we could just eliminate newspapers a great advance would be made, I am sure of it. Newspapers engender lies, hatred, greed, envy, suspicion, fear, malice. We don't need the truth as it is dished up to us in the daily papers. We need peace and solitude and idleness. If we could all go on strike and honestly disavow all interest in what our neighbor is doing we might get a new lease of life. We might learn to do without telephones and radios and newspapers, without machines of any kind, without factories, without mills, without mines, without explosives, without battleships, without politicians, without lawyers, without canned goods, without gadgets, without razor blades even or cellophane or cigarettes or money. This is a pipe dream, I know. People only go on strike for better working conditions, better wages, better opportunities to become something other than they are.

As the Fall came on the rains set in. It was almost impossible to climb up the steep goat path back of the house which led to the highway. After a severe storm there would be wash-outs and all the roads would be blocked by the debris of rocks and trees caused by the landslides. I was marooned for days on end. One day Nancy arrived unexpectedly to get some household belongings. She was returning to Athens by the same boat, that very afternoon. I decided impulsively to return with her.

It was dry in Athens, and unexpectedly hot. It was as though we were going back to Summer again. Now and then the wind blew down from the encircling mountains and then it was as chill as a knife blade. Mornings I would often walk to the Acropolis. I like the base of the Acropolis better than the Acropolis itself. I like the tumbledown shacks, the confusion, the erosion, the anarchic character of the landscape. The archaeologists have ruined the place; they have laid waste big tracts of land in order to uncover a mess of ancient relics which will be hidden away in museums. The whole base of the Acropolis resembles more and

more a volcanic crater in which the loving hands of the archaeologists have laid out cemeteries of art. The tourist comes and
looks down at these ruins, these scientifically created lava beds,
with a moist eye. The live Greek walks about unnoticed or else
is regarded as an interloper. Meanwhile the new city of Athens
covers almost the entire valley, is groping its way up the flanks of
the surrounding mountains. For a country of only seven million
inhabitants it is something of a phenomenon, the city of Athens.
It is still in the throes of birth: it is awkward, confused, clumsy,
unsure of itself; it has all the diseases of childhood and some of
the melancholy and desolation of adolescence. But it has chosen
a magnificent site in which to rear itself; in the sunlight it gleams
like a jewel; at night it sparkles with a million twinkling lights
which seem to be switching on and off with lightning-like speed.
It is a city of startling atmospheric effects: it has not dug itself
into the earth—it floats in a constantly changing light, beats
with a chromatic rhythm. One is impelled to keep walking, to
move on towards the mirage which is ever retreating. When one
comes to the edge, to the great wall of mountains, the light becomes even more intoxicating; one feels as if he could bound up
the side of the mountain in a few giant strides, and then—why
then, if one did get to the top, one would race like mad along
the smooth spine and jump clear into the sky, one clear head-
long flight into the blue and Amen forever. Along the Sacred
Way, from Daphni to the sea, I was on the point of madness several times. I actually did start running up the hillside only to stop
midway, terror-stricken, wondering what had taken possession
of me. On one side are stones and shrubs which stand out with
microscopic clarity; on the other are trees such as one sees in
Japanese prints, trees flooded with light, intoxicated, coryphan-
tic trees which must have been planted by the gods in moments
of drunken exaltation. One should not race along the Sacred
Way in a motor car —it is sacrilege. One should walk, walk as
the men of old walked, and allow one's whole being to become
flooded with light. This is not a Christian highway: it was made
by the feet of devout pagans on their way to initiation at Eleu-

sis. There is no suffering, no martyrdom, no flagellation of the flesh connected with this processional artery. Everything here speaks now, as it did centuries ago, of illumination, of blinding, joyous illumination. Light acquires a transcendental quality: it is not the light of the Mediterranean alone, it is something more, something unfathomable, something holy. Here the light penetrates directly to the soul, opens the doors and windows of the heart, makes one naked, exposed, isolated in a metaphysical bliss which makes everything clear without being known. No analysis can go on in this light: here the neurotic is either instantly healed or goes mad. The rocks themselves are quite mad: they have been lying for centuries exposed to this divine illumination: they lie very still and quiet, nestling amid dancing colored shrubs in a bloodstained soil, but they are mad, I say, and to touch them is to risk losing one's grip on everything which once seemed firm, solid and unshakeable. One must glide through this gully with extreme caution, naked, alone, and devoid of all Christian humbug. One must throw off two thousand years of ignorance and superstition, of morbid, sickly subterranean living and lying. One must come to Eleusis stripped of the barnacles which have accumulated from centuries of lying in stagnant waters. At Eleusis one realizes, if never before, that there is no salvation in becoming adapted to a world which is crazy. At Eleusis one becomes adapted to the cosmos. Outwardly Eleusis may seem broken, disintegrated with the crumbled past; actually Eleusis is still intact and it is we who are broken, dispersed, crumbling to dust. Eleusis lives, lives eternally in the midst of a dying world.

The man who has caught this spirit of eternality which is everywhere in Greece and who has embedded it in his poems is George Seferiades, whose pen name is Seferis. I know his work only from translation, but even if I had never read his poetry I would say this is the man who is destined to transmit the flame. Seferiades is more Asiatic than any of the Greeks I met; he is from Smyrna originally but has lived abroad for many years. He is languorous, suave, vital and capable of surprising feats of

strength and agility. He is the arbiter and reconciler of conflict-
ing schools of thought and ways of life. He asks innumerable
questions in a polyglot language; he is interested in all forms of
cultural expression and seeks to abstract and assimilate what is
genuine and fecundating in all epochs. He is passionate about
his own country, his own people, not in a hidebound chauvinistic way but as a result of patient discovery following upon years
of absence abroad. This passion for country is a special peculiar-
ity of the intellectual Greek who has lived abroad. In other peoples I have found it distasteful, but in the Greek I find it justifiable, and not only justifiable, but thrilling, inspiring. I remember
going with Seferiades one afternoon to look at a piece of land on
which he thought he might build himself a bungalow. There was
nothing extraordinary about the place—it was even a bit shabby
and forlorn, I might say. Or rather it *was,* at first sight. I never had
a chance to consolidate my first fleeting impression; it changed
right under my eyes as he led me about like an electrified jelly-
fish from spot to spot, rhapsodizing on herbs, flowers, shrubs,
rocks, clay, slopes, declivities, coves, inlets and so on. Everything
he looked at was Greek in a way that he had never known before leaving his country. He could look at a headland and read
into it the history of the Medes, the Persians, the Dorians, the
Minoans, the Atlanteans. He could also read into it some fragments of the poem which he would write in his head on the way
home while plying me with questions about the New World.
He was attracted by the Sibylline character of everything which
met his eye. He had a way of looking forwards and backwards, of
making the object of his contemplation revolve and show forth
its multiple aspects. When he talked about a thing or a person
or an experience he caressed it with his tongue. Sometimes he
gave me the impression of being a wild boar which had broken
its tusks in furious onslaughts born of love and ecstasy. In his
voice there was a bruised quality as if the object of his love, his
beloved Greece, had awkwardly and unwittingly mangled the
shrill notes of ululation. The mellifluous Asiatic warbler had
more than once been floored by an unexpected thunderbolt;

his poems were becoming more and more gem-like, more compact, compressed, scintillating and revelatory. His native flexibility was responding to the cosmic laws of curvature and finitude. He had ceased going out in all directions: his lines were making the encircling movement of embrace. He had begun to ripen into the universal poet—by passionately rooting himself into the soil of his people. Wherever there is life to-day in Greek art it is based on this Antaean gesture, this passion which transmits itself from heart to feet, creating strong roots which transform the body into a tree of potent beauty. This cultural transmutation is also evidenced in a physical way by the vast work of reclamation which is going on throughout the country. The Turks, in their fervid desire to desolate Greece, converted the land into a desert and a graveyard; since their emancipation the Greeks have been struggling to reforest the land. The goat has now become the national enemy. He will be dislodged as the Turk was dislodged, in time. He is the symbol of poverty and helplessness. Trees, more trees, that is the cry. The tree brings water, fodder, cattle, produce; the tree brings shade, leisure, song, brings poets, painters, legislators, visionaries. Greece is now, bare and lean as a wolf though she be, the only Paradise in Europe. What a place it will be when it is restored to its pristine verdure exceeds the imagination of man to-day. Anything may happen when this focal spot blazes forth with new life. A revivified Greece can very conceivably alter the whole destiny of Europe. Greece does not need archaeologists—she needs arboriculturists. A verdant Greece may give hope to a world now eaten away by white-heart rot.

My talks with Seferiades really began on the high verandah at Amaroussion when, taking me by the arm, he walked me back and forth in the gathering dusk. Every time I met him he came to me with his whole being, wrapping it around my arm with warmth and tenderness. If I visited him at his chambers it was the same thing: he would open all the doors and windows leading to his heart. Usually he would put on his hat and accompany me to my hotel; it was not just a polite gesture, it was an act of friendship, a demonstration of an enduring love. I shall remember Seferiades and all my Greek friends for this quality which is now so rare among men. I shall remember his sister Jeanne too, and other Greek women whom I met, because of their queenliness. It is a quality we scarcely ever meet with in the modern woman. Like the warm friendliness of the men this quality which all Greek women share to a greater or less degree is the counterpart, or shall I say the corresponding human virtue, which goes with the supernal light. One would have to be a toad, a snail, or a slug not to be affected by this radiance which emanates from the human heart as well as from the heavens. Wherever you go in Greece the people open up like flowers. Cynical-minded people will say that it is because Greece is a small country, because they are eager to have visitors, and so on. I don't believe it. I have been in a few small countries which left quite the opposite impression upon me. And as I said once before, Greece is not a small country—it is impressively vast. No country I have visited has given me such a sense of grandeur. Size is not created by mileage always. In a way which it is beyond the comprehension of my fellow countrymen to grasp Greece is infinitely larger than the United States. Greece could swallow both the United States and Europe. Greece is a little like China or India. It is a world of illusion. And the Greek himself is everywhere, like the Chinaman again. What is Greek in him does not rub off with his ceaseless voyaging. He does not leave little particles of himself distributed all over the lot, as the American does, for example. When the Greek leaves a place he leaves a hole. The American leaves behind him a litter of junk—shoe laces, collar buttons, razor blades, petroleum tins, vaseline jars and so on. The Chinese coolies, as I also said somewhere before, actually feed on the garbage which the Americans throw overboard when they are in port. The poor Greek walks around in the remnants dropped by rich visitors from all parts of the world; he is a true internationalist, disdaining nothing which is made by human hands, not even the leaky tubs discarded by the British mercantile marine. To try to instill in him a sense of national pride, to ask him to become chauvinistic about national industries, fisheries and so forth seems to be a piece of absurdity. What difference does it make to a man whose heart is filled with light whose clothes he is wearing or whether these clothes be of the latest model or pre-war in design? I have seen Greeks walking about in the most ludicrous and abominable garb imaginable—straw hat from the year 1900, billiard cloth vest with pearl buttons, discarded British ulster, pale dungarees, busted umbrella, hair shirt, bare feet, hair matted and twisted—a make-up which even a Kaffir would disdain, and yet, I say it sincerely and deliberately, I would a thousand times rather be that poor Greek than an American millionaire. I remember the old keeper of the ancient fortress at Nauplia. He had done twenty years in that same prison for murder. He was one of the most aristocratic beings I ever met. His face was positively radiant. The pittance on which he was trying to live would not keep a dog, his clothes were in tatters, his prospects were nil. He showed us a tiny patch of earth he had cleared near the rampart where he hoped next year to grow a few stalks of corn. If the government would give him about three cents more a day he would just about be able to pull through. He begged us, if we had any influence, to speak to one of the officials for him. He wasn't bitter, he wasn't melancholy, he wasn't morbid. He had killed a man in anger and he had done twenty years for it; he would do it again, he said, if the same situation arose. He had no remorse, no guilt. He was a marvelous old fellow, stout as an oak, gay, hearty, insouciant. Just three cents more a day and everything would be jake. That was all that was on his mind. I envy him. If I had my choice between being the president of a rubber tire company in America or the prison keeper of the old fortress at Nauplia I would prefer to be the prison keeper, even without the additional three cents. I would take the twenty years in jail too, as part of the bargain. I would prefer to be a murderer with a clear conscience, walking about in tatters and waiting for next year's crop of corn, than the president of the most successful industrial corporation in America. No business magnate ever wore such a benign and radiant expression as this miserable Greek. Of course there is this to remember—the Greek only killed one man, and that in righteous anger, whereas the successful American businessman is murdering thousands of innocent men, women and children in his sleep every day of his life. Here nobody can have a clear conscience: we are all part of a vast interlocking murdering machine. There a murderer can look noble and saintly, even though he live like a dog.

Nauplia. . . . Nauplia is a seaport directly south of Corinth on a peninsula where are located Tiryns and Epidaurus. You can look across the water and see Argos. Above Argos, going north towards Corinth, lies Mycenae. Draw a ring about these places and you mark off one of the most hoary, legendary areas in Greece. I had touched the Peloponnesus before, at Patras, but this is the other side, the magical side. How I got to Nauplia is a long story. I must go back a bit.

I am in Athens. Winter is coming on. People are asking me— have you been to Delphi, have you been to San Turini, have you been to Lesbos or Samos or Poros? I have been practically nowhere, except back and forth to Corfu. One day I had been as far as Mandra, which is past Eleusis on the way to Megara. Fortunately the road was blocked and we had to turn back. I say fortunately because on that day, if we had gone another few miles, I would have lost my head completely. In another way I was doing a great deal of traveling; people came to me at the cafés and poured out their journeys to me; the captain was always returning from a new trajectory; Seferiades was always writing a new poem which went back deep into the past and forward as far as the seventh root race; Katsimbalis would take me on his monologues to Mt. Athos, to Pelion and Ossa, to Leonidion and Monemvasia; Durrell would set my mind whirling with Pythagorean adventures; a little Welshman, just back from Persia, would drag me over the high plateaus and deposit me in Samarkand where I would meet the headless horseman called Death. All the Englishmen I met were always coming back from somewhere, some island, some monastery, some ancient ruin, some place of mystery. I was so bewildered by all the opportunities lying before me that I was paralyzed.

Then one day Seferiades and Katsimbalis introduced me to the painter Ghika. I saw a new Greece, the quintessential Greece which the artist had abstracted from the muck and confusion of time, of place, of history. I got a bifocal slant on this world which was now making me giddy with names, dates, legends. Ghika has placed himself in the center of all time, in that self-perpetuating Greece which has no borders, no limits, no age. Ghika's canvases are as fresh and clean, as pure and naked of all pretense, as the sea and light which bathes the dazzling islands. Ghika is a seeker after light and truth: his paintings go beyond the Greek world. It was Ghika's painting which roused me from my bedazzled stupor. A week or so later we all boarded the boat at Piraeus to go to Hydra where Ghika had his ancestral home. Seferiades and Katsimbalis were jubilant: they had not had a holiday in ages. It was late Fall, which means that the weather was beautifully mild. Towards noon we came within sight of the island of Poros. We had been having a bite on deck—one of those impromptu meals which Katsimbalis loves to put away at any hour of the day or night, when he is in good fettle. I suppose I'll never again experience the warmth of affection which surrounded me that morning as we embarked on our journey. Everybody was talking at once, the wine was flowing, the food was being replenished, the sun which had been veiled came out strong, the boat was rocking gently, the war was on but forgotten, the sea was there but the shore too, the goats were clambering about, the lemon groves were in sight and the madness which is in their fragrance had already seized us and drawn us tightly together in a frenzy of self-surrender.

I don't know which affected me more deeply—the story of the lemon groves just opposite us or the sight of Poros itself when suddenly I realized that we were sailing through the streets. If there is one dream which I like above all others it is that of sailing on land. Coming into Poros gives the illusion of the deep dream. Suddenly the land converges on all sides and the boat is squeezed into a narrow strait from which there seems to be no egress. The men and women of Poros are hanging out of the windows, just above your head. You pull in right under their friendly nostrils, as though for a shave and haircut en route. The loungers on the quay are walking with the same speed as the boat; they can walk faster than the boat if they choose to quicken their pace. The island revolves in cubistic planes, one of walls and windows, one of rocks and goats, one of stiff-blown trees and shrubs, and so on. Yonder, where the mainland curves like a whip, lie the wild lemon groves and there in the Spring young and old go mad from the fragrance of sap and blossom. You enter the harbor of Poros swaying and swirling, a gentle idiot tossed about amidst masts and nets in a world which only the painter knows and which he has made live again because like you, when he first saw this world, he was drunk and happy and carefree. To sail slowly through the streets of Poros is to recapture the joy of passing through the neck of the womb. It is a joy too deep almost to be remembered. It is a kind of numb idiot's delight which produces legends such as that of the birth of an island out of a foundering ship. The ship, the passage, the revolving walls, the gentle undulating tremor under the belly of the boat, the dazzling light, the green snake-like curve of the shore, the beards hanging down over your scalp from the inhabitants suspended above you, all these and the palpitant breath of friendship, sympathy, guidance, envelop and entrance you until you are blown out like a star fulfilled and your heart with its molten smithereens scattered far and wide. It is now, as I write this, just about the same time of day some few months later. The clock and the calendar say so, at any rate. In point of truth it is aeons since I passed through that narrow strait. It will never happen again. Ordinarily I would be sad at the thought, but I am not now. There is every reason to be sad at this moment: all the premonitions which I have had for ten years are coming true. This is one of the lowest moments in the history of the human race. There is no sign of hope on the horizon. The whole world is involved in slaugh-

ter and bloodshed. I repeat—*I am not sad.* Let the world have
its bath of blood—I will cling to Poros. Millions of years may
pass and I may come back again and again on one planet or another, as human, as devil, as archangel (I care not how, which,
what or when), but my feet will never leave that boat, my eyes
will never close on that scene, my friends will never disappear.
That was a moment which endures, which survives world wars,
which outlasts the life of the planet Earth itself. If I should ever
attain the fulfillment which the Buddhists speak of, if I should
ever have the choice of attaining Nirvana or remaining behind
to watch over and guide those to come, I say now let me remain
behind, let me hover as a gentle spirit above the roofs of Poros and look down upon the voyager with a smile of peace and
good cheer. I can see the whole human race straining through
the neck of the bottle here, searching for egress into the world of
light and beauty. May they come, may they disembark, may they
stay and rest awhile in peace. And on a glad day let them push
on, let them cross the narrow strait, on, on, a few more miles—
to Epidaurus, the very seat of tranquillity, the world center of
the healing art.

Some days intervened before I saw with my own eyes the still,
healing splendor of Epidaurus. During that interval I almost lost
my life, but of that I will speak in a moment. Our destination was
Hydra where Ghika and his wife awaited us. Hydra is almost a
bare rock of an island and its population, made up almost exclu-
sively of seamen, is rapidly dwindling. The town, which clusters
about the harbor in the form of an amphitheatre, is immaculate.
There are only two colors, blue and white, and the white is white-
washed every day, down to the cobblestones in the street. The
houses are even more cubistically arranged than at Poros. Aes-
thetically it is perfect, the very epitome of that flawless anarchy
which supersedes, because it includes and goes beyond, all the
formal arrangements of the imagination. This purity, this wild
and naked perfection of Hydra, is in great part due to the spirit of
the men who once dominated the island. For centuries the men
of Hydra were bold, buccaneering spirits: the island produced

nothing but heroes and emancipators. The least of them was an admiral at heart, if not in fact. To recount the exploits of the men of Hydra would be to write a book about a race of madmen; it would mean writing the word DARING across the firmament in letters of fire.

Hydra is a rock which rises out of the sea like a huge loaf of petrified bread. It is the bread turned to stone which the artist receives as reward for his labors when he first catches sight of the promised land. After the uterine illumination comes the ordeal of rock out of which must be born the spark which is to fire the world. I speak in broad, swift images because to move from place to place in Greece is to become aware of the stirring, fateful drama of the race as it circles from paradise to paradise. Each halt is a stepping stone along a path marked out by the gods. They are stations of rest, of prayer, of meditation, of deed, of sacrifice, of transfiguration. At no point along the way is it marked FINIS. The very rocks, and nowhere on earth has God been so lavish with them as in Greece, are symbols of life eternal. In Greece the rocks are eloquent: men may go dead but the rocks never. At a place like Hydra, for example, one knows that when a man dies he becomes part of his native rock. But this rock is a living rock, a divine wave of energy suspended in time and space, creating a pause of long or short duration in the endless melody. Hydra was entered as a pause in the musical score of creation by an expert calligrapher. It is one of those divine pauses which permit the musician, when he resumes the melody, to go forth again in a totally new direction. At this point one may as well throw the compass away. To move towards creation does one need a compass? Having touched this rock I lost all sense of earthly direction. What happened to me from this point on is in the nature of progression, not direction. There was no longer any goal beyond—I became one with the Path. Each station thenceforth marked a progression into a new spiritual latitude and longitude. Mycenae was not greater than Tiryns nor Epidaurus more beautiful than Mycenae: each was different in a degree for which I had lost the circle of comparison. There is only one analogy I can make to explain the nature of this illumi-

nating voyage which began at Poros and ended at Tripolis perhaps two months later. I must refer the reader to the ascension
of Seraphita, as it was glimpsed by her devout followers. It was a
voyage into the light. The earth became illuminated by her own
inner light. At Mycenae I walked over the incandescent dead; at
Epidaurus I felt a stillness so intense that for a fraction of a second I heard the great heart of the world beat and I understood
the meaning of pain and sorrow; at Tiryns I stood in the shadow
of the Cyclopean man and felt the blaze of that inner eye which
has now become a sickly gland; at Argos the whole plain was a
fiery mist in which I saw the ghosts of our own American Indians and greeted them in silence. I moved about in a detached
way, my feet flooded with the earthly glow. I am at Corinth in
a rose light, the sun battling the moon, the earth turning slowly
with its fat ruins, wheeling in light like a waterwheel reflected in
a still pond. I am at Arachova when the eagle soars from its nest
and hangs poised above the boiling cauldron of earth, stunned
by the brilliant pattern of colors which dress the heaving abyss. I
am at Leonidion at sundown and behind the heavy pall of marsh
vapor looms the dark portal of the Inferno where the shades of
bats and snakes and lizards come to rest, and perhaps to pray.
In each place I open a new vein of experience, a miner digging
deeper into the earth, approaching the heart of the star which
is not yet extinguished. The light is no longer solar or lunar; it
is the starry light of the planet to which man has given life. The
earth is alive to its innermost depths; at the center it is a sun in
the form of a man crucified. The sun bleeds on its cross in the
hidden depths. The sun is man struggling to emerge towards
another light. From light to light, from calvary to calvary. The
earth song....

I stayed at Hydra a few days during which time I ran up and
down thousands of steps, visited the home of several admi-
rals, made votive offerings to the saints who protect the island,
said prayers for the dead, the halt and the blind in the little chapel attached to Ghika's house, played ping pong, drank champagne, cognac, *ouzo* and *rezina* at the Old Curiosity Shop, sat
up with a bottle of whiskey talking to Ghika about the monks

in Tibet, began the log of the Immaculate Conception which I finished for Seferiades at Delphi—*and* listened to Katsimbalis, to the Ninth Symphony of his travails and transgressions. Madame Hadji-Kyriakos, Ghika's wife, laid a wonderful table; we rose from the table like wine casks without legs. From the terrace, which was distinctly Oriental in flavor, we could look out on the sea in drunken stupefaction. The house had forty rooms, some of which were buried deep in the earth. The big rooms were like the saloon of an ocean liner; the little rooms were like cool dungeons fitted up by temperamental pirates. The maids were of divine origin and one of them, at least, was descended directly from the Erectheum though she bore the name of a sacred cereal.

One evening, while scaling the broad steps which led to the tip of the island, Katsimbalis began talking of madness. A mist was coming up from the sea and all I could distinguish of him was the huge head which floated above me like the auric egg itself. He was talking of cities, of how he had gotten a mania for Haussmannizing the big cities of the world. He would take the map of London say, or Constantinople, and after the most painstaking study would draw up a new plan of the city, to suit himself. Some cities he rearranged so thoroughly that later he had difficulty finding his way about—I mean in his own imaginative plan. Naturally a great many monuments had to be torn down and new statues, by unheard-of men, erected in their place. While working on Constantinople, for example, he would be seized by a desire to alter Shanghai. By day he would be rebuilding Constantinople and in his sleep he would be remodelling Shanghai. It was confusing, to say the least. Having reconstructed one city he would go on to another and then another. There was no letup to it. The walls were papered with the plans for these new cities. Knowing most of these cities by heart he would often revisit them in his dreams; and since he had altered them throughout, even to such a detail as changing the names of the streets, the result was that he would pass sleepless nights trying to extricate himself and, on awakening, had difficulty recovering his own identity. It was a kind of megalomania, he thought, a sort of glorified constructivism which was a pathologic hangover from his Peloponnesian heritage. We developed the subject further at Tiryns when examining the Cyclopean walls, and again at Mycenae, and for the last time at Nauplia, after climbing the 999 steps leading to the top of the fortress. I came to the conclusion that the Peloponnesians were a race of builders whose spiritual development had been arrested at a formative period and who, consequently, had gone on building automatically, like heavy-handed, heavy-footed sleepwalkers. Nobody knows what these people were trying to create in their sleep; we know only that they preferred to work with the most untractable material. Not a single poet emerged from this race of stone builders. They produced some marvelous "assassinators," legislators and military leaders. When the curtain fell on the scene the house was not only dark but empty. The soil was so saturated with blood that even to-day the crops from the rich plains and valleys are superlatively luxuriant.

When we took the boat for Spetsai Katsimbalis was still talking. The two of us were going on alone. Spetsai was only a few hours away. As I say, Katsimbalis was still talking. As we neared our destination it began to sprinkle a bit. We got into the small boat and were rowed ashore, Katsimbalis remarking that the place looked strange, that perhaps we had pulled in to the opposite side of the island. We got out of the small boat and walked along the quay. Suddenly we were standing in front of a war monument and to my surprise Katsimbalis began to laugh. "I'm crazy," he said, "this isn't Spetsai, this is Ermioni—we're on the mainland." A gendarme came over and spoke to us. He recommended us to go to the other side of the island and there catch a small boat for Spetsai. There was a rattle-trap of a Ford which served as a bus waiting for us. It already had six passengers in it but we managed to squeeze in anyway. As we started off it began to rain. We went through the town of Kranidion at lightning-like speed, half of the car on the sidewalk and the other half in the gutter; we made a sharp turn and descended the mountainside with the engine shut off. The car was falling apart and the young pig on which our feet were resting was squealing like a flea-bitten lunatic. When we got to the little port of Portochelli the rain was coming down in torrents. We waded through mud ankle-deep to get to the tavern at the waterfront. A typical Mediterranean storm was raging. When we inquired if we could get a small boat the card-players looked at us as if we were crazy. We said—"After the storm blows over." They shook their heads. "It will last all day," they said, "and maybe all night." We watched the storm for an hour or more, bored stiff by the prospect of remaining here all night. Wasn't there someone, we inquired, who would take a chance when the storm abated a bit? We let it be known that we would pay double or treble the usual tariff. "By the way," I asked Katsimbalis, "what is the usual price?" He inquired of the barkeeper. "A hundred drachmas," he said, if we were to pay three hundred drachmas that would be handsome. Three hundred drachmas is about two dollars. "You mean that someone would be foolish enough to risk his life for two dollars?" I asked. "What about *us*?" he answered, and then suddenly I realized that it might be a foolhardy thing to tempt someone to sail us over that sea. We sat down and talked it over. "Are you sure you want to risk it?" Katsimbalis asked. "What about you?" I parried. "We may never make it," he said, "it's a gamble. Anyway, it would be a romantic death—*for you*." And then he started to talk about all the English poets who had been drowned in the Mediterranean. "The hell with it," I said, "if you'll come along I'll risk it. Where's that guy who was going to take us?" We asked where the fellow had gone to. "He's gone to take a little nap," they said, "he didn't get any sleep all night." We tried to find another fellow, but there was no one foolish enough to listen to our pleas. "Can you swim?" asked Katsimbalis. The thought of trying to swim in that boiling sea took some of the steam out of me. "Better wait a while," he added. "No use getting drowned immediately." An old tar came up to us and tried to dissuade us from going. "Very treacherous weather," he said. "It may let up for a little while, but not long enough to reach Spetsai. Better stay here overnight. Nobody will take you out in this sea." Katsimbalis looked at me as though to say—"Did you hear that? these fellows know what they're talking about."

A few minutes later the sun came out and with it appeared the fellow who had been taking a nap. We ran out to greet him but he motioned us back with his hand. We stood at the doorway and watched him bail out the boat and hoist the sails. It seemed to take a devil of a time; meanwhile the clouds had gathered again and there came a crack of lightning and a splash of rain. The fellow ducked down into the hatch. We stood and watched the sky some more. It was raining pitchforks again. When it seemed as if all were hopeless suddenly the fellow came up on deck and beckoned to us. The rain had thinned out and the clouds back of us were breaking. "Is it all right to take a chance now?" we asked, none too sure of ourselves. The fellow shrugged his shoulders. "What does he mean by that?" I inquired. To this Katsimbalis also shrugged his shoulders, adding with a malicious smile— "That means that if we're crazy enough to risk our lives he is too." We jumped in and stood up forward, holding on to the mast. "Why don't you go down below?" I said. Katsimbalis didn't want to go below, it made him seasick. "Well, you'll get seasick anyway," I said. "We're in for it now." We had already pushed off and were running close to shore. As we got near the open water a violent gust of wind hit us squarely. The Greek left the tiller to pull down the sails. "Look at that," said Katsimbalis, "these fellows are mad." We were skirting dangerously close to the rocks by the time the fellow had pulled in the sails. The sea was running high—ahead of us was a seething mass of whitecaps. I began to realize just how mad it was when I saw the huge troughs into which we were plunging with terrifying vertigo.

We looked back instinctively at the helmsman to catch a ray of hope from his countenance, but his expression was impassive. "He's probably mad," said Katsimbalis, and with that a wave broke clean over us and drenched us to the skin. The ducking had an exhilarating effect upon us. We were even more exhilarated when we caught sight of a small yacht pulling up on us.

It was only a trifle bigger than our own *benzina* and had about the same speed. Side by side, like two sea horses, the little boats tossed and plunged. I would never have believed that a frail boat could weather such a sea. When we slid down to the bottom of a trough the oncoming wave loomed above us like a white-toothed monster waiting to fall on us belly first. The sky was like the back of a mirror, showing a dull molten glow where the sun vainly strove to beat through. Toward the horizon the lightning was zigzagging back and forth. Now the waves began to strike us from all directions. It took all our strength to hold on to the mast with two hands. We could see Spetsai clearly, the buildings looking ghastly, as if they had vomited up their insides. Oddly enough, neither of us had any fear. I didn't know till afterwards that Katsimbalis had a dread of the sea, being a highlander and not an islander. His face was radiant. Now and then he yelled—"*Homeric*, what?" Good old Katsimbalis! Crazy like all the Greeks. Terrified of the sea he was and yet he had never said a word about it. "We'll have a good meal," he yelled, "if we make it." He had hardly gotten the words out of his mouth when a snarling, whistling spout of water gave us such a clout that I thought we were done for. But the boat was like a cork. Nothing could keel her over or push her down. We looked at each other knowingly, as if to say, "Well, if she weathered that she'll weather anything." We became exultant and shouted crazy words of encouragement as if it were a horse we were riding. "Are you all right back there?" Katsimbalis shouted over his shoulder, hardly daring to look back for fear he would find the man overboard. "*Malista*," came the reply. What a beautiful word for yes, I thought to myself. And then I thought of the first Greek phrase I had learned—"*ligo nero, se para kalo*" ... a little water, please. Water, water ... it was running out of my eyes and ears, down my neck, into my belly-button, between my toes. "Bad for the rheumatism," shouted Katsimbalis. "Not too bad," I yelled, "you'll have a good appetite."

There was a little crowd at the quay when we landed. The gendarme eyed us suspiciously. What had brought us to a place like Spetsai in such weather ... why hadn't we come on the big boat? What was our business? The fact that Katsimbalis was a Greek and had gotten off the big boat by mistake made things look even more suspicious. And what was the crazy American doing—there are no tourists coming to Spetsai in the winter. However, after a few grunts he trundled off. We went to a little hotel nearby and wrote our names in the big book. The proprietor, who was slightly goofy but sympathetic, looked at the names and then said to Katsimbalis—"What regiment were you in during the war? Aren't you my captain?" and he gave his name and the name of the regiment. When we had changed our clothes John the proprietor was waiting for us; he had his little boy by the hand and a baby in his arm. "My children, captain," he said proudly. Mister John steered us to a *taverna* where we could get some excellent fried fish and some *rezina*. On the way he told us in English about his fruit store in New York, at one of the subway entrances uptown. I knew that subway entrance very well because I had once sold a fur-lined coat given to me by a Hindu to a taxi-driver for ten cents one winter's morning at three a.m. just outside Mister John's fruit store. Mister John, who was a little goofy, as I said, found it hard to believe that any native-born American would be so crazy as to do a thing like that. While we were jabbering away in English a fat fellow who had been listening attentively at the next table suddenly turned round and said to me with an impeccable upstate accent—"Where are you from, stranger? I'm from Buffalo." He came over and joined us. His name was Nick. "How is the good old U.S.A.?" he said, ordering another pint of *rezina*. "Jesus, what I wouldn't give to be back there now." I looked at his clothes, obviously American, obviously expensive. "What did you do there?" I asked. "I was a bookie," he said. "You like this suit? I've got seven more of them at the house. Yeah, I brought a supply of everything along. You can't get anything decent here—you see what a dump it is. Jesus, did I have a swell time in Buffalo. When are you going back?" When I told him that I had no intention of returning he gave me a strange smile. "Funny," he said, "you like it here and I like it there. I wish we could swap passports. I'd give a lot to have an American passport right now."

When I awoke the next morning Katsimbalis had already left the hotel, Mister John said I would find him down the road by the Anargyros College. I swallowed Mister John's greasy breakfast and took the road along the waterfront towards the college. The college, as well as most everything else of importance in Spetsai, was donated to the community by the cigarette king. I stood at the entrance admiring the buildings and as I turned to go I saw Katsimbalis approaching with a great flourish of the cane. He had in tow a friend of his—Kyrios Ypsilon, I shall call him, to be discreet. Kyrios Ypsilon was a political exile, I discovered; he had been transferred to Spetsai from some other island because of his poor health. I liked Kyrios Ypsilon at once, the moment I shook hands with him. He spoke French, not knowing any English, but with a German accent. He was as Greek as Greek can be, but he had been educated in Germany. What I liked about him was his keen, buoyant nature, his directness, his passion for flowers and for metaphysics. He escorted us to his room in a big deserted house, the very house in which the famous Bouboulina had been shot. While we chatted he brought out a tin tub and filled it with warm water for his bath. On a shelf near his bed he had a collection of books. I glanced at the titles, which were in five or six languages. There were *The Divine Comedy, Faust, Tom Jones,* several volumes of Aristotle, *The Plumed Serpent,* Plato's Dialogues, two or three volumes of Shakespeare, and so on. A most excellent diet for a prolonged siege. "So you do know a little English?" I said, Oh yes, he had studied it in Germany, but he couldn't speak it very well. "I would like to read Walt Whitman one day," he added quickly. He was sitting in the tub soaping and scrubbing himself vigorously. "To keep up the morale," he said, though neither of us had made any remark about the bath. "One has to have regular habits," he went on, "or else you go to pieces. I do a lot of walking, so that I can sleep at night. The nights are long, you know, when you are not free."

"He's a great fellow," said Katsimbalis, as we were walking

back to the hotel. "The women are crazy about him. He has an interesting theory about love ... get him to talk to you about it sometime."

Talking of love Bouboulina's name came up. "How is it we don't hear more about Bouboulina?" I asked. "She sounds like another Joan of Arc."

"Huh," he snorted, stopping dead in his tracks, "what do you know about Joan of Arc? Do you know anything about her love life?" He ignored my reply to continue about Bouboulina. It was an extraordinary story he told me and I have no doubt that most of it was true. "Why don't you write that story yourself?" I asked him point blank. He pretended that he was nor a writer, that his task was to discover people and present them to the world. "But I never met a man who could tell a story like you," I persisted. "Why don't you try telling your stories aloud—let someone take it down just as you tell it? Couldn't you do that, at least?"

"To tell a good story," he said, "you have to have a good listener. I can't tell a story to an automaton who writes shorthand. Besides, the best stories are those which you don't want to preserve. If you have any arrière-pensée the story is ruined. It must be a sheer gift ... you must throw it to the dogs.... I'm not a writer," he added, "I'm an extemporaneous fellow. I like to hear myself talk. I talk too much—it's a vice." And then he added reflectively: "What good would it do to be a writer, a Greek writer? Nobody reads Greek. If a man can have a thousand readers here he's lucky. The educated Greeks don't read their own writers; they prefer to read German, English, French books. A writer hasn't a chance in Greece."

"But your work could be translated into other languages," I suggested.

"There is no language that can render the flavor and the beauty of modern Greek," he replied. "French is wooden, inflexible, logic-ridden, too precise; English is too flat, too prosaic, too business-like ... you don't know how to make verbs in English." He went on like that, flourishing his cane angrily. He began to recite one of Seferiades' poems, in Greek. "Do you hear that?

The sound of it alone is wonderful, no? What can you give me in English to match that for sheer beauty of resonance?" And suddenly he began to intone a verse from the Bible. "Now that's a little more like it," he said. "But you don't use that language any more—that's a dead language now. The language hasn't any guts to-day. You're all castrated, you've become business men, engineers, technicians. It sounds like wooden money dropping into a sewer. *We've got a language* ... we're still making it. It's a language for poets, not for shopkeepers. Listen to this —" and he began reciting another poem, in Greek. "That's from Sekelianos. I suppose you never even heard the name, what? You never heard of Yannopoulos either, did you? Yannopoulos was greater than your Walt Whitman and all the American poets combined. He was a madman, yes, like all the great Greek fellows. He fell in love with his own country—that's a funny thing, eh? Yes, he became so intoxicated with the Greek language, the Greek philosophy, the Greek sky, the Greek mountains, the Greek sea, the Greek islands, the Greek vegetables, even, that he killed himself. I'll tell you how he killed himself some other time—that's another story. Have you got any writers who would kill themselves because they were too full of love? Are there any French writers or German writers or English writers who feel that way about their country, their race, their soil? *Who are they?* I'll read you some of Yannopoulos when we get back to Athens. I'll read you what he says about the rocks—just the rocks, nothing more. You can't know what a rock is until you've heard what Yannopoulos has written. He talks about rocks for pages and pages; he *invents* rocks, by God, when he can't find any to rave about. People say he was crazy, Yannopoulos. He wasn't crazy—he was *mad*. There's a difference. His voice was too strong for his body: it consumed him. He was like Icarus—the sun melted his wings. He soared too high. He was an eagle. These rabbits we call critics can't understand a man like Yannopoulos. He was out of proportion. He raved about the wrong things, according to them. He didn't have *le sens de mesure*, as the French say. There you are—*mesure*. What a mean little word! They look at the Parthenon and they find the proportions so harmonious. All rot. The human proportions which the Greek extolled were super- human. They weren't *French* proportions. They were divine, be- cause the true Greek is a god, not a cautious, precise, calculating being with the soul of an engineer...."

Our stay at Spetsai was prolonged because the boat for Nau- plia failed to appear. I began to fear that we would be marooned there indefinitely. However, one fine day along about four in the afternoon the boat finally did show up. It was an unserviceable English ferry which rolled with the slightest ripple. We sat on deck watching the sinking sun. It was one of those Biblical sun- sets in which man is completely absent. Nature simply opens her bloody, insatiable maw and swallows everything in sight. Law, order, morality, justice, wisdom, any abstraction seems like a cruel joke perpetrated on a helpless world of idiots. Sunset at sea is for me a dread spectacle: it is hideous, murderous, soul- less. The earth may be cruel but the sea is heartless. There is ab- solutely no place of refuge; there are only the elements and the elements are treacherous.

We were to touch at Leonidion before putting in at Nauplia. I was hoping it would still be light enough to catch a glimpse of the place because it was this grim corner of the Peloponnesus that the Katsimbalis side of the family stemmed from. Unfor- tunately the sun was rapidly setting just behind the wall of rock under which Leonidion lies. By the time the boat dropped an- chor it was night. All I could distinguish in the gloom was a lit- tle cove illuminated by four or five feeble electric bulbs. A dank, chill breath descended from the precipitous black wall above us, adding to the desolate and forbidding atmosphere of the place. Straining my eyes to pierce the chill, mist-laden gloom it seemed to me that I perceived a gap in the hills which my imagination peopled with rude, barbaric tribesmen moving stealthily about in search of forage. I would not have been the least surprised to hear the beat of a tom-tom or a blood-curdling war whoop. The setting was unrelievedly sinister—another death trap. I could well imagine how it must have been centuries ago, when the morning sun pierced the fever-laden mist, disclosing the naked bodies of the slain, their stalwart, handsome figures mutilated by the javelin, the axe, the wheel. Horrible though the image was I could not help but think how much cleaner that than the sight of a shell-torn trench with bits of human flesh strewn about like chicken feed. I can't for the life of me recall by what weird modulation we arrived at the Rue du Faubourg Montmartre, but as the boat pulled out and we installed ourselves at a table in the saloon before a couple of innocent glasses of *ouzo* Katsimbalis was leading me by the hand from café to café along that thoroughfare which is engraved in my memory as perhaps no other street in Paris. At least five or six times it has happened to me now that on taking leave of a strange city or saying good-bye to an old friend this street, which is certainly not the most extraordinary street in the world, has been the parting theme. There is without doubt something sinister and fascinatingly evil about the Rue du Faubourg Montmartre. The first time I walked through it, of an evening, I was literally frightened stiff. There was something in the air which warned one to be on one's guard. It is by no means the worst street in Paris, as I have hinted, but there is something malignant, foul, menacing, which lingers there like a poisonous gas, corroding even the most innocent face until it resembles the ulcer-bitten physiognomy of the doomed and defeated. It is a street that one comes back to again and again. One gets to know it slowly, foot by foot, like a trench which is taken and retaken so many times that one no longer knows if it is a bad dream or a monomania.

In a few hours we would be at Nauplia, within striking distance of such breathtaking places as Argos, Tiryns, Mycenae, Epidaurus, and here we are talking of dingy holes, lye-bitten side streets, dilapidated whores, dwarfs, gigolos, *clochards* of the Faubourg Montmartre. I am trying to visualize my friend Katsimbalis sitting in a certain *bistro* opposite a theatre at midnight. The last time I stood at that bar my friend Edgar was trying to sell me Rudolf Steiner, rather unsuccessfully I must say, because just as he was getting on to group souls and the exact nature of the difference between a cow and a mineral, from the occult standpoint, a chorus girl from the theatre opposite, who was now on the bum, wedged her way in between us and diverted our minds to things less abstruse. We took a seat in the corner near the doorway where we were joined by a dwarf who ran a string of whorehouses and who seemed to derive an unholy pleasure from using the adverb "*malment.*" The story which Katsimbalis was reeling off was one of those stories which begin as a trifling episode and end as an unfinished novel—unfinished because of lack of breath or space or time or because, as happened, he got sleepy and decided to take a nap. This story, which like all his stories I find it impossible to transcribe, lacking the patience and the finesse of a Thomas Mann, haunted me for days. It was not that the subject was so unusual, it was that with a good stretch of sea before us he felt at liberty to make the most extraordinary digressions, to dwell with scrupulous care and attention on the most trivial details. I have always felt that the art of telling a story consists in so stimulating the listener's imagination that he drowns himself in his own reveries long before the end. The best stories I have heard were pointless, the best books those whose plot I can never remember, the best individuals those whom I never get anywhere with. Though it has been practiced on me time and again I never cease to marvel how it happens that, with certain individuals whom I know, within a few minutes after greeting them we are embarked on an endless voyage comparable in feeling and trajectory only to the deep middle dream which the practiced dreamer slips into like a bone into its socket. Often, after one of these suprasensible seances, endeavoring to recapture the thread which had broken, I would work my way back as far as some trifling detail—but between that bespangled point of repair and the mainland there was always an impassible void, a sort of no-man's-land which the wizardry of the artist had encumbered with shell holes and quagmires and barbed wire.

In the case of Katsimbalis there was a quality which, as a writer,

I feel to be of the utmost importance where the art of story-telling is concerned—the complete disregard of the element of time. He never began in the professional way; he began by fumbling about, sparring for an opening, so to speak. The story usually began when he had come to a knothole, when, in order to really launch himself, he would take a tremendous step backward, figuratively, to be sure, saying as he tweaked his nose— "Look here, did you never notice that ..." or "I say, has it ever happened to you that ..." and, not waiting for a yes or a no, his eyes becoming glazed by the surge of inward light, he would actually tumble backwards into the deep well in which all his stories had their source and, gripping the slippery walls of his narrative with finger and toe, he would slowly clamber to the surface, puffing, gasping, shaking himself like a dog to free himself of the last remaining particles of wrack and slime and stardust. Sometimes, in taking the backward plunge, he would hit the bottom with such a thud that he was speechless: one could look into the pupil of his eyes and see him lying there helpless as a starfish, a great sprawling mass of flesh lying face up and counting the stars, counting and naming them in fat, unbroken stupefaction as if to make a colossally unthinkable pattern on which to weave the story which would come to his lips when he would catch his breath again.

The great starfish, as I was saying, was sound asleep before ever we got to Nauplia. He had sprawled out on the bench, leaving me to circle about the Parc Monceau where he had dropped me in a taxi. I was dazed. I went up on deck and paced back and forth, purring to myself, laughing aloud now and then, gesticulating, mimicking his gestures in anticipation of recounting the more succulent fragments of his narrative to my friend Durrell or to Seferiades upon my return to Athens. Several times I slipped back to the saloon to take a look at him, to gaze at that tiny mouth of his which was pried open now in a prolonged mute gasp like the mouth of a fish suffocating with air. Once I approached close to him and bending over I explored the silent cavity with a photographic eye. What an astounding thing is the voice! By what miracle is the hot magma of the earth transformed into that which we call speech? If out of clay such an abstract medium as words can be shaped what is to hinder us from leaving our bodies at will and taking up our abode on other planets or between the planets? What is to prevent us from rearranging all life, atomic, molecular, corporeal, stellar, divine? Why should we stop at words, or at planets, or at divinity? Who or what is powerful enough to eradicate this miraculous leaven which we bear within us like a seed and which, after we have embraced in our mind all the universe, is nothing more than a seed—since to say universe is as easy as to say seed, and we have yet to say greater things, things beyond saying, things limitless and inconceivable, things which no trick of language can encompass. *You* lying there, I was saying to myself, where has that voice gone? Into what inky crevices are you crawling with your ganglionic feelers? Who are you, *what* are you now in drugged silence? Are you fish? Are you spongy root? Are you *you*? If I should bash your skull in now would all be lost—the music, the narcotic vapors, the glissandos, the rugged parentheses, the priapic snorts, the law of diminishing returns, the pebbles between stutters, the shutters you pull down over naked crimes? If I bore into you now with an awl, here at the temple, will there come out with the blood a single tangible clue?

In a few minutes we shall be at Nauplia. In a few minutes he will awake with a start, saying "Huh, I must have dozed off." He always wakes up electrified, as if he were caught committing a crime. He is ashamed to go to sleep. At midnight he is only beginning to feel thoroughly awake. At midnight he goes prowling about in strange quarters looking for someone to talk to. People are collapsing with fatigue: he galvanizes them into attentive listeners. When he is through he pulls out the plug and departs with his vocal apparatus tucked safely away in his diaphragm. He will sit in the dark at a table and stuff himself with bread and olives, with hard-boiled eggs, with herring and cheeses of one sort or another, and while washing it down by his lonesome he will talk to himself, tell himself a story, pat himself on the chest, remind himself to remember to remember it the next time; he will even sing himself a little song in the dark or, if the spirit moves him, get up and do a few bearish paces or urinate through his pants, why not, he's alone, he's happy, he's sad, he's all there is, to himself at least, and who else is there and so forth—*can you see him?* I see him very clearly. It's warm now in Athens and he's had a grand night of it with his cronies. The last one he said good-night to is already home and writing it all down in his diary, having no other existence than this auricular attachment, this appendix of a life in the belly of the whale. The whale is tilting back against a wall under a grape arbor near the niche where Socrates passed his last hours. The whale is again looking for food and drink, trying to spirit it out of a man with a 1905 straw hat brought safely back from America together with fine bed linen, rocking chairs, spittoons and a horned phonograph. The phonograph is standing on a chair in the road and in a moment a canned voice will be screeching a poison song from the time of the Turkish occupation. . . .

In a few minutes we shall be at Nauplia. The whale is now electrified and his memory, which had probably been refreshed by the brief nap, is working with diabolical accuracy on the shreds of a detail which he was too lazy to elaborate on before. The passengers are clearing out and we are caught up and carried along like corks to the forward deck. Near the rail, the first to disembark, are two prisoners escorted by gendarmes with rifles. They are chained to one another by handcuffs. The thought occurs to me that he, Katsimbalis, and myself are also chained to one another, he the teller and I the listener, and that we will go to the end of the world this way, not as prisoners but as willing bondsmen.

Nauplia is dismal and deserted at night. It is a place which has lost caste, like Arles or Avignon. In fact, it is in many ways suggestive of a French provincial town, at night more particularly. There is a military garrison, a fortress, a palace, a cathedral— and a few crazy monuments. There is also a mosque which has been converted into a cinema. By day it is all red tape, lawyers and judges everywhere, with all the despair and futility which follows in the train of these blood-sucking parasites. The fortress and the prison dominate the town. Warrior, jailer, priest—the eternal trinity which symbolizes our fear of life. I don't like Nauplia. I don't like provincial towns. I don't like jails, churches, fortresses, palaces, libraries, museums, nor public statues to the dead.

The hotel was a bit of a madhouse. In the lobby there were engravings of famous Greek ruins and of Indians from the Amazon and the Orinoco. The dining room was plastered with letters from American and English tourists, all praising the comforts of the hotel in extravagant language. The silliest letters were signed by professors from our celebrated universities. Katsimbalis had two beds in his room and I had three. There was no heat because we were the only guests.

We awoke early and hired a car to take us to Epidaurus. The day began in sublime peace. It was my first real glimpse of the Peloponnesus. It was not a glimpse either, but a vista opening upon a hushed still world such as man will one day inherit when he ceases to indulge in murder and thievery. I wonder how it is that no painter has ever given us the magic of this idyllic landscape. Is it too undramatic, too idyllic? Is the light too ethereal to be captured by the brush? This I can say, and perhaps it will discourage the overenthusiastic artist: there is no trace of ugliness here, either in line, color, form, feature or sentiment. It is sheer perfection, as in Mozart's music. Indeed, I venture to say that there is more of Mozart here than anywhere else in the world. The road to Epidaurus is like the road to creation. One stops searching. One grows silent, stilled by the hush of mysterious beginnings. If one could speak one would become melodious. There is nothing to be seized or treasured or cornered off here: there is only a breaking down of the walls which lock the spirit in. The landscape does not recede, it installs itself in the open places of the heart; it crowds in, accumulates, dispossesses. You are no longer riding through something—call it Nature, if you will—but participating in a rout, a rout of the forces of greed, malevolence, envy, selfishness, spite, intolerance, pride, arrogance, cunning, duplicity and so on.

It is the morning of the first day of the great peace, the peace of the heart, which comes with surrender. I never knew the meaning of peace until I arrived at Epidaurus. Like everybody I had used the word all my life, without once realizing that I was using a counterfeit. Peace is not the opposite of war any more than death is the opposite of life. The poverty of language, which is to say the poverty of man's imagination or the poverty of his inner life, has created an ambivalence which is absolutely false. I am talking of course of the peace which passeth all understanding. There is no other kind. The peace which most of us know is merely a cessation of hostilities, a truce, an interregnum, a lull, a respite, which is negative. The peace of the heart is positive and invincible, demanding no conditions, requiring no protection. It just is. If it is a victory it is a peculiar one because it is based entirely on surrender, a voluntary surrender, to be sure. There is no mystery in my mind as to the nature of the cures which were wrought at this great therapeutic center of the ancient world. Here the healer himself was healed, first and most important step in the development of the art, which is not medical but religious. Second, the patient was healed before ever he received the cure. The great physicians have always spoken of Nature as being the great healer. That is only partially true. Nature alone can do nothing. Nature can cure only when man recognizes his place in the world, which is not in Nature, as with the animal, but in the human kingdom, the link between the natural and the divine.

To the infra-human specimens of this benighted scientific age the ritual and worship connected with the art of healing as practiced at Epidaurus seems like sheer buncombe. In our world the blind lead the blind and the sick go to the sick to be cured. We are making constant progress, but it is a progress which leads to the operating table, to the poor house, to the insane asylum, to the trenches. We have no healers—we have only butchers whose knowledge of anatomy entitles them to a diploma which in turn entitles them to carve out or amputate our illnesses so that we may carry on in crippled fashion until such time as we are fit for the slaughterhouse. We announce the discovery of this cure and that but make no mention of the new diseases which we have created en route. The medical cult operates very much like the War Office—the triumphs which they broadcast are sops thrown out to conceal death and disaster. The medicos, like the military authorities, are helpless; they are waging a hopeless fight from the start. What man wants is peace in order that he may live. Defeating our neighbor doesn't give peace any more than curing cancer brings health. Man doesn't begin to live through triumphing over his enemy nor does he begin to acquire health through endless cures. The joy of life comes through peace, which is not static but dynamic. No man can really say that he knows what joy is until he has experienced peace. And without joy there is no life, even if you have a dozen cars, six butlers, a castle, a private chapel and a bomb-proof vault. Our diseases are our attachments, be they habits, ideologies, ideals, principles, possessions, phobias, gods, cults, religions, what you please. Good wages can be a disease just as much as bad wages. Leisure can be just as great a disease as work. Whatever we cling to, even if it be hope or faith, can be the disease which carries us off. Surrender is absolute: if you cling to even the tiniest crumb you nourish the germ which will devour you. As for clinging to God, God long ago abandoned us in order that we might realize the joy of attaining godhood through our own efforts. All this whimpering that is going on in the dark, this insistent, piteous plea for peace which will grow bigger as the pain and the misery increase, where is it to be found? *Peace*, do people imagine that it is something to be cornered, like corn or wheat? Is it something which can be pounced upon and devoured, as with wolves fighting over a carcass? I hear people talking about peace and their faces are clouded with anger or with hatred or with scorn and disdain, with pride and arrogance. There are people who want to fight to bring about peace—the most deluded souls of all. There will be no peace until murder is eliminated from the heart and mind. Murder is the apex of the broad pyramid whose base is the self. That which stands will have to fall. Everything which man has fought for will have to be relinquished before he can begin to live as man. Up till now he has been a sick beast and even his divinity stinks. He is master of many worlds and in his own he is a slave. What rules the world is the heart, not the brain, in every realm our conquests bring only death. We have turned our backs on the one realm wherein freedom lies. At Epidaurus, in the stillness, in the great peace that came over me, I heard the heart of the world beat. I know what the cure is: it is to give up, to relinquish, to surrender, so that our little hearts may beat in unison with the great heart of the world.

I think that the great hordes who made the long trek to Epidaurus from every corner of the ancient world were already cured before they arrived there. Sitting in the strangely silent amphitheatre I thought of the long and devious route by which I had at last come to this healing center of peace. No man could have chosen a more circumlocuitous voyage than mine. Over thirty years I had wandered, as if in a labyrinth. I had tasted every joy, every despair, but I had never known the meaning of peace. En route I had vanquished all my enemies one by one, but the greatest enemy of all I had not even recognized—*myself.* As I entered the still bowl, bathed now in a marble light, I came to that spot in the dead center where the faintest whisper rises like a glad bird and vanishes over the shoulder of the low hill, as the light of a clear day recedes before the velvet black of night. Balboa standing upon the peak of Darien could not have known a greater wonder than I at this moment. There was nothing more to conquer: an ocean of peace lay before me. To be free, as I then knew myself to be, is to realize that all conquest is vain, even the conquest of self, which is the last act of egotism. To be joyous is to carry the ego to its last summit and to deliver it triumphantly. To know peace is total: it is the moment after, when the surrender is complete, when there is no longer even the consciousness of surrender. Peace is at the center and when it is attained the voice issues forth in praise and benediction. Then the voice carries far and wide, to the outermost limits of the universe. Then it heals, because it brings light and the warmth of compassion.

Epidaurus is merely a place symbol: the real place is in the heart, in every man's heart, if he will but stop and search it. Every discovery is mysterious in that it reveals what is so unexpectedly immediate, so close, so long and intimately known. The wise man has no need to journey forth; it is the fool who seeks the pot of gold at the rainbow's end. But the two are always fated to meet and unite. They meet at the heart of the world, which is the beginning and the end of the path. They meet in realization and unite in transcendence of their roles.

The world is both young and old: like the individual, it renews itself in death and ages through infinite births. At every stage there is the possibility of fulfillment. Peace lies at any point along the line. It is a continuum and one that is just as undemonstrable by demarcation as a line is undemonstrable by stringing points together. To make a line requires a totality of being, of will and of imagination. What constitutes a line, which is an exercise in metaphysics, one may speculate on for eternity. But even an idiot can draw a line, and in doing so he is the equal of the professor for whom the nature of a line is a mystery beyond all comprehension.

The mastery of great things comes with the doing of trifles; the little voyage is for the timid soul just as formidable as the big voyage for the great one. Voyages are accomplished inwardly, and the most hazardous ones, needless to say, are made without moving from the spot. But the sense of voyage can wither and die. There are adventurers who penetrate to the remotest parts of the earth, dragging to a fruitless goal an animated corpse. The earth pullulates with adventurous spirits who populate it with death: these are the souls who, bent upon conquest, fill the outer corridors of space with strife and bickering. What gives a phantasmal hue to life is this wretched shadow play between ghoul and ghost. The panic and confusion which grips the soul of the wanderer is the reverberation of the pandemonium created by the lost and the damned.

.

As I was basking on the steps of the amphitheatre the very natural thought came to my head to send a word of cheer to my friends. I thought particularly of my psychoanalyst friends. I wrote out three cards, one to France, one to England, and one to America. I very gently urged these broken-down hacks who called themselves healers to abandon their work and come to Epidaurus for a cure. All three of them were in dire need of the healing art— saviours who were helpless to save themselves. One of them committed suicide before my word of cheer reached him; another died of a broken heart shortly after receiving my card; the third one answered briefly that he envied me and wished he had the courage to quit his work.

The analyst everywhere is fighting a hopeless fight. For every individual whom he restores to the stream of life, "adapted," as they put it, a dozen are incapacitated. There will never be enough analysts to go round, no matter how fast we turn them out. One brief war is enough to undo the work of centuries. Surgery of course will make new advances, though of what use these advances are it is difficult to see. Our whole way of life has to alter. We don't want better surgical appliances, we want a better life. If all the surgeons, all the analysts, all the medicos could be withdrawn from their activity and gathered together for a spell in the great bowl at Epidaurus, if they could discuss in peace and quiet the immediate, drastic need of humanity at large, the answer would be forthcoming speedily, and it would be unanimous: REVOLUTION. A worldwide revolution from top to bottom, in every country, in every class, in every realm of consciousness. The fight is not against disease: disease is a by-product. The enemy of man is not germs, but man himself, his pride, his prejudices, his stupidity, his arrogance. No class is immune, no system holds a panacea. Each one individually must revolt against a way of life which is not his own. The revolt, to be effective, must be continuous and relentless. It is not enough to overthrow governments, masters, tyrants: one must overthrow his own preconceived ideas of right and wrong, good and bad, just and unjust.

We must abandon the hard-fought trenches we have dug ourselves into and come out into the open, surrender our arms, our possessions, our rights as individuals, classes, nations, peoples. A billion men seeking peace cannot be enslaved. We have enslaved ourselves, by our own petty, circumscribed view of life. It is glorious to offer one's life for a cause, but dead men accomplish nothing. Life demands that we offer something more—spirit, soul, intelligence, goodwill. Nature is ever ready to repair the gaps caused by death, but nature cannot supply the intelligence, the will, the imagination to conquer the forces of death. Nature restores and repairs, that is all. It is man's task to eradicate the homicidal instinct, which is infinite in its ramifications and manifestations. It is useless to call upon God, as it is futile to meet force with force. Every battle is a marriage conceived in blood and anguish, every war is a defeat to the human spirit. War is only a vast manifestation in dramatic style of the sham, hollow, mock conflicts which take place daily everywhere even in so-called times of peace. Every man contributes his bit to keep the carnage going, even those who seem to be staying aloof. We are all involved, all participating, willy-nilly. The earth is our creation and we must accept the fruits of our creation. As long as we refuse to think in terms of world good and world goods, of world order, world peace, we shall murder and betray one another. It can go on till the crack of doom, if we wish it to be thus. Nothing can bring about a new and better world but our own desire for it. Man kills through fear—and fear is hydra-headed. Once we start slaying there is no end to it. An eternity would not suffice to vanquish the demons who torture us. *Who put the demons there?* That is for each one to ask himself. Let every man search his own heart. Neither God nor the Devil is responsible, and certainly not such puny monsters as Hitler, Mussolini, Stalin, et alia. Certainly not such bugaboos as Catholicism, Capitalism, Communism. Who put the demons there in our heart to torture us? A good question, and if the only way to find out is to go to Epidaurus, then I urge you one and all to drop everything and go there—at once.

In Greece one has the conviction that *genius* is the norm, not mediocrity. No country has produced, in proportion to its numbers, as many geniuses as Greece. In one century alone this tiny nation gave to the world almost five hundred men of genius. Her art, which goes back fifty centuries, is eternal and incomparable. The landscape remains the most satisfactory, the most wondrous, that our earth has to offer. The inhabitants of this little world lived in harmony with their natural surroundings, peopling them with gods who were real and with whom they lived in intimate communion. The Greek cosmos is the most eloquent illustration of the unity of thought and deed. It persists even to-day, though its elements have long since been dispersed. The image of Greece, faded though it be, endures as an archetype of the miracle wrought by the human spirit. A whole people, as the relics of their achievements testify, lifted themselves to a point never before and never since attained. It was miraculous. It still is. The task of genius, and man is nothing if not genius, is to keep the miracle alive, to live always in the miracle, to make the miracle more and more miraculous, to swear allegiance to nothing, but live only miraculously, think only miraculously, die miraculously. It matters little how much is destroyed, if only the germ of the miraculous be preserved and nurtured. At Epidaurus you are confronted with and permeated by the intangible residue of the miraculous surge of the human spirit. It inundates you like the spray of a mighty wave which broke at last upon the farther shore. To-day our attention is centered upon the physical inexhaustibility of the universe; we *must* concentrate all our thought upon that solid fact because never before has man plundered and devastated to such a degree as to-day. We are therefore prone to forget that in the realm of the spirit there is also an inexhaustibility, that in this realm no gain is ever lost. When one stands at Epidaurus one *knows* this to be a fact. With malice and spite the world may buckle and crack but here, no matter into what vast hurricane we may whip our evil passions, lies an area of peace and calm, the pure distilled heritage of a past which is not altogether lost.

If Epidaurus spells peace Mycenae, which is outwardly as calm and hushed, awakens wholly different thoughts and emotions. At Tiryns the day before I was introduced to the Cyclopean world. We entered the ruins of the once impregnable citadel through a womb-like aperture made, if not by supermen, certainly by giants. The walls of the womb were as smooth as alabaster; they had been polished by thick coats of fleece, for here during the long period of night which settled over this region the shepherds brought their flocks for shelter. Tiryns is prehistoric in character. Little remains of this once formidable pioneer settlement save a few colossal ramparts. Why it should be so I don't know, but to me it seems to antedate, at least in spirit, the cave shelters of the Dordogne region. One feels that the terrain has undergone profound alterations. Supposedly Tiryns was settled by an offshoot from Crete during the Minoan period; if so, the spirit underwent profound transformations, like the land itself. Tiryns is no more like Knossus, for example, than New York is like Rome or Paris. Tiryns represents a relapse, just as America represents Europe in its most degenerate aspects. Crete of the Minoan epochs stands for a culture based upon peace: Tiryns smells of cruelty, barbarism, suspicion, isolation. It is like an H. G. Wells setting for a prehistoric drama, for a thousand years' war between one-eyed giants and blunder-footed dinosaurs.

Mycenae, which follows Tiryns in point of time, is quite another scene. The stillness of it to-day resembles the exhaustion of a cruel and intelligent monster which has been bled to death. Mycenae, and again I give only my impressions and intuitions, seems to have experienced a vast cycle of development and degeneration. It seems to stand outside time, in any historical sense. In some mysterious fashion the same Aegean race which brought the seeds of culture from Crete to Tiryns here evolved to a godlike grandeur, threw out a quick spawn of heroes, Titans, demigods, and then, as if exhausted and dazzled by the unprecedented and divine-like flowering, relapsed into a dark and bloody intestinal conflict which lasted for centuries, ending at a point so far back as to appear mythological to their successors. At Mycenae the gods once walked the earth, of that there can be no question. And at Mycenae the progeny of these same gods produced a type of man who was artistic to the core and at the same time monstrous in his passions. The architecture was Cyclopean, the ornaments of a delicacy and grace unrivalled in any period of art. Gold was abundant and used unstintingly. Everything about the place is contradictory. It is one of the navels of the human spirit, the place of attachment to the past and of complete severance too. It wears an impenetrable air: it is grim, lovely, seductive and repellent. What happened here is beyond all conjecture. The historians and the archaeologists have woven a slim and altogether unsatisfying fabric to cover the mystery. They piece together fragmentary items which are linked in the customary manner to suit their necessitous logic. Nobody has yet penetrated the secret of this hoary scene. It defies the feeble processes of the intellectual mind. We must await the return of the gods, the restoration of faculties which now lie dormant.

It was a Sunday morning when Katsimbalis and I left Nauplia for Mycenae. It was hardly eight o'clock when we arrived at the little station bearing this legendary name. Passing through Argus the magic of this world suddenly penetrated my bowels. Things long forgotten came back with frightening clarity. I was not sure whether I was recalling things I had read as a child or whether I was tapping the universal memory of the race. The fact that these places still existed, still bore their ancient names, seemed incredible. It was like a resurrection and the day we had chosen for the journey was more like Easter than Thanksgiving Day. From the station to the ruins was a walk of several kilometers. As at Epidaurus there was a sublime stillness all about. We walked leisurely towards the encircling hills which rise up from the gleaming Argive plain. A few birds were wheeling overhead in the unbroken vault of blue. Suddenly we came upon a little boy crying as if his heart would break. He was standing in the field beside the road. His weeping had absolutely no relation to the hushed and tranquil world in which he stood; it was as if he had been set down in the green field by a spirit from the outside world. What could a little boy be crying about at such an hour in such a wondrous world? Katsimbalis went over and spoke to him. He was crying because his sister had stolen his money. How much money? Three drachmas. Money, money.... Even here there was such a thing as money. The word money never sounded so preposterous to me before. How could one think such a word in this world of terror and beauty and magic? If he had lost a donkey or a parrot I could have understood. But three drachmas—I just couldn't visualize the meaning of three drachmas. I couldn't believe he was weeping. It was an hallucination. Let him stand there and weep—the spirit would come and fetch him again; he didn't belong, he was an anomaly.

After you pass the little hostelry run by Agamemnon and his wife, which faces a field of Irish green, you become immediately aware that the earth is sown with the bodies and the relics of legendary figures. Even before Katsimbalis opened his mouth I knew they were lying all about us—the earth tells you so. The approach to the place of horror is fantastically inviting. There are smooth green mounds, hummocks, hillocks, tumuli everywhere, and beneath them, not very deep either, lie the warriors, the heroes, the fabulous innovators who without machinery erected the most formidable fortifications. The sleep of the dead is so deep that the earth and all who walk it dream; even the huge carrion birds who wheel above seem drugged and hypnotized. As one rises slowly with the rising terrain the blood thickens, the heart slows down, the mind comes to rest obsessively on the shuddering image of an endless chain of assassinations. There are two distinct worlds impinging on one another—the heroic world of daylight and the claustral world of dagger and poison. Mycenae, like Epidaurus, swims in light. But Epidaurus is all open, exposed, irrevocably devoted to the spirit. Mycenae folds in upon itself, like a fresh-cut navel, dragging its glory down into the bowels of the earth where the bats and the lizards feed upon it gloatingly. Epidaurus is a bowl from which to drink the pure spirit: the blue of the sky is in it and the stars and the winged creatures who fly between, scattering song and melody. Mycenae, after one turns the last bend, suddenly folds up into a menacing crouch, grim, defiant, impenetrable. Mycenae is closed in, huddled up, writhing with muscular contortions like a wrestler. Even the light, which falls on it with merciless clarity, gets sucked in, shunted off, grayed, beribboned. There were never two worlds so closely juxtaposed and yet so antagonistic. It is Greenwich here with respect to everything that concerns the soul of man. Move a hair's breadth either way and you are in a totally different world. This is the great shining bulge of horror, the high slope whence man, having attained his zenith, slipped back and fell into the bottomless pit.

It was still early morning when we slipped through the lion's gate. No sign of a guardian about. Not a soul in sight. The sun is steadily rising and everything is clearly exposed to view. And yet we proceed timidly, cautiously, fearing we know not what. Here and there are open pits looking ominously smooth and slimy. We walk between the huge slabs of stone that form the circular enclosure. My book knowledge is nil. I can look on this mass of rubble with the eyes of a savage. I am amazed at the diminutive proportions of the palace chambers, of the dwelling places up above. What colossal walls to protect a mere handful of people! Was each and every inhabitant a giant? What dread darkness fell upon them in their evil days to make them burrow into the earth, to hide their treasures from the light, to murder incestuously in the deep bowels of the earth? We of the New World, with millions of acres lying waste and millions unfed, unwashed, unsheltered, we who dig into the earth, who work, eat, sleep, love, walk, ride, fight, buy, sell and murder there below ground, are we going the same way? I am a native of New York, the grandest and the emptiest city in the world; I am standing now at Mycenae, trying to understand what happened here over a period of centuries. I feel like a cockroach crawling about amidst dismantled splendors. It is hard to believe that somewhere back in the leaves and branches of the great genealogical tree of life my progenitors knew this spot, asked the same questions, fell back senseless into the void, were swallowed up and left no trace of thought save these ruins, the scattered relics in museums, a sword, an axle, a helmet, a death mask of beaten gold, a beehive tomb, an heraldic lion carved in stone, an exquisite drinking vase. I stand at the summit of the walled citadel and in the early morning I feel the approach of the cold breath from the shaggy gray mountain towering above us. Below, from the great Argive plain the mist is rising. It might be Pueblo, Colorado, so dislocated is it from time and boundary. Down there, in that steaming plain where the automotrice crawls like a caterpillar, is it not possible there once stood wigwams? Can I be sure there never were any Indians here? Everything connected with Argos, shimmering now in the distance as in the romantic illustrations for textbooks, smacks of the American Indian. I must be crazy to think thus, but I am honest enough to admit the thought. Argos gleams resplendent, a point of light shooting arrows of gold into the blue. Argos belongs to myth and fable: her heroes never took on flesh. But Mycenae, like Tiryns, is peopled with the ghosts of antediluvian men, Cyclopean monsters washed up from the sunken ridges of Atlantis. Mycenae was first heavy-footed, slow, sluggish, ponderous, thought embodied in dinosaurian frames, war reared in anthropophagous luxury, reptilian, ataraxic, stunning and stunned. Mycenae swung full circle, from limbo to limbo. The monsters devoured one another, like crocodiles. The rhinoceros man gored the hippopotamic man. The walls fell on them, crushed them, flattened them into the primeval ooze. A brief night. Lurid lightning flashes, thunder cannonading between the fierce shoulders of the hills. The eagles fly out, the plain is scavenged, the grass shoots forth. (This is a Brooklyn lad talking. Not a word of truth in it, until the gods bring forth the evidence.) The eagles, the hawks, the snot-knobbed vultures, gray with greed like the parched and barren mountainsides. The air is alive with winged scavengers. Silence — century upon century of silence, during which the earth puts on a coat of soft green. A mysterious race out of nowhere swoops down upon the country of Argolis. Mysterious only because men have forgotten the sight of the gods. The gods are returning, in full panoply, man-like, making use of the horse, the buckler, the javelin, carving precious jewels, smelting ores, blowing fresh vivid images of war and love on bright dagger blades. The gods stride forth over the sunlit swards, full-statured, fearless, the gaze frighteningly candid and open. A world of light is born. Man looks at man with new eyes. He is awed, smitten by his own gleaming image reflected everywhere. It goes on thus, century upon century swallowed like cough drops, a poem, an heraldic poem, as my friend Durrell would say. While the magic is on the lesser men, the initiates, the Druids of the Peloponnesus, prepare the tombs of the gods, hide them away in the soft flanks of the hillocks and hummocks. The gods will depart one day, as mysteriously as they came, leaving behind the human-like shell which deceives the unbelieving, the poor in spirit, the timid souls who have turned the earth into a furnace and a factory.

We have just come up from the slippery staircase, Katsimbalis and I. We have not descended it, only peered down with lighted matches. The heavy roof is buckling with the weight of time. To breathe too heavily is enough to pull the world down over our ears. Katsimbalis was for crawling down on all fours, on his belly if need be. He has been in many a tight spot before; he has played the mole on the Balkan front, has wormed his way through mud and blood, has danced like a madman from fear and frenzy, killed all in sight including his own men, has been blown skyward clinging to a tree, has had his brain concussed, his rear blunderbussed, his arms hanging in shreds, his face blackened with powder, his bones and sinews wrenched and unsocketed. He is telling me it all over again as we stand midway to earth and sky, the lintel sagging more and more, the matches giving out. "We don't want to miss this," he pleads. But I refuse to go back down into that slimy well of horrors. Not if there were a pot of gold to be filched would I make the descent. I want to see the sky, the big birds, the short grass, the waves of blinding light, the swamp mist rising over the plain.

We come out on the far hillside into a panorama of blinding clarity. A shepherd with his flock moves about on a distant mountainside. He is larger than life, his sheep are covered with golden locks. He moves leisurely in the amplitude of forgotten time. He is moving amidst the still bodies of the dead, their fingers clasped in the short grass. He stops to talk with them, to stroke their beards. He was moving thus in Homeric times when the legend was being embroidered with copperish strands. He added a lie here and there, he pointed to the wrong direction, he altered his itinerary. For the shepherd the poet is too facile, too easily satiated. The poet would say "there *was* ... they *were*...." But the shepherd says *he lives, he is, he does.*... The poet is always a thousand years too late—and blind to boot. The shepherd is eternal, an earth-bound spirit, a renunciator. On these hillsides forever and ever there will be the shepherd with his flock: he will survive everything, including the tradition of all that ever was.

Now we are passing over the little bridge above the sundered vault of Clytemnestra's resting place. The earth is flamy with spirit as if it were an invisible compass we are treading and only the needle quivering luminously as it catches a flash of solar radiance. We are veering towards Agamemnon's tomb over the vault of which only the thinnest patch of earth now rests like a quilt of down. The nudity of this divine cache is magnificent. Stop before the heart glows through. Stoop to pick a flower. Shards everywhere and sheep droppings. The clock has stopped. The earth sways for a fraction of a second, waiting to resume its eternal beat.

I have not yet crossed the threshold. I am outside, between the Cyclopean blocks which flank the entrance to the shaft. I am still the man I might have become, assuming every benefit of civilization to be showered upon me with regal indulgence. I am gathering all of this potential civilized muck into a hard, tiny knot of understanding. I am blown to the maximum, like a great bowl of molten glass hanging from the stem of a glass-blower. Make me into any fantastic shape, use all your art, exhaust your lung-power—till I shall only be a thing fabricated, at the best

a beautiful cultured soul. I know this, I despise it. I stand outside full-blown, the most beautiful, the most cultured, the most
marvelously fabricated soul on earth. I am going to put my foot
over the threshold—*now*. I do so. I hear nothing. I am not even
there to hear myself shattering into a billion splintered smithereens. Only Agamemnon is there. The body fell apart when they
lifted the mask from his face. But he is there, he fills the still beehive: he spills out into the open, floods the fields, lifts the sky a
little higher. The shepherd walks and talks with him by day and
by night. Shepherds are crazy folk. So am I. I am done with civilization and its spawn of cultured souls. I gave myself up when
I entered the tomb. From now on I am a nomad, a spiritual nobody. Take your fabricated world and put it away in the museums, I don't want it, can't use it. I don't believe any civilized
being knows, or ever did know, what took place in this sacred
precinct. A civilized man can't possibly know or understand—
he is on the other side of that slope whose summit was scaled
long before he or his progenitors came into being. They call it
Agamemnon's tomb. Well, possibly someone called Agamemnon was here laid to rest. What of it? Am I to stop there, gaping
like an idiot? I do not. I refuse to rest on that too-too-solid fact.
I take flight here, not as poet, not as recreator, fabulist, mytholo-
gist, but as pure spirit. I say the whole world, fanning out in every direction from this spot, was once alive in a way that no man
has ever dreamed of. I say there were gods who roamed everywhere, men like us in form and substance, but free, electrically
free. When they departed this earth they took with them the one
secret which we shall never wrest from them until we too have
made ourselves free again. We are to know one day what it is to
have life eternal—*when we have ceased to murder*. Here at this
spot, now dedicated to the memory of Agamemnon, some foul
and hidden crime blasted the hopes of man. Two worlds lie juxtaposed, the one before, the one after the crime. The crime contains the riddle, as deep as salvation itself. Spades and shovels
will uncover nothing of any import. The diggers are blind, feel-

ing their way towards something they will never see. Everything that is unmasked crumbles at the touch. Worlds crumble too, in the same way. We can dig in eternally, like moles, but fear will be ever upon us, clawing us, raping us from the rear.

It seems scarcely credible to me now that what I relate was the enchanting work of a brief morning. By noon we were already winding down the road to the little inn. On the way we came across the guardian who, though he had arrived too late, insisted on filling me with facts and dates which are utterly without sense. He spoke first in Greek and then, when he discovered I was an American, in English. When he had finished his learned recital he began talking about Coney Island. He had been a molasses-thrower on the boardwalk. He might just as well have said that he had been a wasp glued to the ceiling of an abandoned chateau for all the interest I showed. Why had he come back? The truth is he hadn't come back. Nobody comes back who has once made the transatlantic voyage westward. He is still throwing molasses on the boardwalk. He came back to incarnate as a parrot, to talk this senseless parrot-language to other parrots who pay to listen. This is the language in which it is said that the early Greeks believed in gods, the word god no longer having any meaning but used just the same, thrown out like counterfeit money. Men who believe in nothing write learned tomes about gods who never existed. This is part of the cultural rigmarole. If you are very proficient at it you finally get a seat in the academy where you slowly degenerate into a full-fledged chimpanzee.

Here is Agamemnon and his spouse. Would we like something à la carte or a full banquet, a royal gorge, so to speak? Where is the wine list? A good cold wine while we wait would be in order. Katsimbalis is smacking his lips; his palate is dry. We flop down on the lawn and Agamemnon brings us a de luxe edition of a book by an English archaeologist. This is the hors d'oeuvre, apparently, for the bloody English tourist. The book stinks of learning: it is about upper and lower strata, breast-plates, chicken bones and grave relics. I chuck it aside when Agamemnon has turned his back. He is a tender fellow, this Agamemnon, and is almost a diplomat from force of habit. His wife has the air of being a good cook. Katsimbalis is dozing off under a big tree. Some German sauerkrauts, disguised as human beings, are sitting at a table under another tree. They look frightfully learned and repulsive; they are swollen like toads.

I am gazing blankly at the field of Irish green. It is a Lawrence Durrell field, heraldic in every sense of the word. Looking blankly into that field I suddenly realize what Durrell was trying to tell me in those long rambling poems he called letters. I used to think, when these heraldic messages arrived at the Villa Seurat on a cold summer's day in Paris, that he had taken a sniff of coke before oiling his pen. Once a big fulsome sheaf which looked like prose fell out of the envelope—it was called "Zero" and it was dedicated to me by this same Lawrence Durrell who said he lived in Corfu. I had heard of chicken tracks and of liver mantic and I once came near grasping the idea of absolute Zero, even though the thermometer has yet to be made which could register it, but not until I sat gazing into the field of Irish green in front of Agamemnon's Inn did I ever get the idea of Zero in the heraldic sense. There never was a field so fieldishly green as this. When you spot anything true and clear you are at Zero. Zero is Greek for pure vision. It means what Lawrence Durrell says when he writes Ionian. It means, and now for example, I can tell you more precisely because what I am trying to describe is happening right before my very eyes ... Two men and a woman are standing in the field. One man has a tape measure in his hand. He is going to measure off the plot of land which he has received for a wedding present. His bride is there to make certain that not a millimeter of land is miscalculated. They are down on all fours. They are arguing about a tiny piece in the southwest corner. Perhaps a twig has diverted the tape measure the fraction of a millimeter. One can't be too careful. Never look a gift horse in the mouth! They are measuring something which heretofore was only a word to me—*land*. The dead heroes, the gold cups, the bucklers, the jewels, the chased daggers—these items have nothing to do with the business in hand. What is vital here is land, just land. I roll it over and over on my tongue — land, land, land. Why yes, *land*, that's it—I had almost forgotten it meant such a simple, eternal thing. One gets twisted, derouted, spavined and indoctrinated shouting "Land of the Free" et cetera. Land is something on which to grow crops, build a home, raise cows and sheep. Land is land, what a grand, simple word! Yes, Lawrence Durrell, zero is what you make it: you take a piece of wet earth and as you squeeze it between your fingers you get two men and a woman standing in a field of Irish green measuring land. The wine has come. I raise my glass. *Salute, Larry me lad, and keep the flag at zero!* In a few more pages we shall revisit Mycenae together and Nancy will lead the way down the bat-slimed stairs to the bottomless well.

PART TWO

OUR GRAND TOUR OF THE PELOPONNESUS WAS CUT short at Mycenae. Katsimbalis had received an urgent call to return to Athens owing to the unexpected discovery of a piece of land which his attorneys had overlooked. The news didn't seem to thrill him. On the contrary he was depressed: more property meant more taxes, more debts—and more headaches. I could have continued my explorations alone, but I preferred to return to Athens with him and digest what I had seen and felt. We took the automotrice at Mycenae, a direct run of five or six hours, if I remember rightly, for the absurd price of a couple of cocktails at the Ritz.

Between the time of my return and my departure for Crete three or four little incidents occurred which I feel impelled to make brief mention of. The first was *Juarez*, the American film which ran for several weeks at one of the leading theatres. Despite the fact that Greece is under a dictatorship this film, which was only slightly modified after the first few showings, was shown night and day to an increasingly packed house. The atmosphere was tense, the applause distinctly Republican. For many reasons the film had acute significance for the Greek people. One felt that the spirit of Venizelos was still alive. In that blunt and magnificent speech which Juarez makes to the assembled plenipotentiaries of the foreign powers one felt that the tragic plight of Mexico under Maximilian had curious and throbbing analogies with the present perilous position of Greece. The only true friend which Greece has at this moment, the only relatively disinterested one, is America. Of that I shall have more to say when I come to Crete, the birthplace of Venizelos as well as of El Greco. But to witness the showing of a film in which all forms of dictatorship are dramatically denounced, to witness it in the midst of an audience whose hands are tied, except to applaud, is an impressive event. It was one of those rare moments when I felt that, in a world which is almost entirely gagged, shackled and manacled, to be an American is almost a luxury.

The second event was a visit to the astronomical observatory in Athens, arranged for Durrell and myself by Theodore Stephanides who, as an amateur astronomer, has made admittedly important astronomical discoveries. The officials received us very cordially, thanks to the generous aid given them by American fellow-workers in this field. I had never looked through the telescope of a bona fide observatory before. Nor had Durrell, I presume. The experience was sensational, though probably not altogether in accord with the expectations of our hosts. Our remarks, which were juvenile and ecstatic, seemed to bewilder them. We certainly did not display the orthodox reactions to the wonders that were unfolded. I shall never forget their utter amazement when Durrell, who was gazing at the Pleiades, suddenly exclaimed—"*Rosicrucian!*" What did he mean by that? they wanted to know. I mounted the ladder and took a look for myself. I doubt if I can describe the effect of that first breathless vision of a splintered star world. The image I shall always retain is that of Chartres, an effulgent rose window shattered by a hand grenade. I mean it in a double or triple sense—of awesome, indestructible beauty, of cosmic violation, of world ruin suspended in the sky like a fatal omen, of the eternality of beauty even when blasted and desecrated. "As above so below," runs the famous saying of Hermes Trismegistus. To see the Pleiades through a powerful telescope is to sense the sublime and awesome truth of these words. In his highest flights, musical and architectural above all, for they are one, man gives the illusion of rivalling the order, the majesty and the splendor of the heavens; in his fits of destruction the evil and the desolation which he spreads seem incomparable until we reflect on the great stellar shake-ups brought on by the mental aberrations of the unknown Wizard. Our hosts seemed impervious to such reflections; they spoke knowingly of weights, distances, substances, etc. They were removed from the normal activities of their fellow men in a quite different way from ourselves. For them beauty was incidental, for us everything. For them the physico-mathematical world palped, calibred, weighed and transmitted by their instruments was reality itself, the stars and planets mere proof of their excellent and infallible reasoning. For Durrell and myself reality lay wholly beyond the reach of their puny instruments which in themselves were nothing more than clumsy reflections of their circumscribed imagination locked forever in the hypothetical prison of logic. Their astronomical figures and calculations, intended to impress and overawe us, only caused us to smile indulgently or to very impolitely laugh outright at them. Speaking for myself, facts and figures have always left me unimpressed. A light year is no more impressive to me than a second, or a split second. This is a game for the feeble-minded which can go on ad nauseam backwards and forwards without taking us anywhere. Similarly I am not more convinced of the reality of a star when I see it through the telescope. It may be more brilliant, more wondrous, it may be a thousand times or a million times bigger than when seen with the naked eye, but it is not a whit more real. To say that this is what a thing *really* looks like, just because one sees it larger and grander, seems to me quite fatuous. It is just as real to me if I don't see it at all but merely imagine it to be there. And finally, even when to my own eye and the eye of the astronomer it possesses the same dimensions, the same brilliance, it definitely does not look the same to us both—Durrell's very exclamation is sufficient to prove that.

But let us pass on—to Saturn. Saturn, and our moon like-
wise, when seen through a magnifying lens, are impressive to the
layman in a way which the scientist must instinctively deplore
and deprecate. No facts or figures about Saturn, no magnifica-
tion, can explain the unreasonably disquieting sensation which
the sight of this planet produces upon the mind of the specta-
tor. Saturn is a living symbol of gloom, morbidity, disaster, fatality. Its milk-white hue inevitably arouses associations with tripe,
dead gray matter, vulnerable organs hidden from sight, loath-
some diseases, test tubes, laboratory specimens, catarrh, rheum,
ectoplasm, melancholy shades, morbid phenomena, incuba and
succuba, war, sterility, anaemia, indecision, defeatism, consti-
pation, antitoxins, feeble novels, hernia, meningitis, dead-letter
laws, red tape, working class conditions, sweat shops, YMCA's,
Christian Endeavor meetings, spiritist seances, poets like T. S.
Eliot, zealots like Alexander Dowie, healers like Mary Baker
Eddy, statesmen like Chamberlain, trivial fatalities like slipping
on a banana peel and cracking one's skull, dreaming of better
days and getting wedged between two motor trucks, drowning
in one's own bathtub, killing one's best friend accidentally, dying of hiccoughs instead of on the battlefield, and so on ad infi-
nitum. Saturn is malefic through force of inertia. Its ring, which
is only paperweight in thickness, according to the savants, is the
wedding ring which signifies death or misfortune devoid of all
significance. Saturn, whatever it may be to the astronomer, is
the sign of senseless fatality to the man in the street. He carries it in his heart because his whole life, devoid of significance
as it is, is wrapped up in this ultimate symbol which, if all else
fails to do him in, this he can count upon to finish him off. Saturn is life in suspense, not dead so much as deathless, i.e. incapable of dying. Saturn is like dead bone in the ear—double mas-
toid for the soul. Saturn is like a roll of wallpaper wrong side out
and smeared with that catarrhal paste which wallpapers find
so indispensable in their metier. Saturn is a vast agglomeration
of those evil looking shreds which one hawks up the morning af-

ter he has smoked several packs of crisp, toasted, coughless, inspiring cigarettes. Saturn is postponement manifesting itself as an accomplishment in itself. Saturn is doubt, perplexity, scepticism, facts for fact's sake and no hokum, no mysticism, understand? Saturn is the diabolical sweat of learning for its own sake, the congealed fog of the monomaniac's ceaseless pursuit of what is always just beyond his nose. Saturn is deliciously melancholic because it knows and recognizes nothing beyond melancholy; it swims in its own fat. Saturn is the symbol of all omens and superstitions, the phony proof of divine entropy, phony because if it were true that the universe is running down Saturn would have melted away long ago. Saturn is as eternal as fear and irresolution, growing more milky, more cloudy, with each compromise, each capitulation. Timid souls cry for Saturn just as children are reputed to cry for Castoria. Saturn gives us only what we ask for, never an ounce extra. Saturn is the white hope of the white race which prattles endlessly about the wonders of nature and spends its time killing off the greatest wonder of all—MAN. Saturn is the stellar impostor setting itself up as the grand cosmocrator of Fate, Monsieur le Paris, the automatic pole-axer of a world smitten with ataraxy. Let the heavens sing its glory—this lymphatic globe of doubt and ennui will never cease to cast its milk-white rays of lifeless gloom.

This is the emotional photograph of a planet whose unorthodox influence still weighs heavily upon the almost extinct consciousness of man. It is the most cheerless spectacle in the heavens. It corresponds to every craven image conceived in the heart of man; it is the single repository of all the despair and defeat to which the human race from time immemorial has succumbed. It will become invisible only when man has purged it from his consciousness.

The third event was of a wholly different order—a jazz seance at the austere bachelor chambers of Seferiades in the Rue Kydathenaion, one of the streets I was instinctively attracted to on

my first exploration of Athens. Seferiades, who is a cross between bull and panther by nature, has strong Virgo traits, speaking astrologically. That is to say, he has a passion for collecting,
as did Goethe who was one of the best Virgo types the world
has ever known. The first shock I had on entering his place on
this particular occasion was that of meeting his most gracious
and most lovely sister, Jeanne. She impressed me immediately
as being of royal descent, perhaps of the Egyptian line—in any
case, distinctly trans-Pontine. As I was gazing at her ecstatically
I was suddenly startled by the sound of Cab Calloway's baboon-
like voice. Seferiades looked at me with that warm Asiatic smile
which always spread over his face like nectar and ambrosia. "Do
you know that piece?" he said, beaming with pleasure. "I have
some others, if you'd care to hear them," and he pointed to a file
of albums about a yard long. "What about Louis Armstrong,
do you like him?" he continued. "Here's a Fats Waller record.
Wait a minute, have you ever heard Count Basie—or Pee Wee
Russell?" He knew every virtuoso of any account; he was a sub-
scriber to "Le Jazz Hot" I soon discovered. In a few moments we
were talking about the Café Boudon in Montmartre where the
great Negro performers of the night clubs repair before and after work. He wanted to hear about the American Negro, about
life behind the scene. What influence did the Negro have upon
American life, what did the American people think of Negro literature? Was it true that there was a Negro aristocracy, a cultural aristocracy which was superior to the white American cultural groups? Could a man like Duke Ellington register at the
Savoy Plaza without embarrassment? What about Caldwell and
Faulkner—was it a true picture of the South which they gave?
And so on. As I've remarked before, Seferiades is an indefatiga-
ble questioner. No detail is too trivial for him to overlook. His
curiosity is insatiable, his knowledge vast and varied. After entertaining me with a selection of the most up-to-date jazz numbers he wanted to know if I should like to hear some exotic music of which he had an interesting variety. While searching for
a record he would ply me with questions about some recondite

English poet or about the circumstances surrounding Ambrose Bierce's disappearance or what did I know about the Greenberg manuscripts which Hart Crane had made use of. Or, having found the record he was looking for he would suddenly switch to a little anecdote about his life in Albania which, in some curiously dissociated way, had to do with a poem by T. S. Eliot or St. Jean Perse. I speak of these divagations of his because they were a refreshing antidote to the sort of obsessive, single-tracked and wholly mirthless order of conversation indulged in by the English literati in Athens. An evening with these buttery-mouthed jakes always left me in a suicidal mood. A Greek is alive to the fingertips; he oozes vitality, he's effervescent, he's ubiquitous in spirit. The Englishman is lymphatic, made for the armchair, the fireside, the dingy tavern, the didactic treadmill. Durrell used to take a perverse delight in observing my discomfiture in the presence of his countrymen: they were one and all like animated cartoons from his "Black Book," that devastating chronicle of the English death. In the presence of an Englishman Katsimbalis would positively dry up. Nobody really hated them—they were simply insufferable.

Later that evening I had the privilege of meeting some Greek women, friends of Seferiades' sister. Here again I was impressed by the absence of those glaring defects which make even the most beautiful American or English woman seem positively ugly. The Greek woman, even when she is cultured, is first and foremost a woman. She sheds a distinct fragrance; she warms and thrills you. Due to the absorption of Greeks from Asia Minor the new generation of Athenian womanhood has improved in beauty and vigor. The ordinary Greek girl whom one sees on the street is superior in every way to her American counterpart; above all she has character and race, a combination which makes for deathless beauty and which forever distinguishes the descendants of ancient peoples from the bastard offshoots of the New World. How can I ever forget the young girl whom we passed one day at the foot of the Acropolis? Perhaps she was ten, perhaps she was fourteen years of age; her hair was reddish gold, her features as noble, as grave and austere as those of the caryatids on the Erectheum. She was playing with some comrades in a little clearing before a clump of ramshackle shanties which had somehow escaped the general demolition. Anyone who has read "Death in Venice" will appreciate my sincerity when I say that no woman, not even the loveliest woman I have ever seen, is or was capable of arousing in me such a feeling of adoration as this young girl elicited. If Fate were to put her in my path again I know not what folly I might commit. She was child, virgin, angel, seductress, priestess, harlot, prophetess all in one. She was neither ancient Greek nor modern Greek; she was of no race or time or class, but unique, fabulously unique. In that slow, sustained smile which she gave us as we paused a moment to gaze at her there was that enigmatic quality which da Vinci has immortalized, which one finds everywhere in Buddhistic art, which one finds in the great caves of India and on the facades of her temples, which one finds in the dancers of Java and of Bali and in primitive races, especially in Africa; which indeed seems to be the culminating expression of the spiritual achievement of the human race, but which to-day is totally absent in the countenance of the Western woman. Let me add a strange reflection—that the nearest approximation to this enigmatic quality which I ever noted was in the smile of a peasant woman at Corfu, a woman with six toes, decidedly ugly, and considered by everyone as something of a monster. She used to come to the well, as is the custom of the peasant women, to fill her jug, to do her washing, and to gossip. The well was situated at the foot of a steep declivity around which there wandered a goat-like path. In every direction there were thick shady olive groves broken here and there by ravines which formed the beds of mountain streams which in Summer were completely dried up. The well had an extraordinary fascination for me; it was a place reserved for the female beast of burden, for the strong, buxom virgin who could carry her jug of water strapped to her back with grace and ease, for the old toothless hag whose curved back was still capable of sustaining a staggering load of firewood, for the widow with her straggling flock of children, for the servant girls who laughed too easily, for wives who took over the work of their lazy husbands, for every species of female, in short, except the grand mistress or the idle English women of the vicinity. When I first saw the women staggering up the steep slopes, like the women of old in the Bible, I felt a pang of distress. The very manner of strapping the heavy jug to the back gave me a feeling of humiliation. The more so because the men who might have performed this humble task were more than likely sitting in the cool of a tavern or lying prone under an olive tree. My first thought was to relieve the young maid at our house of a minor task; I wanted to feel one of those jugs on my own back, to know with my own muscular aches what that repeated journey to the well meant. When I communicated my desire to Durrell he threw up his hands in horror. It wasn't done, he exclaimed, laughing at my ignorance. I told him it didn't matter to me in the least whether it was done or not done, that he was robbing me of a joy which I had never tasted. He begged me not to do it, for his sake—he said he would lose caste, that the Greeks would laugh at us. In short, he made such a point of it that I was obliged to abandon the idea. But on my rambles through the hills I usually made a point of stopping at the well to slake my thirst. There one day I espied the monster with six toes. She was standing in her bare feet, ankle deep in mud, washing a bundle of clothes. That she was ugly I could not deny, but there are all kinds of ugliness and hers was the sort which instead of repelling attracts. To begin with she was strong, sinewy, vital, an animal endowed with a human soul and with indisputable sexual powers. When she bent over to wring out a pair of pants the vitality in her limbs rippled and flashed through the tattered and bedraggled skirt which clung to her swarthy flesh. Her eyes glowed like coals, like the eyes of a Bedouin woman. Her lips were blood red and her strong even teeth as white as chalk. The thick black hair hung over her shoulders in rich, oily strands, as though saturated with olive oil. Renoir would have found her beautiful; he would not have noticed the six toes nor the coarseness of her features. He would have followed the rippling flesh, the full globes of her teats, the easy, swaying stance, the superabundant strength of her arms, her legs, her torso; he would have been ravished by the full, generous slit of the mouth, by the dark and burning glance of the eye, by the massive contours of the head and the gleaming black waves which fell in cascades down her sturdy, columnar neck. He would have caught the animal lust, the ardor unquenchable, the fire in the guts, the tenacity of the tigress, the hunger, the rapacity, the all-devouring appetite of the oversexed female who is not wanted because she has an extra toe.

Anyhow, Renoir apart, there was something in this woman's smile which the sight of the young girl at the base of the Acropolis revived. I said it was the nearest approximation to that enigmatic quality engraved in the countenance of the girl with the reddish gold hair. By that, paradoxical though it may sound, I mean that it was wholly antipodal. The monster might well have been the one to give birth to that startling figure of beauty; she might because in her starved dream of love her embrace had spanned a void beyond the imagination of the most desperately lovelorn woman. All her powers of seduction had been driven back into the coffin of sex where, in the darkness of her loins, passion and desire burned to a thick smoke. Disclaiming all hope of seducing man her lust had turned towards forbidden objects of desire — towards the animals of the field, towards inanimate things, towards objects of veneration, towards mythological deities. Her smile had in it something of the intoxication of parched earth after a sudden and furious downpour; it was the smile of the insatiable one to whom a thousand burning kisses are only the incentive to renewed assaults. In some strange and inexplicable fashion she has remained in my memory as the symbol of that hunger for unbounded love which I sensed in a lesser degree in all Greek women. It is almost the symbol of Greece itself, this unappeasable lust for beauty, passion, love.

•

For twenty years it had been my dream to visit Knossus. I never realized how simple it would be to make the journey. In Greece you have only to announce to someone that you intend to visit a certain place and presto! in a few moments there is a carriage waiting for you at the door. This time it turned out to be an aeroplane. Seferiades had decided that I should ride in pomp. It was a poetic gesture and I accepted it like a poet.

I had never been in a plane before and I probably will never go up again. I felt foolish sitting in the sky with hands folded; the man beside me was reading a newspaper, apparently oblivious of the clouds that brushed the windowpanes. We were probably making a hundred miles an hour, but since we passed nothing but clouds I had the impression of not moving. In short, it was unrelievedly dull and pointless. I was sorry that I had not booked passage on the good ship Acropolis which was to touch at Crete shortly. Man is made to walk the earth and sail the seas; the conquest of the air is reserved for a later stage of his evolution, when he will have sprouted real wings and assumed the form of the angel which he is in essence. Mechanical devices have nothing to do with man's real nature—they are merely traps which Death has baited for him.

We came down at the seaport of Herakleion, one of the principal towns of Crete. The main street is almost a ringer for a movie still in a third-rate Western picture. I found a room quickly in one of the two hotels and set out to look for a restaurant. A gendarme, whom I accosted, took me by the arm and graciously escorted me to a modest place near the public fountain. The meal was bad but I was now within reach of Knossus and too excited to be disturbed about such a trifle. After lunch I went across the street to a café and had a Turkish coffee. Two Germans who had arrived by the same plane were discussing the lecture on Wagner which they were to give that evening; they seemed to be fatuously unaware that they had come with their musical poison to the birthplace of Venizelos. I left to take a quick stroll through the town. A few doors away, in a converted mosque, a cinema announced the coming of Laurel and Hardy. The children who were clustered about the billboards were evidently as enthusiastic about these clowns as the children of Dubuque or Kenosha might he. I believe the cinema was called "The Minoan." I wondered vaguely if there would be a cinema at Knossus too, announcing perhaps the coming of the Marx Brothers.

Herakleion is a shabby town bearing all the earmarks of Turkish domination. The principal streets are filled with open shops in which everything for men's needs is made by hand as in mediaeval times. From the countryside the Cretans come in garbed in handsome black raiment set off by elegant high boots, of red or white leather ofttimes. Next to Hindus and Berbers they are the most handsome, noble, dignified males I have ever seen. They are far more striking than the women: they are a race apart.

I walked to the edge of the town where as always in the Balkans everything comes to an end abruptly, as though the monarch who had designed the weird creation had suddenly become demented, leaving the great gate swinging on one hinge. Here the buses collect like broken-down caterpillars waiting for the dust of the plains to smother them in oblivion. I turned back and dove into the labyrinth of narrow, twisting streets which forms the residential quarter and which, though thoroughly Greek, has the atmospheric flavor of some English outpost in the West Indies. I had long tried to imagine what the approach to Crete would be like. In my ignorance I had supposed that the island was sparsely inhabited, that there was no water to be had except what was brought in from the mainland; I thought that one would see a deserted-looking coast dotted with a few scintillating ruins which would be Knossus, and beyond Knossus there would be a wasteland resembling those vast areas of Australia where the dodo bird, shunned by other feathered species of the bush, forlornly buries his head in the sand and whistles out the other end. I remembered that a friend of mine, a French writer, had been stricken with dysentery here and transported on the back of a donkey to a small boat whence by some miracle he was transported to a passing freighter and returned to the mainland in a state of delirium. I wandered about in a daze, stopping now and then to listen to a cracked record from a horned phonograph standing on a chair in the middle of the street. The butchers were draped in blood-red aprons; they stood before primitive chopping blocks in little booths such as one may still see at Pompeii. Every so often the streets opened up into a public square flanked by insane buildings devoted to law, administration, church, education, sickness and insanity; the architecture was of that startling reality which characterizes the work of the popular primitives such as Bombois, Peyronnet, Kane, Sullivan and Vivin. In the dazzling sunlight a detail such as a grilled gate or a defenceless bastion stands out with hair-raising exactitude such as one sees only in the paintings of the very great or the insane. Every inch of Herakleion is paintable; it is a confused, nightmarish town, thoroughly anomalous, thoroughly heterogeneous, a place-dream suspended in a void between Europe and Africa, smelling strongly of raw hides, caraway seeds, tar and subtropical fruits. It has been brutalized by the Turk and infected with the harmless rose water vaporings of the back pages of Charles Dickens. It has no relation whatever to Knossus or Phaestos; it is Minoan in the way that Walt Disney's creations are American; it is a carbuncle on the face of time, a sore spot which one rubs like a horse while asleep on four legs.

I had in my pocket a card of introduction to the leading literary figure of Crete, a friend of Katsimbalis. Towards evening I found him in the café where the Germans had been hatching their Wagnerian machinations. I shall call him Mr. Tsoutsou as I have unfortunately forgotten his name. Mr. Tsoutsou spoke French, English, German, Spanish, Italian, Russian, Portuguese, Turkish, Arabic, demotic Greek, newspaper Greek and ancient Greek. He was a composer, poet, scholar and lover of food and drink. He began by asking me about James Joyce, T. S. Eliot, Walt Whitman, André Gide, Breton, Rimbaud, Lautréamont, Lewis Carroll, Monk Lewis, Heinrich Georg and Rainer Maria Rilke. I say he asked me about them, much as you would ask about a relative or a mutual friend. He spoke of them as if they were all alive, which they are, thank God. I rubbed my head. He

started off on Aragon—had I read *Le Paysan de Paris?* Did I remember the Passage Jouffroy in Paris? What did I think of Saint-
Jean Perse? Or *Nadja* of Breton? Had I been to Knossus yet? I
ought to stay a few weeks at least—he would take me over the
island from one end to another. He was a very hale and hearty
fellow and when he understood that I liked to eat and drink he
beamed most approvingly. He regretted sincerely that he was
not free for the evening, but hoped to see me the following day;
he wanted to introduce me to the little circle of literati in Herakleion. He was excited by the fact that I came from America and
begged me to tell him something about New York which I found
it almost impossible to do because I had long ceased to identify
myself with that odious city.

I went back to the hotel for a nap. There were three beds
in the room, all of them very comfortable. I read carefully the
sign warning the clients to refrain from tipping the employees.
The room cost only about seventeen cents a night and I became
involved willy-nilly in a fruitless speculation as to how many
drachmas one would give as a tip if one could tip. There were
only three or four clients in the hotel. Walking through the wide
corridors looking for the W. C. I met the maid, an angelic sort
of spinster with straw hair and watery blue eyes who reminded
me vividly of the Swedenborgian caretaker of the Maison Balzac
in Passy. She was bringing me a glass of water on a tray made of
lead, zinc and tin. I undressed and as I was pulling in the blinds
I observed two men and a stenographer gazing at me from the
window of some outlandish commercial house across the way.
It seemed unreal, this transaction of abstract business in a place
like Herakleion. The typewriter looked surrealistic and the men
with sleeves rolled up as in commercial houses everywhere appeared fantastically like the freaks of the Western world who
move grain and corn and wheat around in carload lots by means
of the telephone, the ticker, the telegraph. Imagine what it would
be like to find two businessmen and a stenographer on Easter Island! Imagine how a typewriter would sound in that Oceanic si-

lence! I fell back on the bed and into a deep, drugged sleep. No tipping allowed—that was the last thought and a very beautiful one to a weary traveler.

When I awoke it was dark. I opened the blinds and looked down the forlorn main street which was now deserted. I heard a telegraph instrument clicking. I got into my things and hurried to the restaurant near the fountain. The waiter seemed to expect me and stood ready to translate for me into that Iroquois English which the itinerant Greek has acquired in the course of his wanderings. I ordered some cold fish with the skin on it and a bottle of dark-red Cretan wine. While waiting to be served I noticed a man peering through the large plate-glass window; he walked away and came back again in a few minutes. Finally he made up his mind to walk in. He walked directly up to my table and addressed me—in English. Was I not Mr. Miller who had arrived by plane a few hours ago? I was. He begged leave to introduce himself. He was Mr. So-and-So, the British Vice Consul at Herakleion. He had noticed that I was an American, a writer. He was always happy to make the acquaintance of an American. He paused a moment, as if embarrassed, and then went on to say that his sole motive for introducing himself was to let me know that as long as I remained in Crete I was to consider his humble services entirely at my disposal. He said that he was originally from Smyrna and that every Greek from Smyrna was eternally indebted to the American people. He said that there was no favor too great for me to ask of him.

The natural reply was to ask him to sit down and share a meal with me, which I did. He explained that he would be unable to accept the honor as he was obliged to dine in the bosom of his family, *but*—would I do him the honor of taking a coffee with him and his wife at their home after dinner? As the representative of the great American people (not at all sure of the heroic role we had played in the great disaster of Smyrna) I most graciously accepted, rose, bowed, shook his hand and escorted him to the door where once again we exchanged polite thanks and mutual felicitations. I went back to the table, unskinned the cold fish and proceeded to wet my whistle. The meal was even lousier than at noon, but the service was extraordinary. The whole restaurant was aware that a distinguished visitor had arrived and was partaking with them of their humble food. Mr. Tsoutsou and his wife appeared for just a moment to see how I was faring, commented bravely on the delicious, appetizing appearance of the skinned fish and disappeared with bows and salaams which sent an electric thrill through the assembled patrons of Herakleion's most distinguished restaurant. I began to feel as though something of vast import were about to happen. I ordered the waiter to send the *chasseur* out for a coffee and cognac. Never before had a vice consul or any form of public servant other than a constable or gendarme sought me out in a public place. The plane was responsible for it. It was like a letter of credit.

The home of the vice consul was rather imposing for Herakleion. In truth, it was more like a museum than a home. I felt somewhat hysterical, somewhat disoriented. The vice consul was a good, kind-hearted man but vain as a peacock. He drummed nervously on the arm of the chair, waiting impatiently for his wife to leave off about Paris, Berlin, Prague, Budapest et cetera in order to confide that he was the author of a book on Crete. He kept telling his wife that I was a journalist, an insult which normally I find hard to swallow, but in this case I found it easy not to take offense since the vice consul considered all writers to be journalists. He pressed a button and very sententiously commanded the maid to go to the library and find him a copy of the book he had written on Crete. He confessed that he had never written a book before but, owing to the general state of ignorance and confusion regarding Crete in the mind of the average tourist, he had deemed it incumbent upon him to put down what he knew about his adopted land in more or less eternal fashion. He admitted that Sir Arthur Evans had expressed it all in unimpeachable style hut then there were little things, trifles by comparison of course, which a work of that scope and grandeur could not hope to encompass. He spoke in this pompous, ornate, highly fatuous way about his masterpiece. He said that a journalist like myself would be one of the few to really appreciate what he had done for the cause of Crete et cetera. He handed me the book to glance at. He handed it over as if it were the Gutenberg Bible. I took one glance and realized immediately that I was dealing with one of the "popular masters of reality," a blood-brother to the man who had painted "A Rendezvous with the Soul." He inquired in a pseudo-modest way if the English were all right, because English was not his native tongue. The implication was that if he had done it in Greek it would lie beyond criticism. I asked him politely where I might hope to obtain a copy of this obviously extraordinary work whereupon he informed me that if I came to his office in the morning he would bestow one upon me as a gift, as a memento of this illustrious occasion which had culminated in the meeting of two minds thoroughly attuned to the splendors of the past. This was only the beginning of a cataract of flowery horse shit which I had to swallow before going through the motions of saying good-night. Then came the Smyrna disaster with a harrowing, detailed recital of the horrors which the Turks perpetrated on the helpless Greeks and the merciful intervention of the American people which no Greek would ever forget until his dying day. I tried desperately, while he spun out the horrors and atrocities, to recall what I had been doing at this black moment in the history of Greece. Evidently the disaster had occurred during one of those long intervals when I had ceased to read the newspapers. I hadn't the faintest remembrance of any such catastrophe. To the best of my recollection the event must have taken place during the year when I was looking for a job without the slightest intention of taking one. It reminded me that, desperate as I thought myself then to be, I had not even bothered to look through the columns of the want ads.

Next morning I took the bus in the direction of Knossus. I had to walk a mile or so after leaving the bus to reach the ruins. I was so elated that it seemed as if I were walking on air. At last my dream was about to be realized. The sky was overcast and it sprinkled a bit as I hopped along. Again, as at Mycenae, I felt that I was being drawn to the spot. Finally, as I rounded a bend, I stopped dead in my tracks; I had the feeling that I was there. I looked about for traces of the ruins but there were none in sight. I stood for several minutes gazing intently at the contours of the smooth hills which barely grazed the electric blue sky. This must be the spot, I said to myself, I can't be wrong. I retraced my steps and cut through the fields to the bottom of a gulch. Suddenly, to my left, I discovered a bald pavilion with columns painted in raw, bold colors—the palace of King Minos. I was at the back entrance of the ruins amidst a clump of buildings that looked as if they had been gutted by fire. I went round the hill to the main entrance and followed a little group of Greeks in the wake of a guide who spoke a boustrophedonous language which was sheer Pelasgian to me.

There has been much controversy about the aesthetics of Sir Arthur Evans' work of restoration. I found myself unable to come to any conclusion about it; I accepted it as a fact. However Knossus may have looked in the past, however it may look in the future, this one which Evans has created is the only one I shall ever know. I am grateful to him for what he did, grateful that he had made it possible for me to descend the grand staircase, to sit on that marvelous throne chair the replica of which at the Hague Peace Tribunal is now almost as much of a relic of the past as the original.

Knossus in all its manifestations suggests the splendor and sanity and opulence of a powerful and peaceful people. It is gay—gay, healthful, sanitary, salubrious. The common people played a great role, that is evident. It has been said that throughout its long history every form of government known to man was tested out; in many ways it is far closer in spirit to modern times, to the twentieth century, I might say, than other later epochs of the Hellenic world. One feels the influence of Egypt, the homely human immediacy of the Etruscan world, the wise, communal organizing spirit of Inca days. I do not pretend to know, but I felt, as I have seldom felt before the ruins of the past, that here throughout long centuries there reigned an era of peace. There is something down to earth about Knossus, the sort of atmosphere which is evoked when one says Chinese or French. The religious note seems to be graciously diminished; women played an important, equal role in the affairs of this people; a spirit of play is markedly noticeable. In short, the prevailing note is one of joy. One feels that man lived to live, that he was not plagued by thoughts of a life beyond, that he was not smothered and restricted by undue reverence for the ancestral spirits, that he was religious in the only way which is becoming to man, by making the most of everything that comes to hand, by extracting the utmost of life from every passing minute. Knossus was worldly in the best sense of the word. The civilization which it epitomized went to pieces fifteen hundred years before the coming of the Saviour, having bequeathed to the Western world the greatest single contribution yet known to man—the alphabet. In another part of the Island, at Gortyna, this discovery is immortalized in huge blocks of stone which run over the countryside like a miniature Chinese wall. To-day the magic has gone out of the alphabet; it is a dead form to express dead thoughts.

Walking back to meet the bus I stopped at a little village to get a drink. The contrast between past and present was tremendous, as though the secret of life had been lost. The men who gathered around me took on the appearance of uncouth savages. They were friendly and hospitable, extraordinarily so, but by comparison with the Minoans they were like neglected domesticated animals. I am not thinking of the comforts which they lacked, for in point of comfort I make no great distinction between the life of a Greek peasant, a Chinese coolie and a migratory American jack-of-all-trades. I am thinking now of the lack of those essential elements of life which make possible a real society of human beings. The great fundamental lack, which is apparent everywhere in our civilized world, is the total absence of anything approaching a communal existence. We have become spiritual nomads; whatever pertains to the soul is derelict, tossed about by the winds like flotsam and jetsam. The village of Hagia Triada, looked at from any point in time, stands out like a jewel of consistency, integrity, significance. When a miserable Greek village, such as the one I am speaking of, and the counterpart of which we have by the thousand in America, embellishes its meager, stultified life by the adoption of telephone, radio, automobile, tractor, et cetera, the meaning of the word communal becomes so fantastically distorted that one begins to wonder what is meant by the phrase "human society." There is nothing human about these sporadic agglomerations of beings; they are beneath any known level of life which this globe has known. They are less in every way than the pygmies who are truly nomadic and who move in filthy freedom with delicious security.

As I sipped my glass of water, which had a strange taste, I listened to one of these glorified baboons reminisce about the glorious days he had spent in Herkimer, New York. He had run a candy store there and seemed grateful to America for having permitted him to save the few thousand dollars which he required to return to his native land and resume the degrading life of toil which he was accustomed to. He ran back to the house to fetch an American book which he had kept as a souvenir of the wonderful money-making days. It was a farmer's almanac, badly thumb-marked, fly-bitten, louse-ridden. Here in the very cradle of our civilization a dirty baboon hands me a precious monstrosity of letters—the almanac.

The owner of the almanac and myself were seated at a table off the road in the center of a group of louts who were visibly impressed. I ordered cognac for the crowd and surrendered myself to the interlocutor. A man came over and put his big hairy finger on the photograph of a farm implement. The interlocutor said: "Good machine, he like this." Another one took the book in his hands and went through it with a wet thumb, grunting now and then to signify his pleasure. Interlocutor said: "Very interesting book. He like American books." Suddenly he espied a friend in the background. "Come here" he called. He presented him to

me. "Nick! He work in Michigan. Big farm. He like America too."
I shook hands with Nick. Said Nick: "You New York? Me go
New York once." He made a motion with his hands to indicate
the skyscrapers. Nick spoke animatedly to the others. Suddenly
there was a silence and the interlocutor spoke up. "They want
to know how you like Greece." "It's marvelous," I answered. He
laughed. "Greece very poor country, yes? No money. America
rich. Everybody got money, yes?" I said yes to satisfy him. He
turned to the others and explained that I had agreed—America
was a very rich country, everybody rich, lots of money. "How
long you stay in Greece?" he asked. "Maybe a year, maybe two
years," I answered. He laughed again, as though I were an idiot.
"What your business?" I told him I had no business. "You millionaire?" I told him I was very poor. He laughed, more than
ever. The others were listening intently. He spoke a few words
to them rapidly. "What you have to drink?" he asked. "Cretan
people like Americans. Cretan people good people. You like cognac, yes?" I nodded.

Just then the bus came along. I made as if to go. "No hurry,"
said the interlocutor. "He no go yet. He make water here." The
others were smiling at me. What were they thinking? That I was
a queer bird to come to a place like Crete? Again I was asked
what my business was. I made the motion of writing with a pen.
"Ah!" exclaimed the interlocutor. "Newspaper!" He clapped his
hands and spoke excitedly to the innkeeper. A Greek newspaper
was produced. He shoved it into my hands. "You read that?" I
shook my head. He snatched the paper out of my hand. He read
the headline aloud in Greek, the others listening gravely. As he
was reading I noticed the date—the paper was a month old. The
interlocutor translated for me. "He say President Roosevelt no
want fight. Hitler bad man." Then he got up and seizing a cane
from one of the bystanders he put it to his shoulder and im-
itated a man firing point-blank. Bang-bang! he went, dancing
around and aiming at one after the other. Bang-bang! Everybody
laughed heartily. "Me," he said, jerking his thumb towards his
breast, "me good soldier. Me kill Turks . . . many Turks. Me kill,

kill, kill," and he made a ferocious, blood-thirsty grimace. "Cretan people good soldiers. Italians no good." He went up to one of the men and seized him by the collar. He made as if he were slitting the man's throat. "Italians, bah!" He spat on the ground. "Me kill Mussolini ... like a that! Mussolini bad man. Greek no like Mussolini. We kill all Italians." He sat down grinning and chuckling. "President Roosevelt, he help Greeks, yes?" I nodded. "Greek good fighter. He kill everybody. He no 'fraid of nobody. Look! Me, one man ..." He pointed to the others. "Me one Greek." He pointed to the others, snatching the cane again and brandishing it like a club. "Me kill everybody—German, Italian, Russian, Turk, French. Greek no 'fraid." The others laughed and nodded their heads approvingly. It was convincing, to say the least.

The bus was getting ready to move. The whole village seemed to have gathered to see me off. I climbed aboard and waved goodbye. A little girl stepped forward and handed me a bunch of flowers. The interlocutor shouted Hooray! A gawky young lad yelled *All right!* and they all laughed.

After dinner that evening I took a walk to the edge of the town. It was like walking through the land of Ur. I was making for a brilliantly lit café in the distance. About a mile away, it seemed, I could hear the loudspeaker blasting out the war news—first in Greek, then in French, then in English. It seemed to be proclaiming the news throughout a wasteland. Europe speaking. Europe seemed remote, on some other continent. The noise was deafening. Suddenly another one started up from the opposite direction. I turned back towards the little park facing a cinema where a Western picture was being advertised. I passed what looked like an immense fortress surrounded by a dry moat. The sky seemed very low and filled with tattered clouds through which the moon sailed unsteadily. I felt out of the world, cut off, a total stranger in every sense of the word. The amplifiers increased this feeling of isolation: they seemed to have tuned up to the wildest pitch in order to carry far beyond me—to Abyssinia, Arabia, Persia, Beluchistan, China, Tibet. The waves were passing over my head; they were not intended for Crete, they had been picked up accidentally. I dove into the narrow winding streets which led to the open square. I walked right into a crowd which had gathered outside a tent in which freaks were being exhibited. A man squatting beside the tent was playing a weird melody on the flute, He held the flute up towards the moon which had grown larger and brighter in the interval. A belly-dancer came out of the tent, dragging a cretin by the hand. The crowd giggled. Just then I turned my head and to my astonishment I saw a woman with a vase on her shoulder descending a little bluff in bare feet. She had the poise and grace of a figure on an ancient frieze. Behind her came a donkey laden with jars. The flute was getting more weird, more insistent. Turbaned men with long white boots and black frock coats were pushing towards the open tent. The man beside me held two squawking chickens by the legs; he was rooted to the spot, as if hypnotized. To the right of me was evidently a barracks barred by a sentry box before which a soldier in white skirts paraded back and forth.

There was nothing more to the scene than this, but for me it held the enchantment of a world I was yet to glimpse. Even before I had sailed for Crete I had been thinking of Persia and Arabia and of more distant lands still. Crete is a jumping off place. Once a still, vital, fecund center, a navel of the world, it now resembles a dead crater. The aeroplane comes along, lifts you up by the seat of the pants, and spits you down in Baghdad, Samarkand, Beluchistan, Fez, Timbuktu, as far as your money will take you. All these once marvelous places whose very names cast a spell over you are now floating islets in the stormy sea of civilization. They mean homely commodities like rubber, tin, pepper, coffee, carborundum and so forth. The natives are derelicts exploited by the octopus whose tentacles stretch from London, Paris, Berlin, Tokio, New York, Chicago to the icy tips of Iceland and the wild reaches of Patagonia. The evidences of this so-called civilization are strewn and dumped higgledy-piggledy wherever the long, slimy tentacles reach out. Nobody is being

civilized, nothing is being altered in any real sense. Some are using knives and forks who formerly ate with their fingers; some
have electric lights in their hovels instead of the kerosene lamp
or the wax taper; some have Sears-Roebuck catalogues and a
Holy Bible on the shelf where once a rifle or a musket lay; some
have gleaming automatic revolvers instead of clubs; some are using money instead of shells and cowries; some have straw hats
which they don't need; some have Jesus Christ and don't know
what to do with Him. But all of them, from the top to the bottom, are restless, dissatisfied, envious, and sick at heart. All of
them suffer from cancer and leprosy, in their souls. The most ignorant and degenerate of them will be asked to shoulder a gun
and fight for a civilization which has brought them nothing but
misery and degradation. In a language which they cannot understand the loudspeaker blares out the disastrous news of victory
and defeat. It's a mad world and when you become slightly detached it seems even more mad than usual. The aeroplane brings
death; the radio brings death; the machine gun brings death; the
tinned goods bring death; the tractor brings death; the priest
brings death; the schools bring death; the laws bring death, the
electricity brings death; the plumbing brings death; the phonograph brings death; the knives and forks bring death; the books
bring death; our very breath brings death, our very language, our
very thought, our money, our love, our charity, our sanitation,
our joy. No matter whether we are friends or enemies, no matter whether we call ourselves Jap, Turk, Russian, French, English, German or American, wherever we go, wherever we cast
our shadow, wherever we breathe, we poison and destroy. Hooray! shouted the Greek. I too yell Hooray! Hooray for civilization! *Hooray! We will kill you all, everybody, everywhere. Hooray
for Death! Hooray! Hooray!*

The next morning I paid a visit to the museum where to my
astonishment I encountered Mr. Tsoutsou in the company of
the Nibelungen racketeers. He seemed highly embarrassed to
be discovered in their presence but, as he explained to me later,

Greece was still a neutral country and they had come armed with letters of introduction from men whom he once considered friends. I pretended to be absorbed in the examination of a Minoan chessboard. He pressed me to meet him in the café later in the day. As I was leaving the museum I got the jitterbugs so bad that I made caca in my pants. I thought of my French friend immediately. Fortunately I had in my little notebook a remedy against such ailments; it had been given me by an English traveler whom I met in a bar one night in Nice. I went back to the hotel, changed my clothes, wrapped the old ones in a bundle with the idea of throwing them in a ravine and, armed with the prescription of the English globetrotter, I made for the drug store.

I had to walk a considerable time before I could drop the bundle unobserved. By that time the jitterbugs had come on again. I made for the bottom of the moat near a dead horse swarming with bottle-flies.

The druggist spoke nothing but Greek. Diarrhoea is one of those words you never think to include in a rough and ready vocabulary—and good prescriptions are in Latin which every druggist should know but which Greek druggists are sometimes ignorant of. Fortunately a man came in who knew a little French. He asked me immediately if I were English and when I said yes he dashed out and in a few minutes returned with a jovial-looking Greek who turned out to be the proprietor of a café nearby. I explained the situation rapidly and, after a brief colloquy with the druggist, he informed me that the prescription couldn't be filled but that the druggist had a better remedy to suggest. It was to abstain from food and drink and go on a diet of soggy rice with a little lemon juice in it. The druggist was of the opinion that it was nothing—it would pass in a few days—everybody gets it at first.

I went back to the café with the big fellow—Jim he called himself—and listened to a long story about his life in Montreal where he had amassed a fortune, as a restaurateur, and then lost it all in the stock market. He was delighted to speak English again. "Don't touch the water here," he said. "My water comes from a spring twenty miles away. That's why I have such a big clientele."

We sat there talking about the wonderful winters in Montreal. Jim had a special drink prepared for me which he said would do me good. I was wondering where to get a good bowl of thick soupy rice. Beside me was a man puffing away at a nargileh; he seemed to be in a stony trance. Suddenly I was back in Paris, listening to my occult friend Urbanski who had gone one winter's night to a bordello in Montreal and when he emerged it was Spring. I have been to Montreal myself but somehow the image of it which I retain is not mine but Urbanski's. I see myself standing in his shoes, waiting for a streetcar on the edge of the town. A rather elegant woman comes along bundled in furs. She's also waiting for the streetcar. How did Krishnamurti's name come up? And then she's speaking of Topeka, Kansas, and it seems as if I had lived there all my life. The hot toddy also came in quite naturally. We're at the door of a big house that has the air of a deserted mansion. A colored woman opens the door. It's her place, just as she described it. A warm, cosy place too. Now and then the doorbell rings. There's the sound of muffled laughter, of glasses clinking, of slippered feet slapping through the hall.

I had listened to this story so intently that it had become a part of my own life. I could feel the soft chains she had slipped around him, the too comfortable bed, the delicious, drowsy indolence of the pasha who had retired from the world during a season of snow and ice. In the Spring he had made his escape but I, I had remained and sometimes, like now, when I forget myself, I'm there in a hotbed of roses trying to make clear to her the mystery of Arjuna's decision.

Towards evening I went round to the café to meet Mr. Tsoutsou. He insisted that I accompany him to his studio where he had planned to present me to the little circle of literati. I was wondering about the bowl of rice and how to get it.

The retreat was hidden away in the loft of a dilapidated building which reminded me forcibly of Giono's Biblical birthplace in Manosque. It was the sort of den which St. Jerome might have created for himself during his exile in a foreign land. Outside, in the volcanic hinterland of Herakleion, Augustine ruled; here, amidst the musty books, the paintings, the music, was Jerome's world. Beyond, in Europe proper, another world was going to ruin. Soon one would have to come to a place like Crete to recover the evidences of a civilization which had disappeared. In this little den of Tsoutsou's there was a cross-cut of everything which had gone to make the culture of Europe. This room would live on as the monks lived on during the Dark Ages.

One by one his friends came, poets most of them. French was the common language. Again there came up the names of Eliot, Breton, Rimbaud. They spoke of Joyce as a Surrealist. They thought America was experiencing a cultural renascence. We clashed. I can't stand this idea, which is rooted in the minds of little peoples, that America is the hope of the world. I brought up the names of their own writers, the contemporary poets and novelists of Greece. They were divided as to the merits of this one and that one. They were not sure of their own artists. I deplored that.

Food was served, and wine, and beautiful grapes, all of which I had to refuse. "I thought you liked to eat and drink," said Tsoutsou. I told him I was indisposed. "Oh, come, you can eat a little cold fish," he insisted. "And this wine —you *must* taste it—I ordered it especially for you." The law of hospitality bade me to accept. I raised the glass and drank a toast to the future of Greece. Somebody insisted that I try the wonderful olives—and the famous goat cheese. Not a grain of rice in sight. I saw myself dashing for the bottom of the moat again beside the dead horse with the poisonous fat green flies.

"And what about Sinclair Lewis—surely he was one of America's great writers?"

When I said no they all seemed to be highly dubious of my critical faculties. Who was a great American writer, then, they demanded. I said: "Walt Whitman. He's the only great writer we ever had."

"And Mark Twain?"

"For adolescents," I answered.

They laughed, as the troglodytes had laughed at me the other morning.

"So you think Rimbaud is greater than all the American poets put together?" said one young man challengingly.

"Yes, I do. I think he's greater than all the *French* poets put together too."

This was like throwing a bomb in their midst. As always, the greatest defenders of French tradition are to be found outside France. Tsoutsou was of the opinion that they ought to listen to me at length; he thought my attitude was typical, representative of the American spirit. He applauded as one would applaud a trained seal after it has given a performance with the cymbals. I was somewhat depressed by this atmosphere of futile discussion. I made a long speech in bad French in which I admitted that I was no critic, that I was always passionate and prejudiced, that I had no reverence for anything except what I liked. I told them that I was an ignoramus, which they tried to deny vigorously. I said I would rather tell them stories. I began—about a bum who had tried to hit me up for a dime one evening as I was walking towards the Brooklyn Bridge. I explained how I had said No to the man automatically and then, after I had walked a few yards it suddenly came to me that a man had asked me for something and I ran back and spoke to him. But instead of giving him a dime or a quarter, which I could easily have done, I told him that I was broke, that I had wanted to let him know that, that was all. And the man had said to me—"Do you mean that, buddy? Why, if that's the way it is, I'll be glad to give you a dime myself." And I let him give it to me, and I thanked him warmly, and walked off.

They thought it a very interesting story. So that's how it was in America? Strange country … anything could happen there.

"Yes," I said, "a very strange country," and I thought to myself that it was wonderful not to be there any more and God willing I'd never return to it.

"And what is it about Greece that makes you like it so much?" asked someone.

I smiled. "The light and the poverty," I said. "You're a romantic," said the man.

"Yes," I said, "I'm crazy enough to believe that the happiest man on earth is the man with the fewest needs. And I also believe that if you have light, such as you have here, all ugliness is obliterated. Since I've come to your country I know that light is holy: Greece is a holy land to me."

"But have you seen how poor the people are, how wretchedly they live?"

"I've seen worse wretchedness in America," I said. "Poverty alone doesn't make people wretched."

"You can say that because you have sufficient..."

"I can say it because I've been poor all my life," I retorted. "I'm poor now," I added. "I have just enough to get back to Athens. When I get to Athens I'll have to think how to get more. It isn't money that sustains me— it's the faith I have in myself, in my own powers. In spirit I'm a millionaire—maybe that's the best thing about America, that you believe you'll rise again."

"Yes, yes," said Tsoutsou, clapping his hands, "that's the wonderful thing about America: you don't know what defeat is." He filled the glasses again and rose to make a toast. "To America!" he said, "long may it live!"

"To Henry Miller!" said another, "because he believes in himself."

I got back to the hotel in the nick of time. To-morrow I would surely start the rice diet. I lay in bed watching the men in shirt sleeves across the way. The scene reminded me of similar ones in dingy lofts in the vicinity of the Broadway Central Hotel, New York—Greene or Bleecker Street, for example. The intermediate zone between high finance and grovelling in the bowels of the earth. Paper box representatives ... celluloid collars ... twine ... mousetraps. The moon was scudding through the clouds. Africa not far distant. At the other end of the island a place called Phaestos. As I was dozing off Mlle. Swedenborg knocked at the door to inform me that there had been a telephone call from the prefect of police. "What does he want?" I asked. She didn't know.

I was disturbed. The word police fills me with panic. I got up automatically to search my wallet for the *permis de séjour.* I examined it to make sure that I was *en règle.* What could that bastard want of me? Was he going to ask how much money I had on me? In out of the way places they always think of petty little things to harass you about. "*Vive la France!*" I muttered absent-mindedly. Another thought came to me. I slipped on my bathrobe and wandered from one floor to another to make sure that I could find the W. C. in a hurry if necessary. I felt thirsty. I rang and asked if they had any mineral water. The maid couldn't understand what I meant. "Water, water," I repeated, looking around in vain for a bottle to illustrate what I meant. She disappeared to return with a pitcher of iced water. I thanked her and turned out the lights. My tongue was parched. I got up and wet my lips, fearful lest a stray drop slip down my burning throat.

Next morning I remembered that I had forgotten to call at the vice consul's office for the book he had promised me. I went to his office and waited for him to make his appearance. He arrived beaming with pleasure. He had already written an inscription in the book; he wanted me to be sure to let him know, immediately I had read the book, what I thought of it. I brought up the rice problem as delicately as I could, after he had tried to sell me the idea of visiting the leper colony somewhere on the island. Boiled rice? Nothing could be easier. His wife would fix it for me every day—it would be a pleasure. Somehow I was touched by his alacrity in aiding me. I tried to imagine a French functionary speaking this way—it was just impossible. On the contrary, the image that came to mind was that of the Frenchwoman who ran the *tabac* in a certain neighborhood where I had lived for several years and how one day, when I was short two sous, she had snatched the cigarettes from my hand and shouted to me in a panicky voice that they couldn't possibly give credit to anyone, it would ruin them, and so forth. I thought of a scene in another *bistro*, where I was also a good customer, and how they had refused to lend me the two francs I needed to make the admission to a movie. I remembered how enraged I became when the woman pretended to me that she was not the proprietress but the cashier and how I had taken the change out of my pocket, just to prove to her that I had some money on me, and flinging it into the street I said—"*There*, that's what I think of your lousy francs!" And the waiter had immediately run out into the street and begun searching for the dirty little coins.

A little later, strolling about the town, I stopped into a shop near the museum where they sold souvenirs and postcards. I looked over the cards leisurely; the ones I liked best were soiled and wrinkled. The man, who spoke French fluently, offered to make the cards presentable. He asked me to wait a few minutes while he ran over to the house and cleaned and ironed them. He said he would make them look like new. I was so dumbfounded that before I could say anything he had disappeared, leaving me in charge of the shop. After a few minutes his wife came in. I thought she looked strange for a Greek woman. After a few words had passed I realized that she was French and she, when she learned that I hailed from Paris, was overjoyed to speak with me. We got along beautifully until she began talking about Greece. She hated Crete, she said. It was too dry, too dusty, too hot, too bare. She missed the beautiful trees of Normandy, the gardens with the high walls, the orchards, and so on. Didn't I agree with her? I said NO, flatly. "*Monsieur!*" she said, rising up in her pride and dignity, as if I had slapped her in the face.

"I don't miss anything," I said, pressing the point home. "I think this is marvelous. I don't like your gardens with their high walls; I don't like your pretty little orchards and your well-cultivated fields. I like this . . ." and I pointed outdoors to the dusty road on which a sorely-laden donkey was plodding along dejectedly. "But it's not civilized," she said, in a sharp, shrill voice which reminded me of the miserly tobacconiste in the Rue de la Tombe-Issoire.

"*Je m'en fous de la civilisation européenne!*" I blurted out.

"*Monsieur!*" she said again, her feathers ruffled and her nose turning blue with malice.

Fortunately her husband reappeared at this point with the postcards which he had given a dry-cleaning. I thanked him warmly and bought another batch of cards which I selected at random. I stood a moment looking about, wondering what I might buy to show my appreciation. The woman had overlooked my remarks in her zeal to sell me some trifle. She was holding up a hand-woven scarf and patting it affectionately. "Thank you," I said, "I never wear them." "But it would make a beautiful gift," she said—"from Crete, which you are so enamored of." At this her husband pricked up his ears.

"You like it here?" he asked, looking at me approvingly.

"It's a wonderful place," I said. "It's the most beautiful land I've ever seen. I wish I could live here all my life."

The woman dropped the scarf in disgust. "Come back again," begged the man. "We will have a drink together, yes?" I shook hands with him and gave a cold nod to his wife.

That dried-up prune, I thought to myself. How could a full-blooded Greek live with a thing like that? She was probably be-rating him already for the trouble he had put himself to to please an ignorant foreigner. I could hear her saying in that squeaky, shoe-stringed voice: "*Les Américains, ils sont tous les mêmes; ils ne savent pas ce que c'est la vie. Des barbares, quoi!*"

And out on the hot, dusty road, the flies biting like mad, the sun blistering the warts off my chin, the land of Ur reeling in its auto-intoxicated emptiness, I answer her blithely: "*Oui, tu as raison, salope que tu es. Mais moi je n'aime pas les jardins, les pots de fleurs, la petite vie adoucie. Je n'aime pas la Normandie. J'aime le soleil, la nudité, la lumiére....*"

With that off my chest I let a song go out of my heart, prais-ing God that the great Negro race which alone keeps America from falling apart had never known the vice of husbandry. I let a song go out of my heart to Duke Ellington, that suave, super-civilized, double-jointed cobra with the steel-flanged wrists—and to Count Basie (*sent for you yesterday here you come to-day*), long lost brother of Isidore Ducasse and last direct lineal descen-dant of the great and only Rimbaud.

•

Madame, since you were speaking of gardens, let me tell you once and for all how the Dipsy-Doodle works. Here's a passacaglia to embroider tonight when you're doing the drop stitch. As Joe Dudley of Des Moines says, the drums give a feeling of something present. I'll begin with a one o'clock jump, a maxixe à la Huysmans.

Madame, it's like this.... Once there was a land. And there were no walls and there were no orchards. There was just a Boogie Woogie man whose name was Agamemnon. After a time he gave birth to two sons—Epaminondas and Louis the Armstrong. Epaminondas was for war and civilization and, in his treacherous way (which made even the angels weep), he fulfilled himself, thereby bringing on the white plague which ended in the basement of Clytemnestra's palace where the cesspool now stands. Louis was for peace and joy. *"Peace, it's wonderful!"* he shouted all day long.

Agamemnon, seeing that one of his sons had wisdom, bought him a golden torque, saying unto him: "Go forth now and trumpet peace and joy everywhere!" He said nothing about walls or gardens or orchards. He said nothing about building cathedrals. He said: "Go, my son, and riff it through the land!" And Louis went out into the world, which had already fallen into a state of sadness, and he took with him nothing save the golden torque.

Louis soon found that the world was divided into black and white, very sharp and very bitterly. Louis wanted to make everything golden, not like coins or ikons but like ripe ears of corn, gold like the goldenrod, gold that everybody could look at and feel and roll around in.

When he had walked as far as Monemvasia, which is at the lower end of the Peloponnesus, Louis boarded the gin mill special for Memphis The train was full of white people whom his brother Epaminondas had driven mad with misery. Louis had a great desire to leave the train and run his sore, aching feet through the river Jordan. He wanted to take a riff in the blue, blow his top.

Now it happened that the train came to a stop at Tuxedo Junction, not far from the corner of Munson Street. It was high time because Louis felt a breakdown coming on. And then he remembered what his father, the illustrious Agamemnon, had told him once—to first get tight and quiet as a fiend, *and then blow!* Louis put his thick loving lips to the golden torque and blew. He blew one great big sour note like a rat bustin' open and the tears came to his eyes and the sweat rolled down his neck. Louis felt that he was bringing peace and joy to all the world. He filled his lungs again and blew a molten note that reached so far into the blue it froze and hung in the sky like a diamond-pointed star. Louis stood up and twisted the torque until it became a great shining bulge of ecstasy. The sweat was pouring down him like a river. Louis was so happy that his eyes began to sweat too and they made two golden pools of joy one of which he named the King of Thebes in honor of Oedipus, his nearest of kin, who had lived to meet the Sphinx.

On a certain day it became the Fourth of July, which is Dipsy-Doodle day in Walla Walla. Louis had by this time made a few friends as he went riffin' his way through the new land. One was a Count and another was a Duke. They carried little white rats on their fingertips and when they couldn't stand it any longer, the sad, white gut bucket of a world, they bit with the ends of their fingers and where they bit it was like a laboratory of guinea pigs going crazy with experimentation. The Count was a two-fingered specialist, built small and round like a rotunda, with a little moustache. He always began—*bink-bink!* Bink for poison, bink for arson. He was quiet and steady like, a sort of introverted gorilla who, when he got bogged in the depths of the gerundive, would speak French like a marquis or babble in Polish or Lithuanian. He never started twice the same way. And when he came to the end, unlike other poison and arson men, he always stopped. He stopped sudden like, and the piano sank with him and the little white rats too. Until the next time.

The Duke, on the other hand, always slid down from above in a silver-lined bathrobe. The Duke had been educated in Heaven where at an early age he had learned to play the pearly harp and other vibrafoid instruments of the celestial realm. He was always suave, always composed. When he smiled wreaths of ectoplasm formed around his mouth. His favorite mood was indigo which is that of the angels when all the world is sound asleep.

There were others too of course—Joe the chocolate cherub, Chick who was already sprouting wings, Big Sid, and Fats and Ella and sometimes Lionel the golden boy who carried everything in his hat. There was always Louis, of course, Louis just like he is, with that broad, million dollar smile like the Argive plain itself and smooth, polished nostrils that gleamed like the leaves of the magnolia tree.

On Dipsy-Doodle day they gathered together round the golden torque and they made jam—missionary jam. That is, Chick, who was like peppered lightning, always flashing his teeth, always spitting out dice and doodle balls, Chick would web it to the jungle and back again like a breeze. What for? you say. Why to fetch a big greasy missionary, to boil him in oil, that's what for. Joe, whose business it was to give that reassuring feeling of something present, Joe would keep to the background like a rubber pelvis.

Boil 'em alive, feathers and all—that's how the Dipsy-Doodle works. It's barbarious, Madame, but that's how it is. Ain't no more orchards, ain't no more walls. King Agamemnon say to his son: "Boy, bring that land!" And boy, he bring it back. He bring it back tootlin' and buglin'. He bring back goldenrods and yellow sassafras; he bring back golden cockerels and spaniels red as tigers. No more missionary culturization, no more Pammy Pamondas. Might be Hannibal, M.O., might be Carthage, Illy-Illy. Might be the moon be low, might be a sort of funeralization. Might be nuthin' neither, 'cause I ain't thought to name it yet.

Madame, I'm gonna blow you down so low you're gonna quiver like a snake. I'm gonna take a fat rat-bustin' note and blow you back to Kingdom Come. Hear that tappin' and rappin'? Hear that chicken liver moanin'? That's Boogie Woogie drawin' his breath. That's missionary man foamin' like a stew.

Hear that screamin' high and shrill? That's Meemy the Meemer. She's little and low, sort of built up from the ground. Jam to-day, jam to-morrow. Nobody rare, nobody worry. Nobody die sad no more. 'Cause the old glad land is full of torque. Blow wind! Blow dust in the eye! Blow hot and dry, blow brown and bare! Blow down them orchards, blow down them walls. Boogie Woogie's here again. Boogie Woogie go bink-bink. Bink for poison, bink for arson. He ain't got no feet, he ain't got no hands. Boogie Woogie done swish it up and down the land. Boogie Woogie scream. Boogie Woogie scream again. Boogie Woogie scream again, again, again, again. No walls, no trees, no nuthin'. Tish and pish and pish and tish. Rats movin'. Three rats, four rats, ten rats. One cockerel, one rat. Locomotive make choo-choo. Sun out and the road is hot and dusty. Trees jell, leaves shell. No knees, no hands, no toes between his fingers. Makin' hominy, that's all. He's comin' down the road with a banjo on his knees. He's a-tappin' and a-slappin'. Tappin' the Tappahanna, rappin' the Rappahanna. He's got blood on his fingers and blood in his hair. He's bogged down, kit and boodle, and the blood is on his knees.

Louis's back in the land with a horseshoe round his neck. He's makin' ready to blow a fat rat-bustin' note that'll knock the blue and the gray into a twisted torquemada. Why he wanna do that? To show he's satisfied. All them wars and civilizations ain't brought nobody no good. Just blood everywhere and people prayin' for peace.

In the tomb where they buried him alive lies his father Agamemnon. Agamemnon was a shining god-like man who was indeed a god. He gave birth to two sons who travelled far apart. One sowed misery throughout the world and the other sowed joy.

Madame, I am thinking of you now, of that sweet and fetid stench of the past which you throw off. You are Madame Nostalgia rotting in the cemetery of inverted dreams. You are the black satin ghost of everything which refuses to die a natural death. You are the cheap paper flower carnation of weak and useless womanhood. I repudiate you, your country, your walls, your orchards, your tempered, hand-laundered climate. I call up the malevolent spirits of the jungle to assassinate you in your sleep. I turn the golden torque on you to harass you in your last agonies. You are the white of a rotten egg. You stink.

Madame, there are always two paths to take: one back towards the comfort and security of death, the other forward to nowhere. You would like to fall back amongst your quaint tombstones and familiar cemetery walls. Fall back, then, fall deep and fathomless into the ocean of annihilation. Fall back into that bloody torpor which permits idiots to be crowned as kings. Fall back and writhe in torment with the evolutionary worms. I am going on, on past the last black and white squares. The game is played out, the figures have melted away, the lines are frazzled, the board is mildewed. Everything has become barbarious again.

What makes it so lovely and barbarious? The thought of annihilation. Boogie Woogie came back with blood on his knees. He made a one o'clock jump into the land of Jehoshaphat. They took him for a buggy ride. They poured kerosene on his kinky hair and fried him upside down. Sometimes, when the Count goes *bink-bink*, when he says to himself—what kind of sorrowful tune will I play now?—you can hear the flesh sizzlin' and stretchin'. When he was little and low they bashed him flat with a potato masher. When he was bigger and higher they caught him in the gut with a pitchfork.

Epaminondas sure did a swell job civilizationing everybody with murder and hatred. The whole world has become one great big organism dying of ptomaine poison. It got poisoned just when everything was beautifully organized. It became a gut bucket, the white and wormy gut of a rotten egg that died in the shell. It brought on rats and lice, it brought on trench feet and trench teeth, it brought on declarations and preambles and protocols, it brought on bandy-legged twins and bald-headed eunuchs, it brought on Christian Science and poison gases and plastic underwear and glass shoes and platinum teeth.

Madame, as I understand it, you want to preserve this *Ersatz* which is sadness and propinquity and status quo all rolled into a fat meat ball. You want to put it in the frying pan and fry it when you're hungry, is that it? It comforts you, even though there is no nourishment in it, to call it civilization, isn't that how it is? *Madame*, you are horribly, miserably, woefully, irrefragably mistaken. You were taught to spell a word which makes no sense. There ain't no such thing as civilization. There's one big barbarious world and the name of the rat-catcher is Boogie Woogie. He had two sons and one of them got caught in a wringer and died all mangled and twisted, his left hand thumpin' like a crazy fluke. The other is alive and procreating like a shad roe. He lives in joy barbariously with nothing but the golden torque. He took the gin mill special at Monemvasia one day and when he got to Memphis he rose up and blew a fat rat-bustin' note that knocked the meat ball out of the frying pan.

I'm going to leave you now, *Madame*, to wither in your own trimmed lard. I leave you to fade away to a grease spot. I leave you to let a song go out of my heart. I'm on my way to Phaestos, the last Paradise on earth. This is just a barbarious passacaglia to keep your fingers busy when you fall back on the drop stitch. Should you wish to buy a second-hand sewing machine get in touch with Murder, Death & Blight, Inc. of Oswego, Saskatchewan, as I am the sole, authorized, living agent this side of the ocean and have no permanent headquarters. As of this day forth, in witness whereof, heretofore solemnly sealed and affixed, I do faithfully demit, abdicate, abrogate, evaginate and fornicate all powers, signatories, seals and offices in favor of peace and joy, dust and heat, sea and sky, God and angel, having to the best of my ability performed the duties of dealer, slayer, blighter, bludgeoner and betrayer of the Soiled & Civilized Sewing Machine manufactured by Murder, Death & Blight, Inc. of the Dominions of Canada, Australia, Newfoundland, Patagonia, Yucatan, Schleswig-Holstein, Pomerania and other allied, subjugated provinces registered under the Death and Destruction Act of the planet Earth during the whilomst hegemony of the Homo sapiens family this last twenty-five thousand years.

And now, *Madame*, since by the terms of this contract we have only a few thousand more years to run, I say *bink-bink* and bid you good-day. This is positively the end. *Bink-bink!*

Before the rice diet got properly under way it began to rain, not
heavy rains, but moist, intermittent rains, a half hour's sprinkle,
a thunder shower, a drizzle, a warm spray, a cold spray, an electric needle bath. It went on for days. The aeroplanes couldn't
land because the flying field had become too soggy. The roads
had become a slimy yellow mucus, the flies swarmed in dizzy,
drunken constellations round one's head and bit like fiends. In-
doors it was cold, damp, fungus-bitten; I slept in my clothes
with my overcoat piled on top of the blankets and the windows
closed tight. When the sun came out it was hot, an African heat
which caked and blistered the mud, which made your head ache
and gave you a restlessness which increased as soon as the rain
began to fall. I was eager to go to Phaestos but I kept putting it
off for a change of weather. I saw Tsoutsou again; he told me
that the prefect had been inquiring about me. "He wants to see
you," he said. I didn't dare to ask what for, I said I would pay him
a visit shortly.

Between drizzles and downpours I explored the town more
thoroughly. The outskirts of the city fascinated me. In the sun
it was too hot, in the rain it was creepily cold. On all sides the
town edged off abruptly, like an etching drowned in a plate of
black zinc. Now and then I passed a turkey tied to a doorknob
by a string; the goat was ubiquitous and the donkey. There were
wonderful cretins and dwarves too who wandered about with
freedom and ease; they belonged to the scene, like the cactus,
like the deserted park, like the dead horse in the moat, like the
pet turkeys tied to the doorknobs.

Along the waterfront there was a fang-like row of houses behind a hastily made clearing, strangely reminiscent of certain
old quarters in Paris where the municipality has begun to create
light and air for the children of the poor. In Paris one roams from
quarter to quarter through imperceptible transitions, as if moving through invisible beaded curtains. In Greece the changes are
sharp, almost painful. In some places you can pass through all

the changes of fifty centuries in the space of five minutes. Everything is delineated, sculptured, etched. Even the wastelands have
an eternal cast about them. You see everything in its unique-
ness—*a* man sitting on *a* road under *a* tree: *a* donkey climbing
a path near *a* mountain: *a* ship in *a* harbor in *a* sea of turquoise:
a table on *a* terrace beneath *a* cloud. And so on. Whatever you
look at you see as if for the first time; it won't run away, it won't
be demolished overnight; it won't disintegrate or dissolve or
revolutionize itself. Every individual thing that exists, whether
made by God or man, whether fortuitous or planned, stands out
like a nut in an aureole of light, of time and of space. The shrub
is the equal of the donkey; a wall is as valid as a belfry; a melon
is as good as a man. Nothing is continued or perpetuated beyond its natural time; there is no iron will wreaking its hideous
path of power. After a half hour's walk you are refreshed and exhausted by the variety of the anomalous and sporadic. By comparison Park Avenue seems insane and no doubt is insane. The
oldest building in Herakleion will outlive the newest building
in America. Organisms die; the cell lives on. Life is at the roots,
embedded in simplicity, asserting itself uniquely.

I called regularly at the vice consul's home for my bowl of rice.
Sometimes he had visitors. One evening the head of the merchant tailors' association dropped in. He had lived in America
and spoke a quaint, old-fashioned English. "Gentleman, will you
have a cigar?" he would say. I told him I had been a tailor myself once upon a time. "But he's a journalist now," the vice consul hastily put in. "He's just read my book." I began to talk about
alpaca sleeve linings, bastings, soft rolled lapels, beautiful vicu-
nas, flap pockets, silk vests and braided cutaways. I talked about
these things madly for fear the vice consul would divert the conversation to his pet obsession. I wasn't quite sure whether the
boss tailor had come as a friend or as a favored menial. I didn't
care, I decided to make a friend of him if only to keep the conversation off that infernal book which I had pretended to have
read but which I couldn't stomach after page three.

"Where was your shop, gentleman?" asked the tailor.

"On Fifth Avenue," I said. "It was my father's shop."

"Fifth Avenue—that's a very rich street, isn't it?" he said, where-upon the vice consul pricked up his ears.

"Yes," I said, "we had only the best customers—nothing but bankers, brokers, lawyers, millionaires, steel and iron magnates, hotel keepers, and so on."

"And you learned how to cut and sew?" he said.

"I could only cut pants," I answered. "Coats were too complicated."

"How much did you charge for a suit, gentleman?"

"Oh, at that time we asked only a hundred or a hundred and twenty-five dollars...."

He turned to the vice consul to ask him to calculate what that would be in drachmas. They figured it out. The vice consul was visibly impressed. It *was* a staggering sum in Greek money—enough to buy a small ship. I felt that they were somewhat skeptical. I began talking carload lots—about telephone books, sky-scrapers, tickertape, paper napkins and all the ignominious paraphernalia of the big city which makes the yokel roll his eyes as if he'd seen the Red Sea opening up. The ticker tape arrested the tailor's attention. He had been to Wall Street once, to visit the stock exchange. He wanted to speak about it. He asked me diffidently if there weren't men in the street who ran their own little markets. He began making deaf and dumb signs as they used to do in the curb market. The vice consul looked at him as if he were slightly touched. I came to his rescue. Of course there were such men, thousands of them, all trained in this special deaf and dumb language, I asserted vigorously. I stood up and made a few signs myself, to demonstrate how it was done. The vice consul smiled. I said I would take them inside the stock ex-change, on the floor itself. I described that madhouse in detail, ordering myself slices of Anaconda Copper, Amalgamated Tin, Tel & Tel, anything I could remember of that crazy Wall Street past whether volatile, combustible or analgesic. I ran from one corner of the room to the other, buying and selling like a maniac, standing at the vice consul's commode and telephoning my broker to flood the market, calling my banker to make a loan of fifty thousand immediately, calling the telegraph jakes to take a string of telegrams, calling the grain and wheat trusters in Chicago to dump a load in the Mississippi, calling the Secretary of the Interior to inquire if he had passed that bill about the Indians, calling my chauffeur to tell him to put a new spare tire on the back behind the rumble seat, calling my shirt-maker to curse him for making the neck too tight on the pink and white shirt and what about my initials. I ran across the seat and gobbled a sandwich at the Exchange Buffet. I said hello to a friend of mine who was going upstairs to his office to blow his brains out. I bought the racing edition and stuck a carnation in my button hole. I had my shoes shined, while answering telegrams and telephoning with the left hand. I bought a few thousand railroad stocks absent-mindedly and switched to Consolidated Gas on a hunch that the new pork barrel bill would improve the housewives' lot. I almost forgot to read the weather report; fortunately I had to run back to the cigar store to fill my breast pocket with a handful of Corona-Coronas and that reminded me to look up the weather report to see if it had rained in the Ozark region.

The tailor was listening to me goggle-eyed. "That's the truth," he said excitedly to the vice consul's wife who had just made another bowl of soggy rice for me. And then suddenly it occurred to me that Lindbergh was coming back from Europe. I ran for the elevator and took the express to the 109th floor of a building that hadn't been built yet. I ran to the window and opened it. The street was choked with frantically cheering men, women, boys, girls, horse cops, motorcycle cops, ordinary cops, thieves, bulls, plainclothesmen, Democrats, Republicans, farmers, lawyers, acrobats, thugs, bank clerks, stenographers, floor-walkers, anything with pants or skirts on, anything that could cheer, holler, whistle, stamp, murder or evaginate. Pigeons were flying through the canyon. It was Broadway. It was the year something or other and our hero was returning from his great transcontinental flight. I stood at the window and cheered until I was hoarse. I don't believe in aeroplanes but I cheered anyway. I took a drink of rye to clear my throat. I grabbed a telephone book. I tore it to pieces like a crazed hyena. I grabbed some ticker tape. I threw that down on the flyspecks—Anaconda Copper, Amalgamated Zinc, U. S. Steel—57½, 34, 138, minus two, plus 6¾, 51, going up, going higher, Atlantic Coast Line, Seaboard Air Line, here he comes, he's coming, that's him, that's Lindbergh, Hooray, Hooray, some guy, the eagle of the skies, a hero, the greatest hero of all time....

I took a mouthful of rice to quiet myself.

"How high is the tallest building?" asked the vice consul.

I looked at the tailor. "You answer it," I said.

He guessed about 57 stories.

I said—"A hundred and forty two, not counting the flagpole."

I stood up again to illustrate. Best way is to count the windows. The average skyscraper has roughly 92,546 windows back and front. I undid my belt and put it on again clumsily, as if I were a window-cleaner. I went to the window and sat on the sill outside. I cleaned the window thoroughly. I unhooked myself and went to the next window. I did that for four and a half hours, making roughly 953 windows cleaned, scraped and waterproofed.

"Doesn't it make you dizzy?" asked the tailor.

"No, I'm used to it," I said. "I was a steeplejack once—after I quit the merchant tailoring business." I looked at the ceiling to see if I could do any demonstrating with the chandeliers.

"You'd better eat your rice," said the vice consul's wife.

I took another spoonful by way of politeness and absentmindedly reached for the decanter in which there was the cognac. I was still excited about Lindbergh's homecoming. I forgot that actually, on that day when he landed at the Battery, I was digging a ditch for the Park Department in the County of Catawpa. The Commissioner was making a speech at a bowling club, a speech I had written for him the day before.

The vice consul was completely at home now in the New World. He had forgotten about his contribution to life and letters. He was pouring me another drink.

Had the gentleman tailor ever gone to a ball game, I inquired. He hadn't. Well, he surely must have heard of Christy Mathewson—or Walter Johnson? He hadn't. Had he ever heard of a spitball? He hadn't. Or a home run? He hadn't. I threw the sofa cushions around on the parlor floor—first, second, third base and home plate. I dusted the plate with the napkin. I put on my cage. I caught a fast one right over the plate. Strike! Two more and he's out, I explained. I threw off the mask and ran towards the infield. I looked up through the roof and I saw the ball dropping out of the planet Pluto. I caught it with one hand and threw it to the shortstop. He's out, I said, it was a fly. Three more innings to go. How about a little popcorn? Have a bottle of pop, then? I took out a package of Spearmint and I stuck a rib in my throat. Always buy Wrigley's, I said, it lasts longer. Besides, they spend $5,000,000,963.00 a year for advertising. Gives people work. Keeps the subways clean.... How about the Carnegie Library? Would you like to pay a visit to the library? Five million, six hundred and ninety eight thousand circulating subscribers. Every book thoroughly bound, filed, annotated, fumigated and wrapped in cellophane. Andrew Carnegie gave it to the City of New York in memory of the Homestead Riots. He was a poor boy who worked his way to the top. He never knew a day of joy. He was a very great millionaire who proved that it pays to work hard and save your pennies. He was wrong, but that doesn't make any difference. He's dead now and he left us a chain of libraries which makes the working people more intelligent, more cultured, more informed, in short, more miserable and unhappy than they ever were, bless his heart. Let's go now to Grant's Tomb....

The tailor looked at his watch. It was getting late, he thought. I poured myself a nightcap, picked up the first, second and third bases and looked at the parrot which was still awake because they had forgotten to put the hood over the cage.

"It's been a wonderful evening," I said, shaking hands all around, shaking hands with the maid too by mistake. "You must come and see me when I get back to New York I have a town

house and a country house, you know. The weather is excellent
in the Fall, when the smoke has cleared away. They're building a
new dynamo over near Spuyten Duyvil: it runs by ether waves.
The rice was excellent tonight. And the cognac too...."

To-morrow I'll go to Phaestos, I said to myself, picking my way
through the fang-bitten streets like a laminated water-moccasin.
I had to remind myself that I was in Crete, a quite different Crete
than I had pictured to myself in my dreams. Again I had that feeling of the back pages of Dickens' novels, of a quaint, one-legged
world illumined by a jaded moon: a land that had survived every catastrophe and was now palpitating with a blood beat, a
land of owls and herons and crazy relics such as sailors bring
back from foreign shores. In the moonlight, navigating through
the silent streets like a foundering ship, I felt that the earth was
bearing me through a zone I had never been carried through before. I was a little nearer to the stars and the ether was charged
with their nearness; it was not simply that they were more brilliant, or that the moon which had taken on the color of a yam
had grown swollen and lopsided, but that the atmosphere had
undergone a subtle, perfumed alteration. There was a residue,
an elixir, I might almost say, which had clung to the aura which
the earth gives off and which had increased in essence from repeated journeys through this particular corner of the zodiac. It
was nostalgic; it awakened those ageless hordes of ancestral men
who stand with eyes closed, like trees after the passing of a flood,
in the ever-moving stream of the blood. The blood itself went
through a change, thickening with the remembrance of man-
made dynasties, of animals raised to divination, of instruments
poised to thousand year niceties, of floods lapped up, divested
of secrets, unburdened of treasures. The earth became again that
strange one-legged creature which pegs and wobbles through
diamond-pointed fields, passing faithfully through all the habita-
tions of its solar creation; became that which it will be to the end
and which in becoming transmogrifies the obscene goat into the
stillness of that which always was, since there is no other, not
even the possibility of a simulacrum.

Greece is what everybody knows, even *in absentia,* even as a child or as an idiot or as a not-yet-born. It is what you expect the earth to look like given a fair chance. It is the subliminal threshold of innocence. It stands, as it stood from birth, naked and fully revealed. It is not mysterious or impenetrable, not awesome, not defiant, not pretentious. It is made of earth, air, fire and water. It changes seasonally with harmonious undulating rhythms. It breathes, it beckons, it answers.

Crete is something else. Crete is a cradle, an instrument, a vibrating test tube in which a volcanic experiment has been performed. Crete can hush the mind, still the bubble of thought. I wanted so long and so ardently to see Crete, to touch the soil of Knossus, to look at a faded fresco, to walk where "they" had walked. I had let my mind dwell on Knossus without taking in the rest of the land. Beyond Knossus my mind pictured nothing but a great Australian waste. That Homer had sung of the hundred cities of Crete I didn't know because I could never bring myself to read Homer; that relics of the Minoan period had been found in the tomb of Akhenaton I was ignorant of also. I knew, or believed rather, only that here at Knossus on an island which nowadays scarcely anybody ever thinks to visit there had been initiated some twenty-five or thirty centuries before the dawn of that blight called Christianity a way of life which makes everything that has happened since in this Western World seem pallid, sickly, ghost-ridden and doomed. The Western world, we say, never once thinking to include those other great social experiments which were made in South America and Central America, passing them over always in our rapid historical surveys as if they were accidents, jumping from the Middle Ages to the discovery of America, as if this bastard bloom on the North American continent marked the continuation of the line of true development of man's evolution. Seated on King Minos' throne I felt closer to Montezuma than to Homer or Praxiteles or Caesar or Dante. Looking at the Minoan scripts I thought of the Mayan legends which I had once glimpsed in the British Museum and which stand out in my memory as the most wonderful, the most natural, the most artistic specimens of calligraphy in the long history of letters. Knossus, or what happened there almost fifty centuries ago, is like the hub of a wheel on which many spokes have been fitted only to rot away. The *wheel* was the great discovery; men have since lost themselves in a maze of petty inventions which are merely accessory to the great pristine fact of revolution itself.

The island then was once studded with citadels, the gleaming hub of a wheel whose splendor cast its shadow over the whole known world. In China there was another great revolution going on, in India another, in Egypt another, in Persia another; there were reflections from one to another which intensified the piercing gleams; there were echoes and reverberations. The vertical life of man was constantly churned by the revolutions of these great gleaming wheels of light. Now it is dark. Nowhere throughout the greatly enlarged world is there the least sign or evidence of the turning of a wheel. The last wheel has fallen apart, the vertical life is done with; man is spreading over the face of the earth in every direction like a fungus growth, blotting out the last gleams of light, the last hopes.

I went back to my room determined to plunge into that great unknown tract which we call Crete, anciently the kingdom of Minos, son of Zeus, whose birthplace it was. Since the wheel fell apart, before that too no doubt, every foot of the land has been fought over, conquered and reconquered, sold, bartered, pawned, auctioned off, levelled with fire and sword, sacked, plundered, administered over by tyrants and demons, converted by fanatics and zealots, betrayed, ransomed, traduced by the great powers of our day, desolated by civilized and savage hordes alike, desecrated by all and sundry, hounded to death like a wounded animal, reduced to terror and idiocy, left gasping with rage and impotence, shunned by all like a leper and left to expire in its own dung and ashes. Such is the cradle of our civilization as it was when finally relinquished and bequeathed to its miserable, destitute inhabitants. What had been the birthplace of the greatest of the gods, what had been the cradle and the mother and the inspiration of the Hellenic world, was finally annexed and not so long ago made part of Greece. What a cruel travesty! What a malefic destiny! Here the traveller has to hang his head in shame. This is the Ark left high and dry by the receding waters of civilization. This is the necropolis of culture marking the great crossroads. This is the stone that was finally given Greece to swallow. To be followed up a few years later by another even more terrible gift, the return of a great mutilated member which had been flung with fire and blood into the sea.

I fell into a nightmare. I was being gently and endlessly rocked by the omnipotent Zeus in a burning cradle. I was toasted to a crisp and then gently dumped into a sea of blood. I swam ceaselessly amidst dismembered bodies marked with the cross and the crescent. I came at last to a rock-ribbed shore. It was bare and absolutely deserted of man. I wandered to a cave in the side of a mountain. In the shivery depths I saw a great heart bright as a ruby suspended from the vault by a huge web. It was beating and with each beat there fell to the ground a huge gout of blood. It was too large to be the heart of any living creature. It was larger even than the heart of a god. It is like the heart of agony, I said aloud, and as I spoke it vanished and a great darkness fell over me. Whereupon I sank down, exhausted, and fell into a sob that reverberated from every part of the cave and finally suffocated me.

I awoke and without consulting the sky I ordered a car for the day. Now there were two things I remembered as I set forth in the sumptuous limousine—one, to remember to ask for Kyrios Alexandros at Phaestos and two, to observe whether, as Monsieur Herriot is reported to have said when he climbed to the precincts of the palace, the sky is really closer to the earth than anywhere else on this globe.

We swung through the dilapidated gate in a cloud of dust, scattering chickens, cats, dogs, turkeys, naked children and hoary vendors of sweets to right and left; we burst at full speed into the drab and dun terrain of gutta percha which closes in on the city like mortar filling a huge crack. There were no wolves, buzzards or poisonous reptiles in sight. There was a sun flooded with lemon and orange which hung ominously over the sultry land in that splashing, dripping radiance which intoxicated Van Gogh. We passed imperceptibly from the quick badlands to a fertile rolling region studded with fields of bright-colored crops; it reminded me of that serene steady smile which our own South gives as you roll through the State of Virginia. It set me dreaming, dreaming of the gentleness and docility of the earth when man caresses it with loving hands. I began to dream more and more in the American idiom. I was crossing the continent again. There were patches of Oklahoma, of the Carolinas, of Tennessee, of Texas and New Mexico. Never a great river, never a railroad, however. But the illusion of vast distances, the reality of great vistas, the sublimity of silence, the revelation of light. On the top of a dizzying crag a tiny shrine in blue and white; in the ravine a cemetery of terrifying boulders. We begin to climb, curving around the edges of precipitous drops; across the gulch the earth bulges up like the knees of a giant covered with corduroy. Here and there a man, a woman, the sower, the reaper, silhouetted against billowy clouds of suds. We climb up beyond the cultivated lands, twisting back and forth like a snake, rising to the heights of contemplation, to the abode of the sage, the eagle, the storm cloud. Huge, frenzied pillars of stone, scarred by wind and lightning, grayed to the color of fright, trembling, top-heavy, balanced like macrocosmic fiends, abut the road. The earth grows wan and weird, defertilized, dehumanized, neither brown nor gray nor beige nor taupe nor ecru, the no color of death reflecting light, sponging up light with its hard, parched shag and shooting it back at us in blinding, rock-flaked splinters that bore into the tenderest tissues of the brain and set it whimpering like a maniac.

This is where I begin to exult. This is something to put beside the devastation of man, something to overmatch his bloodiest depredations. This is nature in a state of dementia, nature having lost its grip, having become the hopeless prey of its own elements. This is the earth beaten, brutalized and humiliated by its own violent treachery. This is one of the spots wherein God abdicated, where He surrendered to the cosmic law of inertia. This is a piece of the Absolute, bald as an eagle's knob, hideous as the leer of a hyena, impotent as a granite hybrid. Here nature staggered to a halt in a frozen vomit of hate.

We roll down a crisp, crackling mountainside into an immense plain. The uplands are covered with a sheath of stiff shrub like blue and lavender porcupine quills. Here and there bald patches of red clay, streaks of shale, sand dunes, a field of pea green, a lake of waving champagne. We roll through a village which belongs to no time and no place, an accident, a sudden sprout of human activity because someone sometime or other had returned to the scene of the massacre to look for an old photograph amidst the tumbled ruins and had stayed there from force of inertia and staying there had attracted flies and other forms of animate and inanimate life.

Farther on ... A lone rectangular habitation sunk deep into the ground. A lone pueblo in the midst of a vacuum. It has a door and two windows. It is built like a box. The shelter of some human being. What kind of being? Who lives there? Why? The American scene is behind. We are now traversing the Mesopotamian hinterland. We are riding over dead cities, over elephant bones, over grass-covered sea bottoms. It is beginning to rain a sudden, quick shower that makes the earth steam. I get out and walk through a lake of mud to examine the ruins of Gortyna. I follow the writing on the wall. It tells of laws which nobody obeys any longer. The only laws which last are the unwritten ones. Man is a lawbreaking animal. A timid one, however.

It is high noon. I want to have my lunch in Phaestos. We push on. The rain has stopped, the clouds have broken; the vault of blue spreads out like a fan, the blue decomposing into that ultimate violet light which makes everything Greek seem holy, natural and familiar. In Greece one has the desire to bathe in the sky. You want to rid yourself of your clothes, take a running leap and vault into the blue. You want to float in the air like an angel or lie in the grass rigid and enjoy the cataleptic trance. Stone and sky, they marry here. It is the perpetual dawn of man's awakening.

We glide through a deer run and the car stops at the edge of a

wild park. "Up there," says the man, pointing to a steep bluff—
"Phaestos." He had said the word. It was like magic. I hesitated.
I wanted to prepare myself. "Better take your lunch with you,"
said the man. "They may not have any food up there." I put the
shoe box under my arm and slowly, meditatively, reverently began the pilgrimage.

It was one of the few times in my life that I was fully aware
of being on the brink of a great experience. And not only aware
but grateful, grateful for being alive, grateful for having eyes, for
being sound in wind and limb, for having rolled in the gutter,
for having gone hungry, for having been humiliated, for having
done everything that I did do since at last it had culminated in
this moment of bliss.

I crossed a wooden bridge or two in the depth of the glen and
paused again in the rich mud which was over my shoe tops to
survey the little stretch I had traversed. At the turn of the road I
would begin the laborious ascent. I had the feeling of being surrounded by deer. I had another strong insistent intuition: that
Phaestos was the female stronghold of the Minos family. The
historian will smile; he knows better. But in that instant and forever afterwards, regardless of proofs, regardless of logic, Phaestos became the abode of the queens. Every step I climbed corroborated the feeling.

When I had climbed to the level of the bluff I saw a narrow
path ahead of me leading to the pavilion which has been erected
on the site of the ruins for the convenience of the traveler. Suddenly I espied a man standing at the other end of the path. As
I approached he began bowing and salaaming. That must be
Kyrios Alexandros, I thought.

"God has sent you," he said, pointing heavenward and smiling at me as if in ecstasy. Graciously he relieved me of my coat
and lunch box, informing me rapturously as he trotted along in
front of me what a joy it was to see a human being again. "This
war," he said, wringing his hands and piously raising his eyes in
mute imploration, "this war ... nobody comes here any more.
Alexandros is all alone. Phaestos is dead. Phaestos is forgotten."

He stopped to pick a flower which he handed me. He looked at the flower sadly as if commiserating it on the miserable fate of being left to bloom unnoticed. I had stopped to look backward towards the encircling mountains. Alexandros stood at my side. He waited silently and reverently for me to speak. I couldn't speak. I put my hand on his shoulder and tried to communicate my feelings with moist eyes. Alexandros gave me the look of a faithful dog; he took the hand which I had placed on his shoulder and bending low he kissed it.

"You are a good man," he said. "God sent you to me, to share my loneliness, Alexandros is very happy, very happy. Come," and he took me by the hand and led me round to the front of the pavilion. He did it as if he were about to confer on me the greatest gift that man can give to man. "I give you the earth and all the blessings it contains," said that mute, eloquent look in his eyes. I looked. I said— "God, it's incredible!" I turned my eyes away. It was too much, too much to try to accept at once.

Alexandros had gone inside for a moment, leaving me to pace slowly back and forth on the piazza of the pavilion surveying the grandeur of the scene. I felt slightly demented, like some of the great monarchs of the past who had devoted their lives to the enhancement of art and culture. I no longer felt the need of enrichment; I had reached the apogee, I wanted to give, to give prodigally and indiscriminately of all I possessed.

Alexandros appeared with a rag, a shoe brush and a big rusty knife; he got down on his knees and began manicuring my shoes. I was not in the least embarrassed. I thought to myself let him do as he likes, it gives him pleasure. I wondered vaguely what I might do myself to make men realize what great happiness lies in store for all of us. I sent out a benediction in every direction— to old and young, to the neglected savages in the forgotten parts of the earth, to wild as well as domesticated animals, to the birds of the air, to creeping things, to trees and plants and flowers, to rocks and lakes and mountains. This is the first day of my life, said I to myself, that I have included everybody and everything on this earth in one thought. I bless the world, every inch of it, every living atom, and it is all alive, breathing like myself, and conscious through and through.

Alexandros brought out a table and spread it. He suggested that I walk about the grounds and inspect the ruins. I listened to him as in a trance. Yes, I suppose I ought to stroll about and take it all in. That's what one usually does. I descended the broad steps of the levelled palace and glanced here and there automatically. I hadn't the faintest desire to snoop about examining lintels, urns, pottery, children's toys, votive cells and such like. Below me, stretching away like an infinite magic carpet, lay the plain of Messara, girdled by a majestic chain of mountain ranges. From this sublime, serene height it has all the appearance of the Garden of Eden. At the very gates of Paradise the descendants of Zeus halted here on their way to eternity to cast a last look earthward and saw with the eyes of innocents that the earth is indeed what they had always dreamed it to be: a place of beauty and joy and peace. In his heart man is angelic; in his heart man is united with the whole world. Phaestos contains all the elements of the heart; it is feminine through and through. Everything that man has achieved would be lost were it not for this final stage of contrition which is here incarnated in the abode of the heavenly queens.

I walked about the grounds, taking in the vista from every angle. I described a circle within the enfolding circle of hills. Above me the great vault, roofless, thrown open to infinity. Monsieur Herriot was right and wrong at the same time. One is nearer to the sky, but one is also farther away than ever from that which lies beyond. To reach the sky is nothing—child's play—from this supreme earthly mansion, but to reach beyond, to grasp if only for an instant the radiance and the splendor of that luminous realm in which the light of the heavens is but a faint and sickly gleam is impossible. Here the most sublime thoughts are nullified, stopped in their winged flight by an ever-deepening halo whose effulgence stills the very processes of thought. At its best thought is but speculation, a pastime such as the machine enjoys when it sparks. God has thought everything out in advance. We have nothing to solve: it has all been solved for us. We have but to melt, to dissolve, to swim in the solution. We are soluble fish and the world is an aquarium.

Alexandros was beckoning to me. Lunch was ready. I saw that he had set the table for me alone. I insisted that he set a place for himself. I had difficulty persuading him to do so. I had to put my arm around him, point to the sky, sweep the horizon, include everything in one large gesture before I could induce him to consent to share the meal with me. He opened a bottle of black wine, a heady, molten wine that situated us immediately in the center of the universe with a few olives, some ham and cheese. Alexandros was begging me to stay a few days. He got out the guest book to show me when the last visitor had arrived. The last visitor was a drunken American apparently who had thought it a good joke to sign the Duke of Windsor's name to the register, adding "Oolala, what a night!" I glanced quickly over the signatures and discovered to my astonishment the name of an old friend of mine. I couldn't believe my eyes. I felt like crossing it out. I asked Alexandros if many Americans came to Phaestos. He said yes and from the glow in his eyes I gathered that they left liberal tips. I gathered that they liked the wine too.

I believe the wine was called *mavrodaphne*. If not it should have been because it is a beautiful black word and describes the wine perfectly. It slips down like molten glass, firing the veins with a heavy red fluid which expands the heart and the mind. One is heavy and light at the same time; one feels as nimble as the antelope and yet powerless to move. The tongue comes unloosed from its mooring, the palate thickens pleasurably, the hands describe thick, loose gestures such as one would love to obtain with a fat, soft pencil. One would like to depict everything in sanguine or Pompeiian red with splashes of charcoal and lamp black. Objects become enlarged and blurred, the colors more true and vivid, as they do for the myopic person when he removes his glasses. But above all it makes the heart glow.

I sat and talked with Alexandros in the deaf and dumb language of the heart. In a few minutes I would have to go. I was not unhappy about it; there are experiences so wonderful, so unique, that the thought of prolonging them seems like the basest form of ingratitude. If I were not to go now then I should stay forever, turn my back on the world, renounce everything.

I took a last stroll about the grounds. The sun had disappeared, the clouds were piling up; the brightly carpeted plain of Messara was streaked with heavy patches of shadow and sulphurous gleams of light under the leaden sky. The mountains drew nearer, became massive and ominous in their changing depths of blue. A moment ago the world had seemed ethereal, dream-like, a shifting, evanescent panorama; suddenly it had gathered substance and weight, the shimmering contours massed themselves in orchestral formation, the eagles swooped out of their eyries and hung in the sky like sultry messengers of the gods.

I said good-bye to Alexandros who was now in tears. I turned hastily and started forward along the narrow path which skirts the edge of the cliff. A few paces and Alexandros was behind me; he had quickly gathered a little bouquet of flowers which he pressed upon me. We saluted again. Alexandros remained there, waving to me as I looked back from time to time. I came to the sharp declivity down which I had to wind and twist to the glen. I took a last look back. Alexandros was still there, a tiny speck now, but still waving his arms. The sky had become more menacing; soon everything would be drowned in one vast downpour. I wondered on the way down when I would see it again, if ever. I felt somewhat saddened to think that no one had been with me to share the stupendous gift; it was almost too much to bestow on one lone mortal. It was for that reason perhaps that I had left with Alexandros a princely gratuity—not out of generosity, as he probably assumed, but out of a feeling of guilt. If no one had been there I should still have left something.

Just as I got into the car it began to rain, lightly at first, then more and more heavily. By the time we reached the badlands the earth was a swirling sheet of water; what had been sun-baked clay, sand, barren soil, waste land, was now a series of floating terraces criss-crossed by tawny, turbulent cascades, by rivers flowing in every direction, racing towards the huge steaming sink charged with sullen deposits of earth, broken branches,

boulders, shale, ore, wildflowers, dead insects, lizards, wheelbar-
rows, ponies, dogs, cats, outhouses, yellow ears of corn, birds'
nests, everything which had not the mind nor the feet nor the
roots to resist. On the other side of the mountain, in the same
torrential downpour, we passed men and women with umbrel-
las over their heads seated on diminutive beasts leisurely picking their way down the mountainside. Silent, grave figures moving at a snail's pace, like determined pilgrims on their way to a
holy shrine. The huge twisted sentinels of rock piled one on top
of another like the giddy monuments of matchboxes which Picasso keeps on his mantelpiece had become huge gnarled mush-
rooms dripping with black pigment. In the furious rain their
tilted, toppling forms seemed even more dangerous and menacing than before. Now and then a great mesa rose up, a mass of
delicately veined rock supporting a tiny white sanctuary with a
blue roof. If it were not Crete I could have imagined myself to
be in some weird demonic stretch of Mongolia, some forbidden
pass guarded by evil spirits which lie in wait for the unsuspect-
ing traveler and drive him mad with their three-legged mustangs
and henna-colored corpses that stand like frozen semaphores in
the bleak, moonlit night.

Herakleion was almost dry when we arrived. In the lobby of
the hotel I found Mr. Tsoutsou waiting for me. It was most urgent, he informed me, to pay a visit to the prefect who had been
waiting to see me for the last few days. We went round to his
office at once. There was a beggar woman and two ragged urchins outside his door, otherwise the quarters were empty and
immaculate. We were ushered into his bureau immediately. The
prefect rose from behind a huge, bare desk and came forward
briskly to greet us. Nothing had prepared me to meet such a figure as Stavros Tsoussis turned out to be. I doubt if there is another Greek like him in all Greece. Such alertness, such alacrity,
such punctilio, such suave, steely politeness, such immaculate-
ness. It was as if he had been constantly groomed and attended
during the days and nights that he had been waiting for me to
put in an appearance, as if he had rehearsed his lines over and
over until he had attained the perfection of reeling them off with

a nonchalance that was absolute and terrifying. He was the perfect official, such as one imagines from the cartoons of German officialdom. He was a man of steel through and through, yet bending, compliant, gracious and not in the least officious. The building in which his office was situated was one of those modern cement barracks in which men, papers, rooms and furniture are monotonously the same. Stavros Tsoussis had managed by some undefinable adroitness to transform his bureau, bare though it was, into an alarmingly distinguished tabernacle of red tape. Every gesture of his was fraught with importance; it was as if he had cleared the room of everything which might obstruct his flashing movements, his crisp orders, his terrifically concentrated attention upon the business at hand.

What had he summoned me for? He made that known instantly to Tsoutsou who acted as interpreter. He had asked to see me, immediately upon learning of my arrival, in order first of all to convey his respects to an American author who had graciously deigned to visit such a remote spot as Crete, and secondly to inform me that his limousine, which was waiting outside, was at my disposal should I wish to inspect the island at leisure. Thirdly, he had wished to let me know how deeply he regretted not having been able to reach me sooner because a day or two before he had arranged a banquet in my honor which unfortunately I had evidently not been able to attend. He had wanted me to know what an honor and privilege it was to welcome to his country a representative of such a vast liberty-loving people as the Americans. Greece, he said, would forever be indebted to America, not only for the generous and unselfish aid which she had so spontaneously offered his countrymen in times of anguish, when indeed she seemed to have been deserted by all the civilized nations of Europe, but also because of her unswerving loyalty to those ideals of freedom which were the foundation of her greatness and glory.

It was a magnificent homage and I was for a moment thoroughly overwhelmed. But when he added, almost in the same breath, that he would be pleased to hear what my impressions of Greece were, and particularly Crete, I quickly found my tongue and, turning to Tsoutsou who stood ready to aid me with his own inventive elaborations should I fail, I launched into an equally florid, sweeping testimonial of my love and admiration for his country and his countrymen. I got it out in French because that is the language par excellence for floral wreaths and other decorations. I don't think I had ever before used the French language with such seeming grace and facility; the words rippled off my tongue like pearls, all beautifully garlanded, entwined, interlaced and enchained with deft usages of the verb which ordinarily drive the Anglo-Saxon crazy.

Good, he seemed to say, flashing his lightning-like approval first upon me and then upon the interpreter. Now we can go on to other matters, remaining of course strictly polite, strictly *comme il faut*. You have been where exactly in the course of your brief stay? I explained briefly. Oh, but that is nothing! You must go here, there, everywhere—it is all at your beck and call, and as if to show how easily it might be managed, he nimbly and deftly retreated a pace and a half and, without looking, pressed a button under the desk top, whereupon a flunkey instantly made his appearance, received the peremptory instructions and disappeared. I was dying to ask him where he had received his flawless training, but restrained the impulse until a more favorable moment. What an executive he would have made in a typical American corporation! What a sales director! And here he was in an apparently deserted building, all dressed to go on and do his stuff but no audience, no spectacle, just the usual dull routine of a provincial town at the edge of the world. Never have I seen ability so sadly misplaced. Had he been so inclined—and God only knows what might be the vaulting ambitions of such an individual caught here in a vacuum of futility—he could easily have assumed the dictatorship of the whole Balkans. In a few days I could see him taking over the leadership of the whole Mediterranean world, settling with one bold stroke of the pen the destiny of this great basin for hundreds of years to come. Charming, gracious, hospitable though he was, I was almost terrified of him. For the first time in my life I had found myself in the presence of a man of power, a man who could do anything he set his mind to, a man moreover who would not flinch or balk at the cost of fulfilling his dream. I felt that I was looking at an embryonic despot, a not unkindly one, certainly a most intelligent one, but above all a ruthless one, a man of iron will, a man of one single purpose: the born leader. Beside him Hitler seems a caricature and Mussolini an old-fashioned Ben Greet player. As for the great industrial magnates of America, such as they reveal themselves to be through the movies and the newspapers, why they are but overgrown children, hydrocephalic geniuses playing with dynamite in the sanctimonious arms of the Baptist saints. Stavros Tsoussis could twist them like hairpins between his two fingers.

We withdrew in perfect order after the amenities had come to a natural end. The beggar woman was still at the door with her two ragged urchins. I wondered in vain what that interview would be like, assuming that she ever had the good fortune to get beyond the threshold of that forbidding sanctuary. I gave one of the urchins a few drachmas which he immediately handed to his mother. Tsoutsou, seeing that the mother was about to make an appeal for more substantial aid, gently dragged me away.

I made up my mind that night to leave the next day. I had a hunch that there was money waiting for me in Athens. I notified the Air Line that I would not avail myself of the return ticket. I found that the planes were not running anyway—the landing field was too soggy.

I boarded the boat the next evening. The next morning we were at Canea where we remained until late that afternoon. I spent the time ashore eating and drinking and strolling about the town. The old part of the town was decidedly interesting; it had all the air of a Venetian stronghold which I believe it once was. The Greek part was as usual anomalous, straggling, thoroughly individualistic and eclectic. I had the sensation, only to a more intense degree, which I so often had in Greece—that the moment the power of the invader was halted or suspended, the moment the hand of authority relaxed, the Greek took up

again his very natural, very human, always intimate, always un-
derstandable life of everyday routine. What is unnatural, and
here in such deserted places it speaks so strongly, is the imposing
power of castle, church, garrison, merchant. Power fades away in
ugly decrepitude, leaving little vulture-like knobs of manifested
will here and there to indicate the ravages of pride, envy, malice,
greed, superstition, ritual, dogma. Left to his own resources man
always begins again in the Greek way—a few goats or sheep,
a rude hut, a patch of crops, a clump of olive trees, a running
stream, a flute.

In the night we passed a snow-covered mountain. I think we
stopped again, at Retimo. It was a long, slow journey back by
ship, but a natural, sensible one. There is no better and no more
dilapidated craft than the ordinary Greek boat. It is an ark on
which are gathered together a pair of every kind. I happened
to have chosen the same boat as had taken me once to Corfu;
the steward recognized me and greeted me warmly. He was surprised that I was still knocking about in Greek waters. When I
inquired why he mentioned the war, The war! I had completely
forgotten about the war. The radio was bringing it to us again—
with our meals. Always just enough progress and invention to fill
your mind with fresh horrors. I left the salon to pace the deck.
The wind was up and the boat was pitching and tossing. Some of
the roughest seas in this part of the Mediterranean. Good seas.
Fine rough weather, man-sized, bracing, appetizing. A little boat
in a big sea. An island now and then. A tiny harbor lit up like a
Japanese fairytale. Animals coming aboard, children screaming,
food cooking, men and women washing up in the hold at a little trough, like animals. Fine boat. Fine weather. Stars now and
then soft as geraniums, or hard and splintery like riven pikes.
Homely men walking about in carpet slippers, playing with their
beads, spitting, belching, making friendly grimaces, tossing their
heads back and with a clicking noise saying no when they should
be saying yes. In the rear of the boat the steerage passengers,
sprawled pell-mell over the deck, their possessions spread out

around them, some snoozing, some coughing, some singing, some meditating, some arguing, but whether asleep or awake all joined indiscriminately one to another and giving an impression of life. Not that sterile, sickly, organized life of the tourist third class such as we know on the big ocean liners, but a contaminating, infectious, pullulating, beehive life such as human beings ought to share when they are making a perilous voyage over a great body of water.

I went back to the salon around midnight to write a few lines in the little book which I had promised Seferiades. A man came over and asked me if I weren't an American—he had noticed me at the dinner table, he said. Another Greek from America, only this time an intelligent, entertaining one. He was an engineer doing reclamation work for the government. He had been over every inch of Greek soil. He talked about water supplies, electric equipment, drained marshlands, marble quarries, gold deposits, hotel accommodations, railroad facilities, bridge building, sanitary crusades, forest fires, legends, myths, superstitions, ancient wars and modern wars, piracy, fishing, monastic orders, duck shooting, Easter celebrations, and finally, after talking about long range guns, floating armadas, twin-screwed and double-jointed hurricane bombers, he launched into an account of the massacre at Smyrna of which he had been an eyewitness. In the long list of atrocities to be accredited to the human race it is difficult to say which "incident" is more heinous than the other. To mention the name of Sherman to a Southerner of the United States is to fill him with burning indignation. Even the most ignorant yokel knows that the name Attila is associated with untold horrors and vandalism. But the Smyrna affair, which far outweighs the horrors of the first World War or even the present one, has been somehow soft-pedalled and almost expunged from the memory of present-day man.* The peculiar horror which clings to this catastrophe is due not alone

* For a good account read the "Papers Relating to the Foreign Relations of the U.S., 1922," published by the Department of State in 1938, Vol. 2.

to the savagery and barbarism of the Turks but to the disgraceful, supine acquiescence of the big powers. It was one of the few shocks which the modern world has suffered—the realization that governments, in the pursuit of their selfish ends, can foster indifference, can reduce to impotence the natural spontaneous impulse of human beings in the face of brutal, wanton slaughter. Smyrna, like the Boxer Rebellion and other incidents too numerous to mention, was a premonitory example of the fate which lay in store for European nations, the fate which they were slowly accumulating by their diplomatic intrigues, their petty horse-trading, their cultivated neutrality and indifference in the face of obvious wrongs and injustices. Every time I hear of the Smyrna catastrophe, of the stultification of manhood worked on the members of the armed forces of the great powers who stood idly by under strict command of their leaders while thousands of innocent men, women and children were driven into the water like cattle, shot at, mutilated, burned alive, their hands chopped off when they tried to climb aboard a foreign vessel, I think of that preliminary warning which I saw always in French cinemas and which was repeated doubtless in every language under the sun except the German, Italian and Japanese, whenever a newsreel was shown of the bombing of a Chinese city.* I remember it for the very special reason that at the first showing of the destruction of Shanghai, the streets littered with mutilated bodies which were being hastily shoveled into carts like so much garbage, there arose in this French cinema such a pandemonium as I had never heard before. The French public was outraged. And yet pathetically, humanly enough, they were divided in their indignation. The rage of the just ones was overwhelmed by the rage of the virtuous ones. The latter, curiously enough, were outraged that such barbarous, inhuman scenes could be shown to such well-behaved, law-abiding, peace-loving people as they imagined themselves to he. They wanted to be protected

* Warning to this effect: the public is urgently requested not to display any undue emotion upon the presentation of these horripilating scenes. They might as well have added: remember, these are only Chinese, not French citizens.

from the anguish of enduring such a scene even at the comfortable distance of three or four thousand miles. They had paid to see a drama of love in comfortable seats and by some monstrous and wholly unaccountable faux pas this nasty slice of reality had been shoved before their eyes and their peaceful, idle evening virtually ruined. Such was Europe before the present débâcle. Such is America to-day. And such it will be to-morrow when the smoke has cleared away. And as long as human beings can sit and watch with hands folded while their fellow men are tortured and butchered so long will civilization be a hollow mockery, a wordy phantom suspended like a mirage above a swelling sea of murdered carcasses.

PART III

ON MY RETURN TO ATHENS I FOUND A STACK OF MAIL forwarded from Paris, also several notices from the post office inviting me to call at my earliest convenience for money. The American Express also had money for me, money that had been cabled by friends in America. Golfo the maid, who came from Loutraki where Katsimbalis once owned a gambling casino and who always spoke German to me, was excited by the prospect of my receiving several sums of money at once. So was the night porter, Socrates, and the postman who always had a broad grin when he counted out the money to me. In Greece, as in other places, when you receive a sum of money from abroad you are expected to make little dispensations in every direction. At the same time I was informed indirectly that I might have an excellent room with private bath at one of the best hotels for what I was paying at the Grand. I preferred to stay at the Grand. I liked the maids, the porters, the bellhops and the proprietor himself; I like hotels which are second or third rate, which are clean but shabby, which have seen better days, which have an aroma of the past. I liked the beetles and the huge water bugs which I always found in my room when I turned on the light. I liked the broad corridors and the toilets all jammed together like bath houses at the end of the hall. I liked the dismal courtyard and the sound

of the male choir practicing in a hall nearby. For a few drachmas I could get the bellhop, who was an old Parisian of fourteen years of age, to deliver my letters by hand, a luxury never
before enjoyed. Getting so much money at once I almost lost
my head. I was on the verge of buying a suit of clothes, which I
needed badly, but fortunately the bellhop's uncle who ran a little
shop near the Turkish quarter, couldn't make me a suit quickly
enough. Then I was on the point of buying the bellhop a bicycle, which he claimed would be of inestimable service in running
his little errands, but as he couldn't find one he liked immediately I compromised by giving him some sweaters and a pair of
flannel trousers.

One day Max, who had nothing to do but deliver news bulle-
tins for the British Press Bureau in his car, announced that it was
his birthday and that he was going to squander a small fortune
by inviting all his friends and acquaintances to eat and drink
with him. There was something desperate about this birthday
party. Despite the lavish flow of champagne, the extravagant
abundance of food, the women, the music, the dancing, somehow it never quite came off. The English of course were immediately drunk and in their charming subaqueous way slid off
into their habitual comas. The evening reminded me of a night
I once spent in London at a dance hail with a man from Baghdad. The whole evening he talked insurance to me or else dress
clothes and how to wear them. Max, who couldn't drink because
of his health, kept filling the glasses and sparkled with a reflected
brilliance, like a room lit up with tinkling chandeliers. His idea
of how to bring the festivities to a pleasant termination was to
drive to some Godforsaken ruin and wreck the cars. On a pre-
vious celebration he had actually driven his car up the steps of
the King George Hotel, much to the astonishment of the flun-
keys. I left the party about three in the morning, feeling drunk
but not at all gay.

About this time I received a letter from the American Consulate requesting me to step in and have my passport validated

or invalidated. I went round to the office to make inquiries. Being a native-born I took the matter lightly. Just a bit of red tape, I thought to myself. Had I brought a photograph, I was asked immediately. No, I hadn't thought of that. The porter took me down the street a few blocks to look for a man who usually stood on a certain corner. The apparatus was there but no sign of the man. I had nothing to do so I sat down on the curb and waited patiently. When I got back to the bureau there were several Americanized Greeks waiting to be cross-examined. One sly old peasant who had evidently become prosperous in America amused me. He was talking in Greek to one of the secretaries, a Greek woman. He evidently didn't like her efficient and somewhat superior attitude. He became mulish. He would say neither Yes nor No to the questions put him. He smelled a rat somewhere and he was on his guard. The young woman was almost beside herself. But the more frantic she became the cooler he behaved. She looked at me in despair. I thought to myself it serves you right, what business have you to be tantalizing people with all these stupid questions? Finally it came my turn. What are you doing in Greece? Where is your home? How many dependents have you? Whom do you work for? I was so pleased with the fact that I could answer readily—no home, no dependents, no boss, no aim, et cetera, that when he said "Couldn't you just as well do your writing elsewhere?" I said "Of course, I'm a free man, I can work anywhere, nobody is paying me to write." Whereupon he said—very clever of him—"Well then, I take it you could write in America too, couldn't you?" And I said "Of course, why not? Only I don't care to write in America. I'm writing about Greece now." However, the game was up, as I discovered in a few moments. A brief colloquy with a higher-up and my passport was returned to me invalidated. That meant get home at the earliest possible moment. Clear out!

At first I was angry; I felt that I had been tricked. But after I had walked around the block several times I decided that it was probably an act of fate. At least I was free to clear out. Max was only free to stay and spend his remaining drachmas. The war was spreading. Soon the Balkans would be inflamed. Soon there would be no choice.

I went back the next day to see the American Minister and find out how much time they would accord me. The former director of "The Dial," as he turned out to be, received me cordially. I was delighted to learn of his great sympathy and love for the Greeks. Everything went smoothly. No undue hurry. Only please prepare to leave as soon as possible. I sensed that it was best to comply graciously. So I shook our minister, Mr. Lincoln MacVeagh, cordially by the hand and departed. On the way out I made the sign of the cross in Orthodox fashion.

Winter was coming on; the days were short and sunny, the nights cold and long. The stars seemed more brilliant than ever. Owing to the shortage of coal the heat was turned on for an hour only in the morning and an hour in the evening. I quickly developed sciatica and was reminded that I was getting old. Golfo the maid was very solicitous; Socrates, the night porter, came up every evening to rub me with a Greek horse liniment; the proprietor sent up grapes and mineral waters; Niki with the Nile green eyes came and held my hand; the bellhop brought letters and telegrams. All in all it was a very pleasant illness.

I shall always remember the walks through Athens at night under the autumn stars. Often I would go up to a bluff just under Lykabettos and stand there for an hour or so gazing at the sky. What was wonderful about it was that it was so Greek—not just the sky, but the houses, the color of the houses, the dusty roads, the nakedness, the sounds that came out of the houses. Something immaculate about it. Somewhere beyond the "ammonia" region, in a forlorn district whose streets are named after the philosophers, I would stumble about in a silence so intense and so velvety at the same time that it seemed as if the atmosphere were full of powdered stars whose light made an inaudible noise. Athens and New York are electrically charged cities, unique in my experience. But Athens is permeated with a violet-blue reality which envelops you with a caress; New York has a trip-hammer vitality which drives you insane with restlessness, if you have no inner stabilizer. In both cases the air is like champagne—a tonic, a revivifier. In Athens I experienced the joy of solitude; in New York I have always felt lonely, the loneliness of the caged animal, which brings on crime, sex, alcohol and other madnesses.

At midnight, returning to the hotel, I was frequently intercepted, usually by some wily Greek who knew enough English to strike up a running conversation. Usually he would invite me to join him in taking a coffee, pretending to be overjoyed to meet an American like himself (sic). One evening I ran into a Cretan from Utica, New York. He had come back to do his military service in Greece, so he said. He had a brother in Herakleion who was well off. After much beating about the bush, inquiring after the state of my health and so on, he admitted blushingly that he was short 73 drachmas for the boat fare to Crete. Now 73 drachmas is only about a half dollar in American money and a half dollar is nothing to offer a stranger from Utica who desires to do his military service abroad, especially if like the one I am talking about he has already paid for your coffee, pastry and ice cream, has already offered you his cigarettes and already invited you to make use of his brother's car while in Crete. I hadn't told him that I had just been to Crete, of course. I listened to him in sympathetic silence and acted as naif and ignorant as Americans are supposed to be. As a matter of fact I was really itching to be taken in—otherwise I would have felt cheated, disillusioned about the Greek character. Aside from my experience of the first day nobody in Greece, no Greek certainly, had ever tried to gyp me. And perhaps this one would have been successful had he not been so maladroit. In the first place I happened to know Utica fairly well, having spent one of my honeymoons there, and the street which he described to me as being his home I knew did not exist; in the second place he had made the mistake of telling me that he was taking the "Elsie" to Herakleion, whereas I knew, having just come back on the "Elsie," that this boat would not be returning to Crete for several months; in the third place, having inquired of him what he thought about Phaestos, which is pronounced the same in all languages, including Chinese, he asked me what *it* was, and when I told him it was a place he said he had never heard of it, he even doubted its existence; in the fourth place he couldn't remember the name of the hotel which I ought to stop at when going to Herakleion, and for a man born in Herakleion, which has only two hotels to its name, the sudden loss of memory struck me as rather glaring; in the fifth place he no more resembled a Cretan than a man from Canarsie would, and I very much doubted that he had ever seen the place; in the sixth place he was too free with his brother's car, and cars are not plentiful in Crete where the bullock still draws the plough. None of these factors would have deterred me from handing him the seventy-three drachmas since, being a born American, a half dollar has always seemed to me to be just the right sized coin to throw down a sewer if there is nothing better to be done with it. Only I did want him to know that I knew he was lying. And so I told him so. At this he pretended to be aggrieved. When I pointed out why I thought he had been lying to me he rose up solemnly and said that if I should ever go to Crete and there meet his brother I would regret what I had said—and with that he stalked out looking as injured and wounded as possible. I called the waiter over and asked him if he knew the man. He smiled. "Why, yes," he said, "he's an interpreter." I asked if he had been living a long time in Athens. "He's been here all his life," he said.

There was another one called George, George of Cyprus, who was even less capable. George pretended to be a close friend of the American Minister, our Mr. MacVeagh no less. He had been watching me read a German news weekly at a little kiosk in the same "ammonia" region. He greeted me in German and I answered him in German. He asked me how long I had been in Athens and I told him. He said it was a beautiful night and I agreed, it was indeed. "Where do you go from here?" he asked next and I said "To Persia perhaps." All this in German. "Where do you come from?" he asked. "From New York," I replied. "And you speak nothing but German?" "I can speak English too," I said. "Then why did you speak German to me?" he inquired, with a sly smile. "Because you addressed me in German," I said. "Can you speak Greek?" he asked next. "No," I said, "but I can speak Chinese and Japanese—can you?" He shook his head. "Do you speak Turkish?" I shook my head. "Arabic?" Again I shook my head. "I speak all the languages except Chinese and Japanese," he said, smiling again in his strange way. "You're very intelligent," I said. "Are you an interpreter?" No, he was not an interpreter. He smiled and lowered his eyes. "Have a drink with me?" he said. I nodded.

Seated at the table he began a long roundabout discussion to find out what my occupation was. I told him I had none. "You are a rich man, yes?" he said, his eyes gleaming. "No, I am very poor. I have no money." He laughed in my face, as if the very thought were absurd. "You like women?" he asked suddenly. I said I liked them very much, especially if they were beautiful. "I have a friend—she is very beautiful," he said immediately. "We will go to see her—now, as soon as you have finished your coffee." I told him I didn't care to see her right away because I was going to bed soon. He pretended not to have heard me correctly and went into a long rhapsody about her charms. "She must be very beautiful," I said. "Aren't you jealous of her?" He looked at me as if I were slightly cracked "You are my friend," he said. "She will be honored to see you. Let's go now," and he started to rise from his seat. I sat there as if made of lead and looking up at him I blandly inquired what day it was. He wasn't sure—he thought it was Tuesday. "Ask the waiter," I said. He asked the waiter. It was Tuesday all right. "Well," I said, slowly dragging it out, "I shall be busy until Thursday a week from now, but if you are free Thursday evening, Thursday the 17th, I'll call for you here about ten in the evening and we'll go to see your friend." He laughed. "Come, we'll go there now," he said, taking me by the arm. I remained seated, allowing him to hold my arm which had become as in-ert as a stovepipe. "I'm going to bed in a few minutes," I repeated calmly. "Besides, I have no money—I told you I was poor, you remember?" He laughed. Then he sat down, drawing his chair up closer. "Listen," he said, leaning over in confidential style, "George knows everybody. You don't need any money—you are my guest. We'll stay just a few minutes—it's right near here." "But it's late now," I said, "she may be asleep." He laughed. "Be-sides," I continued, "I told you I was tired. Thursday a week will be fine for me—about ten o'clock." George now dove into his in-side pocket and brought out a packet of letters and a dirty, crum-pled passport. He opened the passport and showed me his pho-tograph, his name, where he was born, etc. I nodded my head. "That's you, George, no?" I said innocently. He tried to pull his chair still closer. "I am an English citizen, you see? I know all the consuls, all the ministers. I will speak to Mr. MacVeagh for you. He will give you the money to go home. He's a very good man." Here he dropped his voice. "You like boys—young boys?" I said I did, sometimes, if they behaved themselves. He laughed again. He knew a place where there were very beautiful boys, very young too. I thought that was very interesting—were they friends of his, I wanted to know. He ignored the question and, dropping his voice, he inquired discreetly if I had enough to pay for the coffee and pastry. I said I had enough to pay for my own share. "You pay for George too?" he said, smiling slyly. I said No flatly. He looked surprised—not injured or aggrieved, but genuinely astounded. I called the waiter over and paid for my check, I got up and started to walk out. I went down the stairs. In a moment—he had been whispering to the waiter—he fol-lowed me to the street. "Well," I said, "it was a pleasant evening. I'll say good-night now." "Don't go yet," he urged, "just two more minutes. She lives right across the street." "*Who?*" I asked inno-cently. "My friend." "Oh," I said, "that's very convenient. Next Thursday a week, then, eh?" I began walking off. He came up close and took me by the arm again. "Give me fifty drachmas, please!" "No," I said, "I'm not giving you anything." I walked a few paces. He crawled up on me again. "Please, thirty drachmas" "No," I said, "no drachmas tonight." "*Fifteen drachmas!*" "No," I repeated, walking away. I got about ten yards away from him. He yelled out: "*Five drachmas!*" "No!" I yelled back, "not one drachma! Good-night!"

It was the first time in my life I had so stubbornly refused anybody. I enjoyed the experience. As I was nearing the hotel an oldish-looking man with long hair and a rather large Bohemian hat darted out of a dark alley and, greeting me in perfect English, held out his hand for alms. I instinctively put my hand in my change pocket and fished out a handful of coins, perhaps fifty or sixty drachmas. He took it, bowed respectfully as he removed his flowing hat and, with a candor and a sincerity that were amazing to behold, he informed me in his impeccable English that grateful as he was for the generous gesture it would not be sufficient for his needs. He asked me if it were possible, and he added that he knew it was a great deal to ask of a stranger, to give him two hundred drachmas more, which was the sum he required to pay his hotel bill. He added that even then he would be obliged to go without food. I immediately pulled out my wallet and handed him two hundred and fifty drachmas. It was now his turn to be astounded. He had asked, but apparently he had never dreamed of getting it. The tears came to his eyes. He began a wonderful speech which I cut short by saying that I had to catch up with my friends who had strolled ahead. I left him in the middle of the street with hat in hand, gazing after me as if I were a phantom.

The incident put me in a good mood. "Ask," said our Lord and Saviour Jesus Christ, "and it shall be given unto you." *Ask*, mind you. Not demand, not beg, not wheedle or cajole. Very simple, I thought to myself. Almost too simple. And yet what better way is there?

Now that my departure had become a certainty Katsimbalis was desperately attempting to organize a few last-minute excursions. It was impossible, with the limited time at my disposal, to even

think of visiting Mt. Athos or Lesbos, or even Mykonos or San-
torini. Delphi yes, perhaps even Delos. Towards lunchtime every day Katsimbalis was at the hotel waiting for me. Lunch lasted
usually until five or six in the afternoon after which we would
repair to a little wine cellar where we would have a few aperi-
tifs in order to whip up an appetite for dinner. Katsimbalis was
now in greater form than ever, though still complaining of arthritis, migraine, bad liver, loss of memory and so on. Wherever
we went we were sure to be joined by some of his numerous
friends. In this ambiance the discussion developed to fantastic
proportions; the newcomer was fitted into the architectural pattern of his talk with the case and dexterity of a mediaeval joiner
or mason. We made sea voyages and inland voyages; we traveled down the Nile, crawled through the pyramids on our bel-
lies, rested awhile in Constantinople, made the rounds of the
cafés in Smyrna, gambled at the casino in Loutraki and again at
Monte Carlo; we lived through the first and second Balkan wars,
got back to Paris in time for the armistice, sat up nights with
the monks at Mr. Athos, went back stage at the Folies Bergère,
strolled through the bazaars of Fez, went crazy with boredom
in Salonika, stopped off at Toulouse and Carcassonne, explored
the Orinoco, floated down the Mississippi, crossed the Gobi
desert, joined the Royal Opera at Sofia, got typhus in Tiflis, put
on a weight-lifting act at the Medrano, got drunk in Thebes and
came back on motorcycles to play a game of dominoes opposite
the Metro station at "Ammonia."

Finally it was decided that we would go to Delphi, the ancient navel of the world. Pericles Byzantis, who was a friend of
Ghika's, had invited us to spend a few days there at the new pavilion for foreign students which the government was opening
up. We pulled up at the museum in Thebes in a beautiful Packard—Ghika, Byzantis and myself. Katsimbalis had decided to
go by bus for some reason or other. By some unaccountable
logic Thebes looked exactly as I had pictured it to look; the inhabitants too corresponded to the loutish image which I had re-

tained since school days. The guide to the museum was a surly brute who seemed suspicious of every move we made; it was all we could do to induce him to unlock the door. Yet I liked Thebes; it was quite unlike the other Greek towns I had visited. It was about ten in the morning and the air was winey; we seemed to be isolated in the midst of a great space which was dancing with a violet light; we were oriented towards another world.

As we rolled out of the town, snaking over the low hills cropped close and kinky like a negro's poll, Ghika who was sitting beside the driver turned round to tell me of a strange dream which he had had during the night. It was an extraordinary dream of death and transfiguration in which he had risen up out of his own body and gone out of the world. As he was describing the wondrous wraiths whom he had encountered in the other world I looked beyond his eye to the undulating vistas which were unrolling before us. Again that impression of a vast, all-englobing space encircling us, which I had noted in Thebes, came over me. There was a terrific synchronization of dream and reality, the two worlds merging in a bowl of pure light, and we the voyagers suspended, as it were, over the earthly life. All thought of destination was annihilated; we were purring smoothly over the undulating ground, advancing towards the void of pure sensation, and the dream, which was hallucinating, had suddenly become vivid and unbearably real. It was just as he was describing the strange sensation he had experienced of suddenly discovering his own body lying prone on the bed, of balancing himself gingerly above it so as to slowly descend and fit himself into it again without the loss of an arm or a toe, that out of the corner of my eye I caught the full devastating beauty of the great plain of Thebes which we were approaching and, unable to control myself, I burst into tears. Why had no one prepared me for this? I cried out. I begged the driver to stop a moment in order to devour the scene with one full sweeping glance. We were not yet in the bed of the plain; we were amidst the low mounds and hummocks which had been stunned motionless by the swift messengers of light. We were in the dead center of that soft silence which absorbs even the breathing of the gods. Man had nothing to do with this, nor even nature. In this realm nothing moves nor stirs nor breathes save the finger of mystery; this is the hush that descends upon the world before the coming of a miraculous event. The event itself is not recorded here, only the passing of it, only the violet glow of its wake. This is an invisible corridor of time, a vast, breathless parenthesis which swells like the uterus and having bowelled forth its anguish relapses like a run-down clock. We glide through the long level plain, the first real oasis I have ever glimpsed. How am I to distinguish it from those other irrigated Paradises known to man? Was it more lush, more fertile, did it groan with a heavier weight of produce? Was it a thriving honeycomb of activity? I cannot say that I was made aware of any of these factors. The plain of Thebes was empty, empty of man, empty of visible produce. In the belly of this emptiness there throbbed a rich pulse of blood which was drained off in black furrowed veins. Through the thick pores of the earth the dreams of men long dead still bubbled and burst, their diaphanous filament carried skyward by flocks of startled birds.

To the left of us ran the range leading to Parnassus, grim, silent, hoary with legend. Strange that all the time I was in Paris, all that joy and misery associated with Montparnasse, I never once thought of the place from which the name derives. On the other hand, though no one had ever counselled me to go there, Thebes had been in my mind ever since the day I landed in Athens. By some unaccountable quirk the name Thebes, just as Memphis in Egypt, always brought to life a welter of fantastic memories and when, in the chill morgue of the museum there, I espied that most exquisite stone drawing so like one of Picasso's illustrations, when I saw the rigid Egyptian-like colossi, I felt as if I were back in some familiar past, back in a world which I had known as a child. Thebes, even after one has visited it, remains in the memory very much like the vague, tremulous reveries which attend a long wait in the antechamber of a dentist's office. Waiting to have a tooth extracted one often gets involved in the plan of a new book; one fairly seethes with ideas. Then comes the torture, the book is expunged from the consciousness; days pass in which nothing more brilliant is accomplished than sticking the tongue in a little cavity of the gum which seems enormous. Finally that too is forgotten and one is at work again and perhaps the new book is begun, but not as it was feverishly planned back in the cauterized waiting-room. And then, of a night when one tosses fitfully, plagued by swarms of irrelevant thoughts, suddenly the constellation of the lost tooth swims over the horizon and one is in Thebes, the old childhood Thebes from which all the novels have issued, and one sees the plan of the great life's work finely etched on a tablet of stone—and this is the book one always meant to write but it is forgotten in the morning, and thus Thebes is forgotten and God and the whole meaning of life and one's own identity and the identities of the past and so one worships Picasso who stayed awake all night and kept his bad tooth. This you know when you pass through Thebes, and it is disquieting, but it is also inspiring and when you are thoroughly inspired you hang yourself by the ankles and wait for the vultures to devour you alive. Then the real Montparnasse life begins, with Diana the huntress in the background and the Sphinx waiting for you at a bend in the road.

We stopped for lunch at Levadia, a sort of Alpine village nestling against a wall of the mountain range. The air was crisp and exhilarating, balmy in the sun and chill as a knife in the shade. The doors of the restaurant were opened wide to suck in the sunlit air. It was a colossal refectory lined with tin like the inside of a biscuit box; the cutlery, the plates, the tabletops were ice cold; we ate with our hats and overcoats on.

From Levadia to Arachova was like a breathless ride on the scenic railway through a tropical Iceland. Seldom a human being, seldom a vehicle; a world growing more and more rarefied, more and more miraculous. Under lowering clouds the scene became immediately ominous and terrifying: only a god could survive the furious onslaught of the elements in this stark Olympian world.

At Arachova Ghika got out to vomit. I stood at the edge of

a deep canyon and as I looked down into its depths I saw the shadow of a great eagle wheeling over the void. We were on the very ridge of the mountains, in the midst of a convulsed land which was seemingly still writhing and twisting. The village itself had the bleak, frostbitten look of a community cut off from the outside world by an avalanche. There was the continuous roar of an icy waterfall which, though hidden from the eye, seemed omnipresent. The proximity of the eagles, their shadows mysteriously darkening the ground, added to the chill, bleak sense of desolation. And yet from Arachova to the outer precincts of Delphi the earth presents one continuously sublime, dramatic spectacle. Imagine a bubbling cauldron into which a fearless band of men descend to spread a magic carpet. Imagine this carpet to be composed of the most ingenious patterns and the most variegated hues. Imagine that men have been at this task for several thousand years and that to relax for but a season is to destroy the work of centuries. Imagine that with every groan, sneeze or hiccough which the earth vents the carpet is grievously ripped and tattered. Imagine that the tints and hues which compose this dancing carpet of earth rival in splendor and subtlety the most beautiful stained glass windows of the mediaeval cathedrals. Imagine all this and you have only a glimmering comprehension of a spectacle which is changing hourly, monthly, yearly, millennially. Finally, in a state of dazed, drunken, battered stupefaction you come upon Delphi. It is four in the afternoon, say, and a mist blowing in from the sea has turned the world completely upside down. You are in Mongolia and the faint tinkle of bells from across the gully tells you that a caravan is approaching. The sea has become a mountain lake poised high above the mountaintops where the sun is sputtering out like a rum-soaked omelette. On the fierce glacial wall where the mist lifts for a moment someone has written with lightning speed in an unknown script. To the other side, as if borne along like a cataract, a sea of grass slips over the precipitous slope of a cliff. It has the brilliance of the vernal equinox, a green which grows between the stars in the twinkling of an eye.

Seeing it in this strange twilight mist Delphi seemed even more sublime and awe-inspiring than I had imagined it to be. I actually felt relieved, upon rolling up to the little bluff above the pavilion where we left the car, to find a group of idle village boys shooting dice: it gave a human touch to the scene. From the towering windows of the pavilion, which was built along the solid, generous lines of a mediaeval fortress, I could look across the gulch and, as the mist lifted, a pocket of the sea became visible—just beyond the hidden port of Itea. As soon as we had installed our things we looked for Katsimbalis whom we found at the Apollo Hotel—I believe he was the only guest since the departure of H. G. Wells under whose name I signed my own in the register though I was not stopping at the hotel. He, Wells, had a very fine, small hand, almost womanly, like that of a very modest, unobtrusive person, but then that is so characteristic of English handwriting that there is nothing unusual about it.

By dinnertime it was raining and we decided to eat in a little restaurant by the roadside. The place was as chill as the grave. We had a scanty meal supplemented by liberal portions of wine and cognac. I enjoyed that meal immensely, perhaps because I was in the mood to talk. As so often happens, when one has come at last to an impressive spot, the conversation had absolutely nothing to do with the scene. I remember vaguely the expression of astonishment on Ghika's and Katsimbalis' faces as I unlimbered at length upon the American scene. I believe it was a description of Kansas that I was giving them; at any rate it was a picture of emptiness and monotony such as to stagger them. When we got back to the bluff behind the pavilion, whence we had to pick our way in the dark, a gale was blowing and the rain was coming down in bucketfuls. It was only a short stretch we had to traverse but it was perilous. Being somewhat lit up I had supreme confidence in my ability to find my way unaided. Now and then a flash of lightning lit up the path which was swimming in mud. In these lurid moments the scene was so harrowingly desolate that I felt as if we were enacting a scene from Macbeth. "Blow wind and crack!" I shouted, gay as a mud-lark, and at that moment I slipped to my knees and would have rolled down a gully had not Katsimbalis caught me by the arm. When I saw the spot next morning I almost fainted.

We slept with the windows closed and a great fire roaring in the huge stove. At breakfast we congregated about a long communion table in a hall that would have done credit to a Dominican monastery. The food was excellent and abundant, the view from the window superb. The place was so enormous, the floor so inviting, that I couldn't resist the temptation to do some fancy skating in my shoes. I sailed in and out the corridors, the refectory, the salon, the studios, delivering glad tidings from the ruler of my ninth house, Mercury himself.

It was now time to inspect the ruins, extract the last oracular juices from the extinct navel. We climbed up the hill to the theatre whence we overlooked the splintered treasuries of the gods, the ruined temples, the fallen columns, trying vainly to recreate the splendor of this ancient site. We speculated at length on the exact position of the city itself which is as yet undiscovered. Suddenly, as we stood there silently and reverently, Katsimbalis strode to the center of the bowl and holding his arms aloft delivered the closing lines of the last oracle. It was an impressive moment, to say the least. For a second, so it seemed, the curtain had been lifted on a world which had never really perished but which had rolled away like a cloud and was preserving itself intact, inviolate, until the day when, restored to his senses, man would summon it back to life again. In the few seconds it took him to pronounce the words I had a long glimpse down the broad avenue of man's folly and, seeing no end to the vista, experienced a poignant feeling of distress and of sadness which was in no way connected with my own fate but with that of the species to which by accident I happen to belong. I recalled other oracular utterances I had heard in Paris, in which the present war, horrible as it is, was represented as but an item in the long catalogue of impending disasters and reversals, and I remembered the skeptical way in which these utterances were received. The world which passed away with Delphi passed away as in a sleep. It is the same now. Victory and defeat are meaningless in the light of the wheel which relentlessly revolves. We are moving into a new latitude of the soul, and a thousand years hence men will wonder at our blindness, our torpor, our supine acquiescence to an order which was doomed.

We had a drink at the Castellian Spring where I suddenly remembered my old friend Nick of the Orpheum Dance Palace on Broadway because he had come from a little village called Castellia in the valley beyond the mountains. In a way my friend Nick was largely responsible for my being here, I reflected, for it was through his terpsichorean instrumentations that I met my wife June and if I hadn't met her I should probably never have become a writer, never have left America, never have met Betty Ryan, Lawrence Durrell and finally Stephanides, Katsimbalis and Ghika.

After wandering about amidst the broken columns we ascended the tortuous path to the stadium on high. Katsimbalis took off his overcoat and with giant strides measured it from end to end. The setting is spectacular. Set just below the crest of the mountain one has the impression that when the course was finished the charioteers must have driven their steeds over the ridge and into the blue. The atmosphere is superhuman, intoxicating to the point of madness. Everything that is extraordinary and miraculous about Delphi gathers here in the memory of the games which were held in the clouds. As I turned to go I saw a shepherd leading his flock over the ridge; his figure was so sharply delineated against the sky that he seemed to be bathed in a violet aura; the sheep moved slowly over the smooth spine in a golden fuzz, as though somnolently emerging from the dead pages of a forgotten idyll.

In the museum I came again upon the colossal Theban statues which have never ceased to haunt me and finally we stood

before the amazing statue of Antinous, last of the gods. I could
not help but contrast in my mind this most wonderful idealiza-
tion in stone of the eternal duality of man, so bold and simple,
so thoroughly Greek in the best sense, with that literary creation
of Balzac's, *Seraphita*, which is altogether vague and mysterious and, humanly speaking, altogether unconvincing. Nothing
could better convey the transition from light to darkness, from
the pagan to the Christian conception of life, than this enigmatic
figure of the last god on earth who flung himself into the Nile. By
emphasizing the soulful qualities of man Christianity succeeded
only in disembodying man; as angel the sexes fuse into the sublime spiritual being which man essentially is. The Greeks, on
the other hand, gave body to everything, thereby incarnating
the spirit and eternalizing it. In Greece one is ever filled with the
sense of eternality which is expressed in the here and now; the
moment one returns to the Western world, whether in Europe
or America, this feeling of body, of eternality, of incarnated spirit
is shattered. We move in clock time amidst the debris of vanished worlds, inventing the instruments of our own destruction,
oblivious of fate or destiny, knowing never a moment of peace,
possessing not an ounce of faith, a prey to the blackest superstitions, functioning neither in the body nor in the spirit, active not
as individuals but as microbes in the organism of the diseased.

That night, at the dinner table in the big hall, while listening
to Pericles Byzantis, I made up my mind to return to Athens the
next day. He had just been urging me to stay, and indeed there
was every reason for me to stay, but I had the feeling that something awaited me in Athens and I knew I would not stay. Next
morning at breakfast, to his great amazement, I told him of my
decision. I told him very frankly that I could give no good reason for my departure—except that best of all reasons, imperious
desire. I had had the distinction of being the very first foreigner
to enjoy the privileges of the new pavilion and my abrupt leave-
taking was undoubtedly a poor way of expressing my gratitude,
but so it was. Ghika and Katsimbalis quickly decided to return
with me. I hope that when he reads what happened to me upon

my return to Athens the good Kyrios Byzantis will forgive my rude behavior and not consider it as typically American.

The return at top speed was even more impressive to me than our coming. We passed through Thebes in the late afternoon, Katsimbalis regaling me with a story of his mad motorcycle trips from Thebes to Athens after he had had a skinful. It seemed to me that we had just skirted the vicinity of the great battlefield of Platea and were perhaps facing Mount Kithaeron when suddenly I became aware of a curious trap-like formation through which we were whirling like a drunken cork. Again we had come to one of those formidable passes where the invading enemy had been slaughtered like pigs, a spot which must be the solace and the joy of defending generals everywhere. Here it was, it would not surprise me to discover, that Oedipus had met the Sphinx. I was profoundly disturbed, shaken to the roots. And by what? By associations born of my knowledge of ancient events? Scarcely, since I have but the scantiest knowledge of Greek history and even that is thoroughly confused, as is all history to me. No, as with the sacred places so with the murderous spots—the record of events is written into the earth. The real joy of the historian or the archaeologist when confronted with a discovery must lie in the fact of confirmation, corroboration, not in surprise. Nothing that has happened on this earth, however deeply buried, is hidden from man. Certain spots stand out like semaphores, revealing not only the clue but the event—provided, to be sure, they are approached with utter purity of heart. I am convinced that there are many layers of history and that the final reading will be delayed until the gift of seeing past and future as one is restored to us.

I thought, when I got back to my hotel and found that money had been cabled me for my return to America, that that was what had drawn me back to Athens, but in the morning when I found Katsimbalis waiting for me with a mysterious smile upon his face I discovered that there was another, more important reason. It was a cold wintry day with a stiff wind blowing down from the encircling hills. It was a Sunday. Somehow everything had undergone a radical change. A boat was leaving in about ten days and the knowledge that I would take that boat had already brought the journey to an end.

Katsimbalis had come to propose a visit to an Armenian sooth-sayer whom he and several of his friends had already consulted. I consented with alacrity, never having been to a soothsayer in my life. Once in Paris I had been on the verge of doing so, having witnessed the hallucinating effect of such an experience upon two of my close friends. I was of the opinion that nothing more could be expected than a good or bad reading of one's own mind.

The abode of this particular soothsayer was in the Armenian refugee quarter of Athens, a section of the city I had not yet seen. I had heard that it was sordid and picturesque but nothing I had heard about it had quite prepared me for the sight which greeted my eyes. By no means the least curious feature of this neighborhood is its duality. Around the rotten yolk of the egg lies the immaculate new shell of the community which is to be. For almost twenty years these miserable refugees have been waiting to move into the new quarters which have been promised them. These new homes which the government has provided and which now stand ready for occupancy (rent free, I believe), are models in every sense of the word. The contrast between these and the hovels in which the refugees have somehow managed to survive for a generation is fantastic, to say the least. From the rubbish heap a whole community provided shelter for itself and for its animals, its pets, its rodents, its lice, its bedbugs, its microbes. With the march of civilization such pustulant, festering agglomerations of humanity are of course no unusual sight. The more staggering the world cities become in elegance and proportion, in power and influence, the more cataclysmic the upheavals, the vaster the armies of footloose, destitute, homeless, penniless individuals who, unlike the miserable Armenians of Athens, are not even privileged to dig in the dung-heaps for the scraps with which to provide themselves with shelter but are forced to keep on the march like phantoms, confronted in their own land with rifles, hand grenades, barbed wire, shunned like lepers, driven out like the pest.

The home of Aram Hourabedian was buried in the heart of the labyrinth and required much questioning and manoeuvring before we could locate it. When at last we found the little sign announcing his residence we discovered that we had come too early. We killed an hour or so strolling about the quarter, marvelling not so much at the squalor but at the pathetically human efforts that had been made to adorn and beautify these miserable shacks. Despite the fact that it had been created out of the rubbish heap there was more charm and character to this little village than one usually finds in a modern city. It evoked books, paintings, dreams, legends: it evoked such names as Lewis Carroll, Hieronymus Bosch, Breughel, Max Ernst, Hans Reichel, Salvador Dali, Goya, Giotto, Paul Klee, to mention but a few. In the midst of the most terrible poverty and suffering there nevertheless emanated a glow which was holy; the surprise of finding a cow or a sheep in the same room with a mother and child gave way instantly to a feeling of reverence. Nor did one have the slightest desire to laugh at seeing a squalid hut surmounted by an improvised solarium made of pieces of tin. What shelter there was was shared alike and this shelter included provision for the birds of the air and the animals of the field. Only in sorrow and suffering does man draw close to his fellow man; only then, it seems, does his life become beautiful. Walking along a sunken planked street I stopped a moment to gaze at the window of a bookshop, arrested by the sight of those lurid adventure magazines which one never expects to find in a foreign land but which flourish everywhere in every land, in every tongue almost. Conspicuous among them was a brilliant red-covered volume of Jules Verne, a Greek edition of "Twenty Thousand Leagues Under the Sea." What impressed me at the moment was the thought that the world in which this fantastic yarn lay buried was far more fantastic than anything Jules Verne had imagined. How could anyone possibly imagine, coming out of the sky from another planet in the middle of the night, let us say, and finding himself in this weird community, that there existed on this earth other beings who lived in towering skyscrapers the very materials of which would baffle the mind to describe? And if there could be such a gulf between two worlds lying in such proximity what might be the gulf between the present world and the world to come? To see even fifty or a hundred years ahead taxes our imagination to the utmost; we are incapable of seeing beyond the repetitious cycle of war and peace, rich and poor, right and wrong, good and bad. Look twenty thousand years ahead: do you still see battleships, skyscrapers, churches, lunatic asylums, slums, mansions, national frontiers, tractors, sewing machines, canned sardines, little liver pills, etc. etc.? How will these things be eradicated? How will the new world, brave or poor, come about? Looking at the beautiful volume of Jules Verne I seriously asked myself the question—*how will it come about?* I wondered, indeed, if the elimination of these things ever seriously occupies our imagination. For as I stood there daydreaming I had the impression that everything was at a standstill, that I was not a man living in the twentieth century but a visitor from no century seeing what he had seen before and would see again and again, and the thought that that might be possible was utterly depressing.

It was the soothsayer's wife who opened the door for us. She had a serene, dignified countenance which at once impressed me favorably. She pointed to the next room where her husband sat a table in his shirtsleeves, his head supported by his elbows. He was apparently engaged in reading a huge, Biblical book. As we entered the room he rose and shook hands cordially. There was nothing theatrical or ostentatious about him; indeed he had more the air of a carpenter pursuing his rabbinical studies than any appearance of being a medium. He hastened to explain that he was not possessed of any extraordinary powers, that he had simply been a student of the Kabbala for many years and that he had been instructed in the art of Arabian astrology. He spoke Arabic, Turkish, Greek, Armenian, German, French, Czech and several other languages and had until recently been in the service of the Czechoslovak consulate. The only information he demanded was the date, hour and place of my birth, my first name and my mother's and father's first names. I should say that before he had put these questions to me he remarked to Katsimbalis that I was decidedly a Capricorn of the Jupiterian type. He consulted the books, made his computations slowly and methodically and then, raising his eyes, began to talk. He spoke to me in French, but now and then, when things became too complicated, he addressed himself to Katsimbalis in Greek and the latter translated it back to me in English. Linguistically, to say the least, the situation was rather interesting. I felt unusually calm, steady, sure of myself, aware as he talked of every object in the room and yet never for a moment distracted. It was the living room we were seated in and it was extremely clean and orderly, the atmosphere reminding me strongly of the homes of poor rabbis whom I had visited in other cities of the world.

He began by telling me that I was approaching a new and most important phase of my life, that up to the present I had been wandering in circles, that I had created many enemies (by what I had written) and caused much harm and suffering to others. He said that I had led not only a dual life (I believe he used the word schizophrenic) but a multiple life and that nobody really understood me, not even my closest friends. But soon, he said, all this was to cease. At a certain date, which he gave me, I would find a clear, open path ahead of me; before dying I would bring great joy to the world, to everybody in the world, he emphasized, and my greatest enemy would bow down before me and beg my forgiveness. He said that I would enjoy before my death the greatest honors, the greatest rewards which man can confer upon man. I would make three trips to the Orient where, among other things, I would meet a man who would understand me as no one had and that this meeting was absolutely indispensable for the both of us. That on my last visit to the Orient I would never return, neither would I die, but vanish in the light. I interrupted him here to ask if he meant by that that I would be immortal, through my works or my deeds, and he answered solemnly and most significantly that he did not, that he meant simply and literally that I would never die. At this I confess I felt startled and I glanced at Katsimbalis, without saying a word, to make sure that I had heard correctly.

He went on to tell me that there were signs and indications given which he himself could not understand but which he would relate to me exactly as they were given. Not at all surprised by this I begged him to do so, adding that I would understand quite well myself. He was particularly baffled, and impressed, it seemed, by the fact that I had all the signs of divinity and at the same time my feet were chained to the earth. He paused to explain himself to Katsimbalis in Greek, obviously quite moved and obviously fearful to offer an interpretation of which he was not certain. Turning to me again he made it clear, both by his speech and by his words, that he considered it a rare privilege to be in the presence of such a one as myself. He confessed that he had never seen the indications for such a splendid career as now lay before me. He asked me pertinently if I had not escaped death several times. "In fact," he added, hardly waiting for confirmation, "you have always miraculously escaped whenever a situation became desperate or unbearable. You always will. You lead a charmed life. I want you to remember my words, when danger confronts you again—that however perilous the situation you must never give up, you will be saved. You are like a ship with two rudders: when one gives out the other will function. In addition, you are equipped with wings: you can take flight when those about you must perish. You are protected. You have had only one enemy—*yourself.*" And with this he rose, came round to me and seizing my hand raised it to his lips.

I give the gist of his words, omitting numerous details concerning my relations with others which would be of no interest to the reader without knowledge of the personalities and relationships involved. Everything he told me about the past was startlingly accurate and for the most part were about things which no one in Greece, not even Durrell or Katsimbalis, could possibly have had any knowledge about. We chatted a few moments before taking leave and during the course of the conversation he begged me, since I was returning to America, to look up his brother in Detroit from whom he hoped to get aid. There was one touch, incidentally, which I forgot and which is worth relating, because it struck me as so Armenian. In telling me of the fame and glory, the honors and rewards I would receive, he remarked in a puzzled way —"But I see no money!" At this I laughed outright. Money has been the one thing I have never had, and yet I have led a rich life and in the main a happy one. Why should I need money now—or later? When I have been desperately in need I have always found a friend. I go on the assumption that I have friends everywhere. I shall have more and more as time goes on. If I were to have money I might become careless and negligent, believing in a security which does not exist, stressing those values which are illusory and empty. I have no misgivings about the future. In the dark days to come money will be less than ever a protection against evil and suffering.

I was of course profoundly impressed by the interview. More than anything I felt chastened. Aside from the enigmatic reference to my not dying nothing he had predicted for my future astounded inc. I have always expected everything of the world and have always been ready to give everything. I had also, even before leaving Paris, the conviction that I would eventually break the vicious chain of cycles which, as he said, were usually of seven years' duration. I had left Paris before the war knowing that my life there had come to an end. The decision to take a vacation for one year, to abstain from writing during that time, the very choice of Greece which, as I see it now, was the only country which could have satisfied my inner needs, all this was significant. In the last year or two in Paris I had been hinting to my friends that I would one day give up writing altogether, give it up voluntarily—at the moment when I would feel myself in possession of the greatest power and mastery. The study of Balzac, which was my final work in Paris, had only corroborated a thought which had begun to crystallize in me, namely that the life of the artist, his devotion to art, is the highest and the last phase of egotism in man. There are friends who tell me that I will never stop writing, that I can't. But I did stop, for a good interval while in Greece, and I know that I can in the future, any time I wish, and for good. I feel under no compulsion to do any particular thing. I feel, on the contrary, a growing liberation, supplemented more and more by a desire to serve the world in the highest possible way. What that way is I have not yet determined, but it seems clear to me that I shall pass from art to life, to exemplify whatever I have mastered through art by my living. I said I felt chastened. It is true that I also felt exalted. But above all I felt a sense of responsibility such as I had never known before. A sense of responsibility towards myself, let me hasten to add. Without tasting the rewards which he had spoken of I had nevertheless enjoyed them in advance, enjoyed them imaginatively, I mean. During all the years that I have been writing I have steeled myself to the idea that I would not really be accepted, at least to my own countrymen, until after my death. Many times, in writing, I have looked over my own shoulder from beyond the grave, more alive to the reactions of those to come than to those of my contemporaries. A good part of my life has, in a way, been lived in the future. With regard to all that vitally concerns me I am really a dead man, alive only to a very few who, like myself, could not wait for the world to catch up with them. I do not say this out of pride or vanity, but with humility not untouched with sadness. Sadness is perhaps hardly the right word either, since I neither regret the course I have followed nor desire things to be any different than they are. I know now what the world is like and knowing I accept it, both the good and the evil. To live creatively, I have discovered, means to live more and more unselfishly, to live more and more *into* the world, identifying oneself with it and thus influencing it at the core, so to speak. Art, like religion, it now seems to me, is only a preparation, an initiation into the way of life. The goal is liberation, freedom, which means assuming greater responsibility. To continue writing beyond the point of self-realization seems futile and arresting. The mastery of any form of expression should lead inevitably to the final expression—mastery of life. In this realm one is absolutely alone, face to face with the very elements of creation. It is an experiment whose outcome nobody can predict. If it be successful the whole world is affected and in a way never known before. I do not wish to boast, nor do I wish to say that I am yet ready to make such a grave step, but it is in this direction that my mind is set. It was my belief before meeting the Armenian, and it still is, that when the honors and rewards shall be conferred upon me I shall not be present to receive them, that I shall be living alone and unknown in some remote part of the world carrying on the adventure which began with the effort to realize myself in words. I know that the greatest dangers lie ahead; the real voyage has only begun. As I write these lines it is almost a year since that moment in Athens which I have just described. May I add that since coming to America everything that has happened to me, one fulfillment, one realization after another, has occurred with an almost clock-like precision. Indeed, I am almost terrified for now, contrary to my life in the past, I have but to desire a thing and my wishes are gratified. I am in the delicate position of one who has to be careful not to wish for something he really does not desire. The effect, I must say, has been to make me desire less and less. The one desire which grows more and more is to give. The very real sense of power and wealth which this entails is also somewhat frightening—because the logic of it seems too utterly simple. It is not until I look about me and realize that the vast majority of my fellow men are desperately trying to hold on to what they possess or to increase their possessions that I begin to understand that the wisdom of giving is not so simple as it seems. Giving and receiving are at bottom one thing, dependent upon whether one lives open or closed. Living openly one becomes a medium, a transmitter; living thus, as a river, one experiences life to the full, flows along with the current of life, and dies in order to live again as an ocean.

The holidays were approaching and everybody was urging

me to postpone my departure until after Christmas. The boat was due to sail in two or three days. Just when I had given up all hope I received word that the boat had been detained at Gibraltar and that we would not be able to sail for at least a week, possibly ten days. Durrell, who had borrowed Max's car for the holidays, decided to take a trip to the Peloponnesus and insisted that I accompany him and Nancy. If the boat were to sail in a week there was a good chance that I would miss it. Nobody could say for certain when it would sail. I decided to risk the chance that it would be delayed beyond a week.

Between times I went again to Eleusis with Ghika. It was a late afternoon when he called for me in his car. By the time we reached Daphni the sun was setting in violent splendor. I put it down in my memory as a green sunset. Never was the sky more clear, nor more dramatic. We were racing to reach the ruins before dark, but in vain. We arrived to find the gates locked. After a little persuasion, however, the guardian permitted us to enter. Lighting one match after another Ghika led me rapidly from one spot to another. It was a weird spectacle and one which I shall never forget. When we had finished we walked through the shabby streets to the shore of the bay facing Salamis. There is something sinister and oppressive about this scene at night. We walked up and down the quay, buffeted by the strong winds, and talked of other days. There was an ominous silence all about and the twinkling lights of the new Eleusis gave to the place an even shabbier atmosphere than the light of day. But as we rolled back to Athens we were rewarded by an electrical display which for me is without a parallel among the cities of the world. The Greek is just as enamored of electric light as he is of sunlight. No soft shades, as in Paris or New York, but every window ablaze with light, as if the inhabitants had just discovered the marvels of electricity. Athens sparkles like a chandelier; it sparkles like a chandelier in a bare room lined with tiles. But what gives it its unique quality, despite the excessive illumination, is the softness which it retains in the midst of the glare. It is as if the sky, becoming more liquescent, more tangible, had lowered itself to fill every crevice with a magnetic fluid. Athens swims in an electric effluvia which comes directly from the heavens. It affects not only the nerves and sensory organs of the body but the inner being. On any slight eminence one can stand in the very heart of Athens and feel the very real connection which man has with the other worlds of light. At the end of Anagnastopolou Street, where Durrell lived, there is a bluff which enables one to overlook a great part of the city; night after night, upon leaving him, I have stood there and fallen into a deep trance, intoxicated by the lights of Athens and the lights above. At Sacré-Coeur, in Paris, it is another feeling that one gets; from the towering height of the Empire State Building, in New York, still another. I have looked over Prague, Budapest, Vienna, over the harbor at Monaco, all beautiful and impressive at night, but I know no city to compare with Athens when the lights go on. It seems ridiculous to say so, yet I have the feeling that in Athens the miraculous light of day never entirely vanishes; in some mysterious way this soft, peaceful city never wholly lets the sun out of its grasp, never quite believes that the day is done. Often, when I had said good-night to Seferiades in front of his home in Kydathenaion Street, I would wander over to the Zapion and stroll about in the dazzling starlight, repeating to myself as if it were an incantation: "you are in another part of the world, in another latitude, you are in Greece, in Greece, do you understand?" It was necessary to repeat the Greece because I had the strange feeling of being at home, of being in a spot so familiar, so altogether like home should be that from looking at it with such intense adoration it had become a new and strange place. For the first time in my life, too, I had met men who were like men ought to be—that is to say, open, frank, natural, spontaneous, warm-hearted. These were the types of men I had expected to meet in my own land when I was growing up to manhood. I never found them. In France I found another order of human beings, a type whom I admired and respected but whom I never felt close to. In every possible way that I can think of Greece presented itself to me as the very center of the universe, the ideal meeting place of man with man in the presence of God. It was the first voyage I had ever made which was wholly satisfactory, in which there was no slightest trace of disillusionment, in which I was offered *more* than I had expected to find. The last nights in the Zapion, alone, filled with wonderful memories, were like a beautiful Gethsemane. Soon all this would be gone and I would be walking once more the streets of my own city. The prospect no longer filled me with dread. Greece had done something for me which New York, nay, even America itself, could never destroy. Greece had made me free and whole. I felt ready to meet the dragon and to slay him, for in my heart I had already slain him. I walked about as if on velvet, rendering silent homage and thanksgiving to the little band of friends whom I had made in Greece. I love those men, each and every one, for having revealed to me the true proportions of the human being. I love the soil in which they grew, the tree from which they sprang, the light in which they flourished, the goodness, the integrity, the charity which they emanated. They brought me face to face with myself, they cleansed me of hatred and jealousy and envy. And not least of all, they demonstrated by their own example that life can be lived magnificently on any scale, in any clime, under any conditions. To those who think that Greece to-day is of no importance let me say that no greater error could be committed. To-day as of old Greece is of the utmost importance to every man who is seeking to find himself. My experience is not unique. And perhaps I should add that no people in the world are as much in need of what Greece has to offer as the American people. Greece is not merely the antithesis of America, but more, the solution to the ills which plague us. Economically it may seem unimportant, but spiritually Greece is still the mother of nations, the fountainhead of wisdom and inspiration.

Only a few days remain. The day before Christmas I am sitting in the sun on the terrace of the King George Hotel, waiting for Durrell and Nancy to appear with the car. The weather is dubious; heavy rains may set in. We were to have left at ten in the morning; it is now two o'clock. Finally they arrive in Max's flimsy little English car which looks like an overgrown bug. The car is not working right, the brakes particularly. Durrell is laughing, as usual. Laughing and swearing at the same time. He is going to run the car into the ground. He hopes I will miss the boat. Will we wait a moment until he buys a newspaper and a sandwich? He follows the war news closely. I haven't read a newspaper since I left Paris; I don't intend to read one until I get to New York, where I know I will get an eyeful.

The first thing I realize, as we speed along, is that it is no longer Autumn. The car is an open car with a shed over it. In the sun it is pleasant, but once it gets dark it will be uncomfortable. Riding along the side of the mountain overlooking the sea Durrell suddenly asks me what I think of when the name Corinth is mentioned. I answer immediately: "Memphis." "I think of something fat, reddish and sensuous," he says. We are going to put up in Corinth for the night and then move on to Sparta. At the canal we stop a moment. First touch of red; something distinctly Egyptian about the Corinth canal. We enter the new city of Corinth in the late afternoon. It is anything but attractive. Broad avenues, low box-like houses, empty parks—new in the worst sense of the word. We choose a hotel with central heating, take time out for a cup of tea, and start off for old Corinth to get a glimpse of the ruins before dark. Old Corinth is several miles away, built on a piece of rising ground overlooking a waste land. In the light of a wintry afternoon the site takes on a prehistoric aspect. Above the ruins rises the Acrocorinth, a sort of Aztec mesa on which, one might easily believe, the bloodiest sacrificial rites were performed.

Once amidst the ruins the whole impression changes. The great plinth of the Acrocorinth now looms up soft and ingratiating, a giant megalith which has grown a coat of wool. Every minute that passes sheds a new luster, a new tenderness, upon the scene. Durrell was right: there is something rich, sensuous and rosy about Corinth. It is death in full bloom, death in the midst of voluptuous, seething corruption. The pillars of the Roman temple are fat; they are almost Oriental in their proportions, heavy, squat, rooted to the earth, like the legs of an elephant stricken with amnesia. Everywhere this lush, overgrown, over-ripe quality manifests itself, heightened by a rose-colored light flush from the setting sun. We wander down to the spring, set deep in the earth like a hidden temple, a mysterious place suggesting affinities with India and Arabia. Above us is the thick wall which surrounds the old site. A marvelous atmospheric duet is taking place in the sky; the sun, which has become a ball of fire, is now joined by the moon, and in the flood of swiftly shifting harmonics created by the conjunction of these two luminaries the ruins of Corinth glow and vibrate with supernatural beauty. Only one effect is withheld—a sudden rain of starlight.

The way back leads through another world, for in addition to the darkness there is a mist rising from the sea. A string of tiny, twinkling lights marks the coastline across the gulf where the mountains roll up peacefully and somnolently. Corinth, new Corinth, is engulfed in a cold sweat which penetrates to the bone.

Looking for a restaurant a little later we decide to take a brisk walk through the town first. There is nothing to do but follow one of the broad avenues leading nowhere. It is Christmas Eve, but there is nothing here to indicate that anyone is aware of it. Approaching a lonely house lit up by a smoky kerosene lamp we are suddenly arrested by the queer strains of a flute. We hasten our steps and stand in the middle of the wide street to take in the performance. The door of the house is open, revealing a room filled with men listening to an uncouth figure playing the flute. The man seems to be exalted by his own music, a music such as I have never heard before and probably never will again. It seems like sheer improvisation and, unless his lungs give out, there promises to be no end to it. It is the music of the hills, the wild notes of the solitary man armed with nothing but his instrument. It is the original music for which no notes have been written and for which none is necessary. It is fierce, sad, obsessive, yearning and defiant. It is not for men's ears but for God's. It is a duet in which the other instrument is silent. In the midst of the performance a man approaches us on a bicycle, dismounts and doffing his hat inquires respectfully if we are strangers, if we had arrived perhaps just to-day. He is a telegraph messenger and he has a message in his hand for an American woman, he says. Durrell laughs and asks to see the message. It is a Christmas greeting to the Countess von Reventlow (Barbara Hutton). We read it—it is in English—and pass it back to him. He goes off, peering like a scout into the darkness, ready no doubt to intercept the next tall woman with golden hair whom he sees dressed like a man. The incident reminded me of my own days in the telegraph service, of a winter's night when I came upon a messenger walking the streets of New York in a daze with a fistful of undelivered messages. Noticing the blank stare in his eyes I led him back to the office he had come from, where I learned that he had been missing for two days and nights. He was blue with cold and chattering like a monkey. When I opened his coat to see if he had any messages in his inside pockets I discovered that under the coarse suit he was naked. In one of his pockets I found a program of musical compositions which he had evidently printed himself since almost the entire list of pieces indicated him as being the composer. The incident came to a close in the observation ward at Bellevue where he was pronounced insane.

In the restaurant, which was spacious and draughty, we had a delicious greasy meal of the sort which usually turns the Anglo-Saxon's stomach. When the plates are ice cold I admit, of course, that some of the charm of the Greek cuisine is nullified, but the English, being the worst cooks in the world, ought to be the last to complain. With the aid of a few bottles of wine we made the best of a rather cheerless Christmas Eve gathering. The high spot of the festivity—the other diners had left—was the elaborate formulation of quixotic messages on postcards to various celebrities throughout the world. We returned to the hotel, which was now as warm as toast, and went promptly to bed.

In the morning we set out for Mycenae which the Durrells

had not yet visited. The air was crisp, the road free and clear, and we were all in good spirits. The Peloponnesus affects everyone in much the same way, I imagine. The best way that I can express it is to say that it is like a soft, quick stab to the heart. Durrell, who was raised near the Tibetan frontier in India, was tremendously excited and confessed that at times he had the impression of being back in India, in the hill country. As we neared Mycenae he was even more impressed. Always voluble and articulate, I observed with pleasure that he was silenced.

This time, being equipped with a flashlight, we decided to descend the slippery staircase to the well. Durrell went first, Nancy next, and I followed gingerly behind. About halfway down we halted instinctively and debated whether to go any farther. I experienced the same feeling of terror as I had the first time with Katsimbalis, more, if anything, since we had descended deeper into the bowels of the earth. I had two distinct fears — one, that the slender buttress at the head of the stairs would give way and leave us to smother to death in utter darkness, and two, that a misstep would send me slithering down into the pit amidst a spawn of snakes, lizards and bats. I was tremendously relieved when Durrell, after much persuasion, consented to abandon the descent. I was thankful that I was first now instead of last. When we reached the surface I was in a cold sweat and mentally still going through the motion of kicking off the demons who were trying to drag me back into the horror-laden mire. Thinking back on it now, after a lapse of months, I honestly believe that I would rather be shot than forced to descend that staircase alone. In fact, I think I would die of heart failure before ever reaching the bottom.

We had now to go through Argos, which I had only seen from the distance before, and over the mountains to Tripolis. To rise from the lush Argive plain to the first tier of mountain ranges is a dramatic experience of another order. The road is fairly narrow, the curves sharp and perilous, the drop precipitous. Buses travel over this road, driven it would seem by maniacs, for the Greek, as I have said before, is by nature reckless and foolhardy. The clouds were gathering for a storm and we had only begun to cross the broken spine that lay ahead. The question in our minds was—would the brakes hold out? We asked ourselves that while straddling an overhanging ledge on a hairpin turn, waiting jitteringly for a bus to pass without grazing our fenders. Finally, rolling around the edge of a huge soup tureen which Durrell assured me was Arcady, it began to pour and as it increased an icy wind, chill as the hand of death, smote us full force. Meanwhile, juggling the loose wheel with the dexterity of a mountebank, Durrell expatiated on the merits of Daphnis and Chloë. The rain was coming in from the sides and back, the engine began to snort and chug, the windshield wipers stopped functioning, my hands were frozen and the water was dripping off my hat and down my back. I was scarcely in a mood to hear about Daphnis and Chloë; I was thinking, on the contrary, how comfortable it would be standing on that slippery staircase at Mycenae.

Once over the top of the range we could see the broad plateau on which Tripolis rests. Suddenly the rain ceased and a rainbow appeared, the most heartening, frivolous, gamboling rainbow I have ever seen, to be followed shortly by a second one, both of which seemed within our grasp and yet always tantalizingly out of reach. We chased them at breakneck speed down the long winding ravines that lead to the level of the plateau.

We had lunch at a marvelous hotel, drank some more wine, shook ourselves like dogs and started off again in the direction of Sparta. It started to rain again, a torrential downpour which, with brief interruptions, was to continue for three days steadily. If I had to do the trip again I would ask for nothing better than another such downpour. The whole countryside was magically transformed by the tawny flood which created lakes and rivers of spectacular beauty. The land became more and more Asiatic in appearance, enhancing the sense of voyage and heightening our already keen expectations. As we came within view of the valley of the Eurotas the rain ceased and the soft wind from the south brought a warmth and fragrance which was distinctly pleasurable. To the right of the long Spartan plain extended the snow-capped range of the Taygetos which runs unbroken right to the tip of the peninsula. The fragrance of the oranges grew more and more powerful as we approached Sparta. It was about four in the afternoon when we entered the city. The principal hotel, which covered almost a square block, was full up. We had to walk about for an hour or so before we could find rooms. Durrell thought it a wretched place; I found it quite the contrary. It is true, there is nothing very ancient about the appearance of Sparta; it is probably no better than Corinth, and yet, probably because it is a meridional town, it seemed more cheerful, more animated and more alluring to me than Corinth. It has a vulgar, pushing, somewhat aggressive air, as though it had been influenced by the return of Americanized Greeks. We were of course immediately spotted as English and greeted in English at every turn, a practice which the English abhor but which an American like myself is not over-sensitive about. As a matter of fact I rather enjoy these casual greetings, being avidly curious always about the explorations of my fellow men, and particularly the Greeks who have a genius for penetrating to the most remote and outlandish places. What Durrell could not comprehend, never having been to America, is that the uncouth language and manners of these too friendly Greeks are thoroughly familiar, natural and acceptable to the American, having been acquired solely through contact with the native American. The Greek is not naturally thus; he is, according to my experience, soft-spoken, gentle and considerate. I saw in these Spartans the traces of the very things which I deplore in my own countrymen; I felt like congratulating them, individually and collectively, upon their good sense in returning to their native land.

Having some time to kill before dinner we took a spin out to Mystras, the Byzantine village whose ruins are the chief attraction for visitors to Sparta. The boulder-studded bed of the Eurotas had not yet become the swirling cataract which it would be on the morrow. It was now a rather swift, icy stream darting like a black snake through its shallow, gleaming bed. For some reason or other we did not enter the ruins, but sat in the car looking out over the broad plain. On the way back we passed a friend of Durrell's—without stopping. The greeting impressed me as most nonchalant and casual. "What's the matter," I inquired, "are you on the outs with him?" Durrell seemed surprised by my remark. No, he wasn't on the outs with the fellow—what made me think so? "Well, isn't it a bit unusual to run into an old friend in an odd corner of the world like this?" I asked. I don't remember the exact words he used in answer to this but substantially they were these: "What would we do with an Englishman here? They're bad enough at home. Do you want to spoil our holiday?" His words set me to meditating. In Paris, I recalled, I had never been keen to meet an American. But that was because I considered Paris my home and at home, however mistaken the idea may be, one feels that he has a right to be rude, intolerant and unsociable. But away from home, especially in an utterly strange place, I have always felt good about running into a compatriot, even though he might prove to be an incurable bore. In fact, once out of familiar bounds, boredom and enmity and prejudice usually cease with me. If I were to encounter my worst enemy, in Samarkand, let us say, I am certain I would go up to him and hold out my hand. I would even put up with a little insult and injury in order to win his good graces. I don't know why, except perhaps that just being alive and breathing in some different part of the world makes enmity and intolerance seem the absurd things which they are. I remember a meeting with a Jew who detested me in America, because he considered me an anti-Semite. We had encountered one another in a railway station in Poland after a lapse of several years. The moment he laid eyes on me his hatred vanished. I not only felt glad to see him again but eager to make amends for having, whether rightly or wrongly, wittingly or unwittingly, inspired his hostility. Had I met him in New York, where we had formerly known each other, it is highly improbable that our reactions would have been the same. The reflection, I admit, is a sad commentary on human limitations. It gives rise to even worse reflections, such as for example, the stupidity which permits rival factions to go on fighting one another even when confronted with a common enemy.

Back in town, seated in a suffocating café of railway station proportions, we were again greeted by a friend, a Greek this time, an official of some sort whom Durrell had known in Patras. He was soon gotten rid of in polite, friendly fashion. No injury was intended, I am certain, for Durrell is if anything un-English in this respect, yet somehow I felt as if we were building a wall of ice around ourselves. If it had been London or New York I would have felt annoyed by the noisy gaiety of the crowd, but being in Sparta I was intensely interested in this Christmas atmosphere. Had I been alone I would undoubtedly have introduced myself to some congenial-looking group and participated in the merriment, however idiotic it may have been. But the English don't do that; the English look on and suffer because of their inability to let go. My remarks unfortunately give a wholly false picture of Durrell who is normally the most easy-going, amiable, jovial, forthright and outright fellow imaginable. But Christmas is a morbid day for sensitive Anglo-Saxons and driving a dilapidated car over dangerous roads in the rain doesn't help to put one back on velvet. Myself I have never known what it is to pass a merry Christmas. For the first time in my life I was ready for it—in Sparta. But it was not to be. There was only one thing to do—eat and go to bed. And pray that the rain would let up by morning.

Durrell, whom I could see now was caving in with fatigue, refused to look about for a restaurant. We walked out of the café and down into a smoky cellar which was cold and damp. A radio was going full blast with triple amplifiers, megaphones, cowbells and dinner horns. To add to Durrell's discomfiture the program was from a German broadcasting station which was bombarding us with melancholy Christmas carols, lying reports of German victories, moth-eaten Viennese waltzes, broken-down Wagnerian arias, snatches of demented yodeling, blessings for Herr Hitler and his wretched gang of murderers, et cetera. To cap it all the food was abominable. But the lights were splendiferous! In fact, the illumination was so brilliant that the food began to look hallucinatingly enticing. To me at least it was really beginning to look like Christmas—that is to say, sour, moth-eaten, bilious, crapulous, worm-eaten, mildewed, imbecilic, pusillanimous and completely gaga. If a drunken Greek had come running in with a cleaver and begun chopping off our hands I would have said "Bravo! Merry Christmas to you, my gay little man!" But the only drunken Greek I saw was a little fellow at the next table who suddenly turned very white and without a word of warning puked up a heaping dishful of bright vomit and then quietly lowered his heavy head into it with a dull splash. Again I could scarcely blame Durrell for being disgusted. By this time his nerves were on edge. Instead of leaving immediately we remained to carry on a foolish discussion about the relative merits of various peoples. Crossing the square with its quaint arcades a little later, in a fine drizzle, Sparta seemed even more appealing to me than at first blush. It seemed very like Sparta, is what I thought—which is a meaningless phrase and yet exactly what I mean. Sparta, when I had thought about it previously, had always appeared in my mind as a very blue and white hamlet tucked away like some forgotten outpost in the midst of a fertile plain. If you think about it at all, Sparta must give rise to an image exactly the contrary of Athens. In fact, the whole Peloponnesus seems inevitably to awaken a suggestion of notness. Against the brilliant, diamond-pointed Attica one posits an obstinate sloth which resists not for any good reason but for the perverted pleasure of resisting. Rightly or wrongly, Sparta stands out in the mind's eye as an image of cantankerous, bovine righteousness, a foul behemoth of virtue, adding nothing to the world despite its advanced eugenic ideals. This image now comes to rest in the mud, sleepy as a turtle, contented as a cow, useless as a sewing machine in a desert. You can like Sparta now because, after centuries of obsolescence, it is no longer a menace to the world. It is now exactly the quaint, rather ugly, rather shabbily attractive hamlet which you imagined it to be. Being neither disillusioned nor undeceived you can accept it for what it is, glad that it is neither more nor less than it seems. Our own Faulkner could settle down and write a huge book about its negative aspects, its un-thisness and its not-thatness. In the rain, in the morbid gaiety of a Byzantine hangover, I saw the one positive fact about it, that it *is*, that it is Sparta, and being Sparta therefore Greek, which is sufficient in itself to redeem all the antithetical anomalies of the Peloponnesus. Inwardly, I confess, I felt perversely gay about Sparta for it had at last revealed to me the Englishman in Durrell, the least interesting thing about him, to be sure, but an element not to be overlooked. At the same time I was aware that never in my life had I felt so thoroughly American, which is a curious fact and perhaps not devoid of significance. All of which, anyhow, presented itself to the consciousness as a long-forgotten Q.E.D. out of the Euclidian history of the world.

It rained all night and in the morning, when we came down to the breakfast table, it was still pouring. Durrell, still feeling somewhat English, insisted on having a couple of boiled eggs for breakfast. We sat in a little nook overlooking the square. Nancy and I had almost finished our tea and toast when the eggs arrived. Durrell turned the egg cup upside down and gently chipped the first egg. It was hardly boiled and already quite cool, he complained aloud, ringing for the waitress who happened to be the proprietor's wife. "Please boil it a little longer," he said— "the two of them." We waited ten or fifteen minutes. The same performance and the same result. Only this time the egg was too badly chipped to be sent back again. However, determined to have his eggs, Durrell rang again. He explained elaborately, with ill-suppressed rage, that he wanted his eggs medium boiled. "Don't bother with that one," he said, "just have this one done a little more—and quickly, please, I can't sit here all morning." The woman left, promising to do her best. Again we waited, this time longer than before. Nancy and I had ordered more tea and toast. We smoked a couple of cigarettes. Finally I got up to look out of the window, hearing some strange noise below, and as I was gazing out I espied the woman crossing the square with an umbrella over her head and carrying the egg in her hand. "Here it comes," I said. "Here comes what?" said Durrell, "Why the egg! She's carrying it in her hand."

"What's the meaning of all this?" Durrell demanded, taking the cool egg and smashing the shell. "We have no stove," said the woman. "I had to take it to the baker's to have it boiled. Is it hard enough now?"

Durrell was at once apologetic. "It's just right," he said, cracking it vigorously with the back of his spoon. And as he smiled gratefully up at her he added in English—"The damned idiot, couldn't she have told us that in the first place? It's as hard as a rock, b'Jesus."

We started back in the rain, stopping here and there on the edge of a precipice to take snapshots. The car was working badly, gasping and wheezing as if on its last legs. About three miles outside of Tripolis, in the midst of a veritable cloudburst accompanied by hail and thunder and lightning, the road flooded like a rice field, the car suddenly gave a violent shudder and stopped dead. We might as well have been fifty miles away; there was absolutely no traffic and no way of getting assistance. To step out of the car was to wade in up to one's knees. I was to get the train for Athens at Tripolis and there was only one train to get. If I were to miss it I would miss the boat which was due to leave the next day. It was so obvious that the car had given its last spark of life that we sat there laughing and joking about our plight without thinking to make the slightest effort to start her again. After ten or fifteen minutes of it the laughter died away. It looked as if we were doomed to sit there all afternoon, maybe all night. "Why don't you try to do something?" said Nancy. Durrell was saying, as he usually did when Nancy proffered her advice—"Why don't you shut up?"—but instinctively he had made a few automatic motions. To our amazement we heard the thing spitting. "The bloody thing's going," he said, and sure enough, as he stepped on the gas she jumped like a kangaroo and was off. We art wed at the door of the hotel at top speed and were greeted by a porter with a huge umbrella. The car looked as if it were going to be carried away in the flood and deposited on top of Mt. Ararat.

The train was due to leave at four o'clock, so we had time for a last meal together. Durrell did his best to persuade me to stay overnight, convinced that the boat would not leave on schedule. "Nothing goes according to schedule in this bloody country," he assured me. In my heart I was hoping that some convenient accident would detain me. If I were to miss the boat I might not get another for a month and in that time Italy might declare war on Greece and thus shut me off in the Mediterranean, a most delightful prospect. Nevertheless I went through the motions of leaving. It was up to Fate now, I thought to myself. Durrell and Nancy were going to Epidaurus and then to Olympia. I would be going back to jail.

The horse and carriage were at the door waiting for me. Durrell and Nancy stood on the steps waving good-bye. The sleigh bells began to ring, the flaps came down over my eyes and we started off in a teeming mist which was made of rain and tears. "Where will we meet again?" I asked myself. Not in America, not in England, not in Greece, thought I. If anywhere it will be in India or Tibet. And we are going to meet haphazardly—on the road—as Durrell and his friend had met on the way to Mystras. The war will not only change the map of the world but it will affect the destiny of everyone I care about. Already, even before the war had broken out, we were scattered to the four winds, those of us who had lived and worked together and who had no thought to do anything but what we were doing. My friend X, who used to be terrified at the very mention of war, had volunteered for service in the British Army; my friend Y, who was utterly indifferent and who used to say that he would go right on working at the Bibliothèque Nationale war or no war, joined the Foreign Legion; my friend Z, who was an out-and-out pacifist, volunteered for ambulance service and has never been heard of since; some are in concentration camps in France and Germany, one is rotting away in Siberia, another is in China, another in Mexico, another in Australia. When we meet again some will be blind, some legless, some old and white-haired, some demented, some bitter and cynical. Maybe the world will be a better place to live in, maybe it'll be just the same, maybe it'll be worse than it is now—who knows? The strangest thing of all is that in a universal crisis of this sort one instinctively knows that certain ones are doomed and that others will be spared. With some, usually the shining, heroic figures, one can see death written in their faces; they glow with the knowledge of their own death. Others, whom one would normally think of as worthless, in the military sense, you feel nevertheless will become hardened veterans, will go through hell's fire unscathed and emerge grinning, perhaps to settle down in the old routine and amount to nothing. I saw the effect of the last war on some of my friends in America; I can see the effect which this one will produce even more clearly. One thing is certain, I thought to myself—the chaos and confusion which this war is engendering will never be remedied in our lifetime. There will be no resuming where we left off. The world we knew is dead and gone. The next time we meet, any of us, it will be on the ashes of all that we once cherished.

The scene at the railway station was one of utter confusion. Word had just been received that the train would be an hour or two late—there had been a washout up the line somewhere, nobody knew exactly where. The rain came down relentlessly and unceasingly, as if all the cocks in the celestial plumbing system had been opened and the monkey wrench thrown away. I sat down on a bench outside and prepared myself for a long siege. In a few minutes a man approached me and said "Hello, what you doing here? You an American?" I nodded and smiled. "Helluva country this, eh?" he said. "Too poor, that's what's the matter. Where you come from—Chicago?"

He sat down beside me and began to chew my ear off about the wonderful efficiency of the American railways. A Greek, naturally, who had lived in Detroit. "Why I come back to this country I don't know," he went on. "Everybody poor here—you can't make no money here. Soon we go to war. I was a damn fool to leave America. What you think of Greece—you like it? How long you stay here? You think America go to war?"

I decided to get out of his clutches as soon as possible. "Try to find out when the train will arrive," I said, dispatching him to the telegraph office. He didn't budge. "What's the use," he said, "nobody knows when the train will come. Maybe to-morrow morning." He began to talk about automobiles, what a wonderful car the Ford was, for instance.

"I don't know anything about cars," I said.

"That's funny," he said, "and you an American."

"I don't like cars."

"But just the same, when you want to get somewhere...."

"I don't want to get anywhere."

"That's funny," he said. "You like the train better maybe, yes?"

"I like the donkey better than the train. I like to walk too."

"My brother just like that," he said. "My brother say, 'Why you want a car?' My brother, he never been in a car in his life. He stay here in Greece. He live in the mountains—very poor, but he say he don't care just so long as he have enough to eat."

"He sounds like an intelligent man," I said.

"Who, my brother? No, he know nothing. He can't read or write; he can't even sign his own name."

"That's fine," I said, "then he must be a happy man."

"My brother? No, he's very sad. He lose his wife and three children. I want him to go to America with me, but he say 'What I go to America for?' I tell him he make lots of money there. He say he don't want to make money. He just want to eat every day, that's all. Nobody got ambition here. America everybody want to be a success. Maybe some day your son be President of the United States, yes?"

"Maybe," I said, just to please him.

"In America everybody got a chance—poor man too, yes?"

"Sure."

"Maybe I go back again and make big money, what you think?"

"Nothing like trying," I answered.

"Sure, that's what I tell my brother. You must work. In America you work like a son of a bitch—but you get paid for it. Here you work and work and work and what you got? Nothing. A piece of bread maybe. What kind of life is that? How you going to succeed?"

I groaned.

"You make lots of money in New York, I bet, yes?"

"No," I said, "I never made a cent."

"What you mean?" he said. "You couldn't find job in New York?"

"I had lots of jobs," I answered.

"You don't stay long on one job, that's it, yes?"

"That's right," I said.

"Maybe you don't find the right job. You got to try many jobs—till you find the right one. You got to save your money. Maybe you have bad luck sometimes—then you have something for a rainy day, yes?"

"That's it," I said.

"Sometimes you get sick and you lose all your money. Sometimes a friend he take your money away from you. But you never give up, right? You stick it out. You try again."

"That's the idea," I grunted.

"You got a good job waiting for you in New York?"

"No," I said, "I haven't any job."

"Not so many jobs now as before," he said. "In 1928 lots of jobs. Now everybody poor. I lose ten thousand dollars in stock market. Some people lose more. I say never mind, try again. Then I come to this country to see my brother. I stay too long. No money here. Only trouble.... You think Italy make trouble soon for Greece?"

"I don't know," I said.

"You think Germany win—or France?"

"I couldn't say."

"I think United States should go in the war. United States clean up those sons of bitches quick, yes? If United States make war on Germany I fight for United States."

"That's the stuff," I said.

"Sure, why not?" he continued. "I no like to fight, but United

States good country. Everybody get square deal, rich or poor. Uncle Sam afraid of nobody. We raise ten million, twenty million soldiers—like that! We kill those sons of bitches like dogs, yes?"

"You said it, brother."

"I say to myself Uncle Sam he give me gun, he send me over to fight, I fight for him. Greek people no like Italians. Greek people like America. Everybody like America...."

"I like you too," I said, getting up and shaking hands with him, "but now I've got to leave you—I must make pipi."

"That's all right, I'll wait for you," he said.

You'll have a long wait, I thought to myself, as I disappeared inside the station. I got out on the other side of the station and walked around in the rain. When I returned I saw that the train was due to arrive at eight o'clock. A string of cars was standing at the platform waiting for the other section to arrive. Towards seven o'clock a bellhop from the hotel arrived and handed me a note. It was from Durrell, urging me to come back to the hotel and have dinner with them. The train wouldn't arrive until after ten, he informed me. I thought it over and decided against it, more because I hated to say good-bye a second time than for any other reason.

I got into one of the coaches and sat there in the dark. Towards nine-thirty a train pulled in from the opposite direction and everybody got excited. But when we tried to climb aboard we found that it was an excursion train that had been hired by a club. As I stood on the platform of the special I learned that it was leaving for Athens in a few minutes. I was wondering if I couldn't persuade them to take me along when a man came up to me and spoke to me in Greek. I answered in French that I couldn't speak Greek, that I was an American and that I was very anxious to get to Athens as soon as possible. He called a young lady over who spoke English and when she learned that I was an American tourist she got excited and told me to wait, saying she thought she could fix it for me. I stood there a few minutes congratulating myself on my good luck. The young lady returned accompanied by a grave, melancholy-looking man with an officious air. He asked me very courteously why it was important for me to get back to Athens quickly, why couldn't I wait for the other train which was due now in a little while, he was certain. I answered very courteously that there was no good reason except fear. He assured me there was nothing to be worried about. The other train was due in a few minutes and he had not the slightest doubt that it would leave in good time. He hesitated a moment and then cautiously, as if giving me a straw to grasp at, he inquired politely and with the utmost tact, as if unwilling to wrest the secret from me, whether I did not have a more urgent reason for wishing to leave ahead of time. There was something about his manner which warned me that it would be better not to invent a false reason. Something told me that he suspected me of being more than just a tourist. Beneath that suave, courteous exterior I divined the police inspector. True, I had in my pocket a letter from the Bureau of Tourisme which Seferiades had given me when I went to Crete, but experience has taught me that when a man is suspicious of you the better your credentials are the worse it is for you. I backed quietly down the steps, thanking him for his courtesy and excusing myself for the inconvenience I had caused him. "Your bags?" he said, with a flash of the eye. "I have none," I said, and quickly disappeared in the crowd.

As soon as the train had pulled out I came out on the platform of the station and dove into the buffet where I put away some tender bits of lamb and a few cognacs. I felt as though I had narrowly missed going to jail. Two prisoners who were handcuffed came in escorted by soldiers. I learned later that they had murdered the man who had violated their sister. They were good men, mountaineers, and they had surrendered without resistance. I went outside and got up an appetite watching a tender lamb being rolled on a spit. I had some more cognac. Then I got inside a coach and fell into conversation with a Greek who had lived in Paris. He was even more of a bore than the guy from Detroit. He was an intellectual who liked all the wrong things. I extricated myself as gracefully as possible and paced up and down in the rain again.

When the train did roll in at midnight I could scarcely believe my eyes. Of course it didn't pull out until about two in the morning—I didn't expect it to do any better. I had changed my ticket for a first-class compartment, thinking thereby to gain a little sleep before morning. There was only one man in the compartment with me and he soon began to doze off. I had a whole bench to myself, an upholstered one with white doilies over it. I stretched out full length and closed my eyes. Presently I felt something crawling over my neck. I sat up and brushed off a fat cockroach. As I sat there, gazing stupidly ahead of me, I noticed a file of cockroaches climbing the wall opposite. Then I took a glance at my fellow traveler. To my disgust I saw that they were crawling at a good pace over the lapel of his coat, onto his tie and down inside his vest. I got up and nudged him, pointing to the cockroaches. He made a grimace, brushed them off and with a smile fell back to sleep again. Not me. I was as wide awake as if I had just swallowed a half dozen cups of coffee. I felt itchy all over, I went outside and stood in the corridor. The train was going downhill, not just fast as trains do when they go downhill, but as if the engineer had gone to sleep and left the throttle wide open. I felt anxious. I wondered whether it would be wise to wake my companion up and warn him that something was wrong. Finally I realized that I didn't know how to express the thought in Greek and I gave up the idea. I clung to the open window with two hands and prayed to Christ and all the little angels that we'd hit the bottom without going off the track. Somewhere before Argos I felt the brakes being applied and realized with a sigh of relief that the engineer was at his post. As we came to a stop I felt a gush of warm, fragrant air. Some urchins in bare feet swarmed around the train with baskets of fruit and soda water. They looked as if they had been routed out of bed—little tots, about eight or ten years of age. I could see nothing but mountains about and overhead the moon scudding through the clouds. The warm air seemed to be coming up from the sea, rising slowly and steadily, like incense. A pile of old ties were going up in flames, casting a weird light on the black mountains yonder.

At the hotel in Athens I found a note from the American Express saying that the boat had been held up another twenty-four hours. Golfo the maid was overjoyed to see me. My socks and shirts were lying on the bed, all beautifully mended during my absence. After I had taken a bath and a nap I telephoned Katsimbalis and Seferiades to have a last dinner together. Captain Antoniou unfortunately was taking his boat to Saloniki. Ghika was unable to come, but promised to take me to the boat on the morrow. Theodore Stephanides was in Corfu putting his X-ray laboratory in shape. Durrell and Nancy, either they were marooned in the hotel at Tripolis or they were sitting in the amphitheatre at Epidaurus. There was one other person whose presence I missed and that was Spiro of Corfu. I didn't realize it then, but Spiro was getting ready to die. Only the other day I received a letter from his son telling me that Spiro's last words were: "New York! New York! I want to find Henry Miller's house!" Here is how Lillis, his son, put it in his letter: "My poor father died with your name in his mouth which closed forever. The last day, he had lost his logic and pronounced a lot of words in English as: 'New York! New York! where can I find Mr. Miller's house?' He died as poor as he always was. He did not realize his dream to be rich. This year I finish the Commercial School of Corfu but I am unemployed. And this is a result of the miserable war. Who knows when I shall find a job to be able to feed my family. Anyway such is the life and we can do nothing to it ..."

No, Lillis is quite right—we can do nothing to it! And that is why I look back on Greece with such pleasure. The moment I stepped on the American boat which was to take me to New York I felt that I was in another world. I was among the go-getters again, among the restless souls who, not knowing how to live their own life, wish to change the world for everybody. Ghika, who had brought me to the quay, came on board to have a look at the strange American boat which lay at anchor in the port of Piraeus. The bar was open and we had a last drink together. I felt as though I were already back in New York: there was that clean, vacuous, anonymous atmosphere which I know so well and detest with all my heart. Ghika was impressed with the luxurious appearance of the boat; it answered to the picture which he had built up in his mind. Myself, I felt depressed. I was sorry I hadn't been able to take a Greek boat.

I was even more depressed when I found that I was to have opposite me at the table a Greek surgeon who had become an American citizen and who had spent some twenty years or so in America. We hit it off badly right from the start. Everything he said I disagreed with; everything he liked I detested. I never met a man in my life whom I more thoroughly despised than this Greek. Finally, about the end of the second day, after he had gotten me aside to finish a discussion which had begun at the dinner table, I told him frankly that despite his age, his experience of life, which was vast, despite his status, despite his knowledge, despite the fact that he was a Greek, I considered him an ignorant fool and that I wanted nothing more to do with him. He was a man approaching seventy, a man who was evidently respected by those who knew him, a man who had been distinguished for bravery on the field of battle and who had been honored for his contribution to medical science; he was also a man who had travelled to every nook and corner of the world. He was somebody and in his declining years he lived in the realization of that fact. My words therefore produced a veritable shock in him. He said he had never been spoken to that way in his life. He was insulted and outraged. I told him I was glad to hear it, it would do him good.

From that moment on of course we never addressed a word to one another. At meals I looked straight through him, as if he were a transparent object. It was embarrassing for the others, more so because we were both well liked, but I would no more think of conciliating that pest than I would of jumping off the boat. Throughout the voyage the doctor would air his views which everybody would listen to with attention and respect and then I would air mine, taking a perverse delight in demolishing everything he said, yet never answering him directly but talking as if he had already left the table. It's a wonder we didn't get dyspepsia before the voyage was out.

Coming back to America I am happy to say I have never run into a type like that again. Everywhere I go I see Greek faces and often I stop a man in the street and ask him if he isn't a Greek. It heartens me to have a little chat with a stranger from Sparta or Corinth or Argos. Only the other day, in the lavatory of a big hotel in New York, I struck up a friendly conversation with the attendant who proved to be a Greek from the Peloponnesus. He gave me a long and instructive talk about the construction of the second Parthenon. Lavatories are usually underground and the atmosphere, one would imagine, is scarcely conducive to good talk, but I had a wonderful conversation in this particular hole and I've made a mental note to come back at intervals and resume intercourse with my new-found friend. I know a night elevator runner in another hotel who is also interesting to talk to. The fact is, the more humble the employment the more interesting I find the Greek to be.

The greatest single impression which Greece made upon me is that it is a man-sized world. Now it is true that France also conveys this impression, and yet there is a difference, a difference which is profound. Greece is the home of the gods; they may have died but their presence still makes itself felt. The gods were of human proportion: they were created out of the human spirit. In France, as elsewhere in the Western world, this link between the human and the divine is broken. The skepticism and paralysis produced by this schism in the very nature of man provides the clue to the inevitable destruction of our present civilization. If men cease to believe that they will one day become gods then they will surely become worms. Much has been said about a new order of life destined to arise on this American continent. It should be borne in mind, however, that not even a beginning has been visioned for at least a thousand years to come.

The present way of life, which is America's, is doomed as surely as is that of Europe. No nation on earth can possibly give birth to a new order of life until a world view is established. We have learned through bitter mistakes that all the peoples of the earth are vitally connected, but we have not made use of that knowledge in an intelligent way. We have seen two world wars and we shall undoubtedly see a third and a fourth, possibly more. There will be no hope of peace until the old order is shattered. The world must become small again as the old Greek world was—small enough to include everybody. Until the very last man is included there will be no real human society. My intelligence tells me that such a condition of life will be a long time in coming, but my intelligence also tells me that nothing short of that will ever satisfy man. Until he has become fully human, until he learns to conduct himself as a member of the earth, he will continue to create gods who will destroy him. The tragedy of Greece lies not in the destruction of a great culture but in the abortion of a great vision. We say erroneously that the Greeks humanized the gods. It is just the contrary. The gods humanized the Greeks. There was a moment when it seemed as if the real significance of life had been grasped, a breathless moment when the destiny of the whole human race was in jeopardy. The moment was lost in the blaze of power which engulfed the intoxicated Greeks. They made mythology of a reality which was too great for their human comprehension. We forget, in our enchantment with the myth, that it is born of reality and is fundamentally no different from any other form of creation, except that it has to do with the very quick of life. We too are creating myths, though we are perhaps not aware of it. But in our myths there is no place for the gods. We are building an abstract, dehumanized world out of the ashes of an illusory materialism. We are proving to ourselves that the universe is empty, a task which is justified by our own empty logic. We are determined to conquer and conquer we shall, but the conquest is death.

People seem astounded and enthralled when I speak of the effect which this visit to Greece produced upon me. They say they envy me and that they wish they could one day go there them-selves. Why don't they? Because nobody can enjoy the experi-ence he desires until he is ready for it. People seldom mean what they say. Anyone who says he is burning to do something other than he is doing or to be somewhere else than he is is lying to himself. To desire is not merely to wish. To desire is to become that which one essentially is. Some men, reading this, will inevi-tably realize that there is nothing to do but act out their desires. A line of Maeterlinck's concerning truth and action altered my whole conception of life. It took me twenty-five years to fully awaken to the meaning of his phrase. Other men are quicker to coordinate vision and action. But the point is that in Greece I finally achieved that coordination. I became deflated, restored to proper human proportions, ready to accept my lot and pre-pared to give of all that I have received. Standing in Agamem-non's tomb I went through a veritable re-birth. I don't mind in the least what people think or say when they read such a state-ment. I have no desire to convert anyone to my way of thinking. I know now that any influence I may have upon the world will be a result of the example I set and not because of my words. I give this record of my journey not as a contribution to human knowledge, because my knowledge is small and of little account, but as a contribution to human experience. Errors of one sort and another there undoubtedly are in this account but the truth is that something happened to me and *that* I have given as truth-fully as I know how.

My friend Katsimbalis for whom I have written this book, by way of showing my gratitude to him and his compatriots, will I hope forgive me for having exaggerated his proportions to that of a Colossus. Those who know Amaroussion will realize that there is nothing grandiose about the place. Neither is there any-thing grandiose about Katsimbalis. Neither, in the ultimate, is there anything grandiose about the entire history of Greece. But there is something colossal about any human figure when that individual becomes truly and thoroughly human. A more hu-man individual than Katsimbalis I have never met. Walking with him through the streets of Amaroussion I had the feeling that I was walking the earth in a totally new way. The earth became more intimate, more alive, more promising. He spoke frequently of the past, it is true, not as something dead and forgotten however, but rather as something which we carry within us, something which fructifies the present and makes the future inviting. He spoke of little things and of great with equal reverence; he was never too busy to pause and dwell on the things which moved him; he had endless time on his hands, which in itself is the mark of a great soul. How can I ever forget that last impression he made upon me when we said farewell at the bus station in the heart of Athens? There are men who are so full, so rich, who give themselves so completely that each time you take leave of them you feel that it is absolutely of no consequence whether the parting is for a day or forever. They come to you brimming over and they fill you to overflowing. They ask nothing of you except that you participate in their superabundant joy of living. They never inquire which side of the fence you are on because the world they inhabit has no fences. They make themselves invulnerable by habitually exposing themselves to every danger. They grow more heroic in the measure that they reveal their weaknesses. Certainly in those endless and seemingly fabulous stories which Katsimbalis was in the habit of recounting there must have been a good element of fancy and distortion, yet even if truth was occasionally sacrificed to reality the man behind the story only succeeded thereby in revealing more faithfully and thoroughly his human image. As I turned to go, leaving him sitting there in the bus, his alert, round eye already feasting itself upon other sights, Seferiades who was accompanying me home remarked with deep feeling: "He is a great fellow, Miller, there is no doubt about it: he is something extraordinary ... a human phenomenon, I should say." He said it almost as if he Seferiades were saying farewell and not me. He knew Katsimbalis as well as one man can know another, I should imagine; he was sometimes impatient with him, sometimes irritated beyond words, sometimes downright furious, but even if he were one day to become his bitterest enemy I could not imagine him saying one word to reduce the stature or the splendor of his friend. How wonderful it was to hear him say, knowing that I had just left Katsimbalis—"Did he tell you that story about the coins he found?" or whatever it might be. He asked with the enthusiasm of a music lover who, learning that his friend has just bought a gramophone, wishes to advise him of a record which he knows will bring his friend great joy. Often, when we were all together and Katsimbalis had launched into a long story, I caught that warm smile of recognition on Seferiades' face—that smile which informs the others that they are about to hear something which has been proved and tested and found good. Or he might say afterwards, taking me by the arm and leading me aside: "Too bad he didn't give you the whole story tonight; there is a wonderful part which he tells sometimes when he's in very good spirits— it's a pity you had to miss it." It was also taken for granted by everybody, it seemed to me, that Katsimbalis not only had a right to improvise as he went along but that he was expected to do so. He was regarded as a virtuoso, a virtuoso who played only his own compositions and had therefore the right to alter them as he pleased.

There was another interesting aspect of his remarkable gift, one which again bears analogy to the musician's talent. During the time I knew him Katsimbalis' life was relatively quiet and unadventurous. But the most trivial incident, if it happened to Katsimbalis, had a way of blossoming into a great event. It might be nothing more than that he had picked a flower by the roadside on his way home. But when he had done with the story that flower, humble though it might be, would become the most wonderful flower that ever a man had picked. That flower would remain in the memory of the listener as the flower which Katsimbalis had picked; it would become unique, not because there was anything in the least extraordinary about it, but because Katsimbalis had immortalized it by noticing it, because he had put into that flower all that he thought and felt about flowers, which is like saying—a universe.

I choose this image at random but how appropriate and accurate it is! When I think of Katsimbalis bending over to pick a flower from the bare soil of Attica the whole Greek world, past, present and future, rises before me. I see again the soft, low mounds in which the illustrious dead were hidden away; I see the violet light in which the stiff scrub, the worn rocks, the huge boulders of the dry river beds gleam like mica; I see the miniature islands floating above the surface of the sea, ringed with dazzling white bands I see the eagles swooping out from the dizzy crags of inaccessible mountaintops, their somber shadows slowly staining the bright carpet of earth below; I see the figures of solitary men trailing their flocks over the naked spine of the hills and the fleece of their beasts all golden fuzz as in the days of legend; I see the women gathered at the wells amidst the olive groves, their dress, their manners, their talk no different now than in Biblical times; I see the grand patriarchal figure of the priest, the perfect blend of male and female, his countenance serene, frank, full of peace and dignity; I see the geometrical pattern of nature expounded by the earth itself in a silence which is deafening. The Greek earth opens before me like the Book of Revelation. I never knew that the earth contains so much; I had walked blindfolded, with faltering, hesitant steps; I was proud and arrogant, content to live the false, restricted life of the city man. The light of Greece opened my eyes, penetrated my pores, expanded my whole being. I came home to the world, having found the true center and the real meaning of revolution. No warring conflicts between the nations of the earth can disturb this equilibrium. Greece herself may become embroiled, as we ourselves are now becoming embroiled, but I refuse categorically to become anything less than the citizen of the world which I silently declared myself to be when I stood in Agamemnon's tomb. From that day forth my life was dedicated to the recovery of the divinity of man. Peace to all men, I say, and life more abundant!

FINIS

APPENDIX

Just as I had written the last line the postman delivered me a characteristic letter from Lawrence Durrell dated August 10th, 1940. I give it herewith to round off the portrait of Katsimbalis.

"*The peasants are lying everywhere on deck eating watermelons; the gutters are running with the juice. A huge crowd bound on a pilgrimage to the Virgin of Tinos. We are just precariously out of the harbour, scouting the skyline for Eyetalian Subs. What I really have to tell you is the story of the Cocks of Attica: it will frame your portrait of Katsimbalis which I have not yet read but which sounds marvelous from all accounts. It is this. We all went up to the Acropolis the other evening very drunk and exalted by wine and poetry; it was a hot black night and our blood was roaring with cognac. We sat on the steps outside the big gate, passing the bottle, Katsimbalis reciting and G—— weeping a little, when all of a sudden K. was seized with a kind of fit. Leaping to his feet he yelled out—"Do you want to hear the cocks of Attica, you damned moderns?" His voice had a hysterical edge to it. We didn't answer and he wasn't waiting for one. He took a little run to the edge of the precipice, like a faery queen, a heavy black faery queen, in his black clothes, threw back his head, clapped the crook of his stock into his wounded arm, and sent out the most blood-curdling clarion I have ever heard. Cock-a-doodle-doo. It echoed all over the city—a sort of dark bowl dotted with lights like cherries. It ricochetted from hillock to hillock and wheeled up under the walls of the Parthenon … We were so shocked that we were struck dumb. And while we were still looking at each other in the darkness, lo, from the distance silvery clear in the darkness a cock drowsily answered—then another, then another. This drove K. wild. Squaring himself, like a bird about to fly into space, and flapping his coat tails, he set up a terrific scream—and the echoes multiplied. He screamed until the veins stood out all over him, looking like a battered and ravaged rooster in profile, flapping on his own dunghill. He screamed himself hysterical and his audience in the valley increased until all over Athens like bugles they were calling and calling, answering him. Finally between laughter and hysteria we had to ask him to stop. The whole night was alive with cockcrows—all Athens, all Attica, all Greece, it seemed, until I almost imagined you being woken at your desk late in New York to hear these terrific silver peals: Katsimbaline cockcrow in Attica. This was epic—a great moment and purely Katsimbalis. If you could have heard these cocks, the frantic psaltery of the Attic cocks! I dreamt about it for two nights afterwards. Well, we are on our way to Mykonos, resigned now that we have heard the cocks of Attica from the Acropolis. I wish you'd write it—it is part of the mosaic...."*

LARRY

THE ROAD FROM DELPHI:
HENRY MILLER AND GREECE
by Ian S. MacNiven

FOR ALMOST FIVE YEARS LAWRENCE DURRELL HAD BEEN urging Henry Miller to come to Greece, and in this he had a strong ally in Betty Ryan, the lovely young American artist who lived downstairs from Miller at 18 Villa Seurat. In Henry's words, "she seduced me with her faithful, ravishing descriptions of Greece." And his Paris artist friend and neighbor Mayo, *nom de peinture* of Antoine Malliarakis, urged him further, "Miller, you will like Greece." In October 1938 Henry got as far as Marseilles, but in a war-induced panic he considered hopping the next ship for America instead, then returned to Paris. Finally, in May 1939, he stored his manuscripts and books and headed south again. This time he made it, and stayed for five months.

Henry Miller would never be the same again.

Greece is a dangerous land for a seeker, a visionary. Miller arrives primed for a revelation, for an epiphany. Not, to be sure, one that has anything to do with Christianity: Delphi, he considers, is the pre-Christian Navel of the World. His approach to it is indirect. He begins with Eleusis, site of the Elusinian Mysteries, traveling "along the Sacred Way, from Daphni to the sea." It is definitely "not a Christian highway," he says, "no suffering, no martyrdom, no flagellation.... Everything speaks now, as it did centuries ago, of illumination, of blinding, joyous illumination." He convinces himself that he is gripped by holy ecstacy, like a Corybant: "I was on the point of madness several times.... running up the hillside only to stop midway, terror-stricken, wondering what had taken possession of me." The book that emerged from his sojourn in Greece, *The Colossus of Maroussi*, while supposedly a portrait of his new friend George Katsimbalis, is more importantly an account of his own possession by the spirit of Greece. It was a Greece in which the ancient land he intuited blended almost seamlessly with the Greece he experienced. Indeed, his main diatribes were directed against those who wished to change Greece in their own image—Greeks returned from America who sang to him the wonders of Chicago over the "backwardness" of Greece, and the resident English: "An evening with these buttery-mouthed jakes always left me in a suicidal mood," he raged.

By the time he arrived in Greece, Miller had an underground reputation as a controversial author largely unread because his books could not be published in the English-speaking world. Readers of contraband copies of the two *Tropics* such as George Orwell or Durrell considered him a ground-breaking leader in free expression, one who had advanced honesty of expression beyond the also-banned *Lady Chatterley's Lover*. Others, including George Bernard Shaw, branded him a pornographer, one who used "verbatim reports of bad language." Increasingly, however, Miller thought of himself as a visionary, a mystic, a holy man bent on purging the dross from existence. Looking back over his life from the vantage point of his eighty-fifth year, Miller would write, "It is strange that the countries I most wanted to visit I have never seen—India, Tibet, China, Japan, Iceland. But I have lived with them in my mind." Miller, after seeing Delphi, could better imagine India, China, Tibet, and *Devachan*, that mythic locus that he would rhapsodize over for most of his life. Earlier he had written, "When I go to Delphi I shall consult my own oracles." These oracles, internalized, guided the course of his life and writing.

Within days after landing at Piraeus, Henry travels by boat to Corfu and a rendezvous with Larry and Nancy Durrell. They head north to wild Kalami below Mount Pantokrator, where they "baptized themselves anew in the raw" at the isolated shrine of Agios Arsenios, and Henry finds himself adopting an easy amalgam of Christian and pagan Greek attitudes. He is fascinated by the arduous life of the Corfiot peasants, and wants to join the women carrying water from the springs so that he can like them *feel* the ache of muscles, the throb and pulse of stressed arteries. Larry sternly dissuades him: he would lose face with the natives. Then the Greek army is mobilized, and Miller and the Durrells move back and forth between Corfu and Athens. In Athens, Durrell's great doctor friend Theodore Stephanides takes Larry and Henry to the observatory to view the Pleiades: "Rosicrucian!" exclaims Larry, another visionary.

Of course, the basic text for the impact of Greece on Miller is the *Colossus*. But there is also "First Impressions of Greece," drafted earlier. Miller had come to Greece with the fantasy that he could give himself a year's vacation after twenty years of continuous writing and scrambling to get by in Paris, yet writing had become perhaps even more necessary to him than discovery, food, and drink as stimulative to companionship and visions. In fact, it was tied up with all these. At the home of the painter Niko Ghika, with George and Aspasia Katsimbalis and the future Nobel laureate George Seferis, Henry notes: "Ripe, fecundating atmosphere—for conversation, dream, work, leisure, indolence, friendship and everything. Everywhere the ancestral spirit. The whiskey excellent, especially favorable for discussions about Blavatsky and Tibet." He opens a fresh notebook and writes:

Island of Hydra—11/5/39

The birthplace of the immaculate conception. An island built by a race of artists. Everything miraculously produced out of nothingness. Each house related to the other, as though by an unseen architect. Everything white as snow yet colorful. The whole town is like a dream creation: a dream born out of a rock.

It was to be a dream trip, yet one grounded in reality. Henry gave the notebook to Seferis, inscribed "For his most sensitive majesty, King George Seferis of Smyrna!"

Part of this reality, merging repeatedly into dream, is the voice of Katsimbalis, talking, "a living organ, a voice pealing heavy sonorous notes." Listening to his evocations, not only of Greece but also of Paris, of Shanghai (which Katsimbalis had never visited), Henry remarks prophetically in "First Impressions," "I feel as though I may suddenly bifurcate and no longer tell my own story but his." They are linked together as brothers, Henry claims, "handcuffed for eternity." Together they visit many of the stupendous places of classical antiquity. Henry tries to see everything in human terms: "Epidaurus is merely a place symbol: the real place is in the heart." His is a human-centered universe; mankind's antagonists lie within himself: "the enemy of man is not germs, but man himself, his pride, his prejudices, his stupidity, his arrogance." In fact, "every war is a defeat to the human spirit." They explore Agamemnon's Mycenae, where Henry refuses to descend with Katsimbalis the "slippery staircase" to Erebus, the claustrophobic descent into the deep cistern that kept Mycenae alive during sieges. Miller has flinched, and Part I of *Colossus* ends at Mycenae.

In Part II Henry flies alone to Crete with the purpose of seeing Knossos ("Knossus," in his spelling). His experience of Crete seems oddly disembodied: it might as well have been entitled Forty Days in the Wilderness. It is a digression on the path to Delphi. There are no revelations. The eponymous Colossus is absent. So is, for Henry, that vivid spirit which he found everywhere in mainland Greece and its close-lying islands.

Life seems to begin again when Miller returns to Athens, and in Part III the spirit of the first part is reborn. Katsimbalis meets him every day for an enthralling lunch that blends into dinner. Finally, Pericles Byzantis, Ghika's friend, offers accommodation at a new government pavilion for foreign students at Delphi. "It was decided," Henry writes impersonally, as if he had surrendered all personal initiative, that Ghika and Byzantis would take him to Delphi. Katsimbalis would meet them there.

Henry records the trip faithfully. They ride in a "beautiful" Packard; stop at the Thebes museum; as the plain of Thebes rolls past and facing rearward over the front seat, Ghika recounts at length the dream of death and transfiguration that he had experienced the night before; they pause for lunch at Levadia; Ghika gets out to vomit at Arachova (perhaps seeing Greece in receding frames while facing backwards has unsettled his stomach). "From Arachova to the outer precincts of Delphi the earth presents one continuously sublime, dramatic spectacle. Imagine a bubbling cauldron into which a fearless band of men descend to spread a magic carpet. Imagine this carpet to be composed of the most ingenious patterns and the most variegated hues. Imagine that men have been at this task for several thousand years...." Miller spends half a page creating a fantastic picture of color and subtlety. "Finally, in a state of dazed, drunken, battered stupefaction you come upon Delphi." Through the "twilight mist" Delphi appears "even more sublime and awe-inspiring than I had imagined it to be." They find Katsimbalis, have a "scanty meal," generously supplemented with wine and cognac, that Henry enjoys "immensely," being "in the mood to talk"—he confides this as though it were an unusual state for him. With Delphi outside the windows, what does he discourse on? Kansas! And how empty and monotonous it is. His companions are astounded, but for Henry this is a mere subliminal image, the equivalent of an artist applying a turpentine-diluted wash to a canvas before attempting a masterpiece.

After a night of fierce rains, "It was now time to inspect the ruins, extract the last oracular juices from the extinct navel.... the splintered treasuries of the gods, the ruined temples, the fallen columns.... Suddenly, as we stood there silently and reverently, Katsimbalis strode to the center of the bowl and holding his arms aloft delivered the closing lines of the last oracle." Miller does not say which "last oracle" this might be, but surely he had in mind the response, by tradition the last response ever vouchsafed by the Pythia, given to Julian the Apostate, the fourth-century Roman emperor attempting to revive classical Greek culture:

> Tell to the king that the carven hall is fallen in decay;
> Apollo has no chapel left, no prophesying bay,
> No talking spring. The stream is dry that had so much to say.

Apollo is dead. The time to revive Greek culture has passed. Henry tries to thrust this deadly conclusion away: "For a second, so it seemed, the curtain had been lifted on a world which had never really perished but which had rolled away like a cloud and was preserving itself intact, inviolate, until the day when, restored to his senses, man would summon it back to life again." Miller applies this oracular voice to his own predicament, as a drifter in the immense tragedy sweeping a world at war. Henry's optimism is incurable, however. "I recalled other oracular utterances I had heard in Paris, in which the present war, horrible as it is, was represented as but an item in the long catalogue of impending disasters and reversals, and I remembered the sceptical way in which these utterances were received." Henry prefers a longer view. "Victory and defeat are meaningless in the light of the wheel which relentlessly revolves. We are moving into a new latitude of the soul, and a thousand years hence men will wonder at our blindness, our torpor, our supine acquiescence to an order which was doomed."

Miller, Ghika, and Katsimbalis drink from the sacred Castellian Spring, and Henry sees his presence at Delphi as part of a fated Plan, a continuum that has led him from 1923 to this moment. His friend Nick at the Orpheum Dance Palace on Broadway had been born near Delphi, and through his "terpsichorean instrumentations" Henry had met June who became his wife; without her goading and inspiration he would never have become a writer, nor left America, nor met Betty Ryan or Durrell, who propelled him to Greece and into the company of Seferis, Ghika, and Katsimbalis—and so on to Delphi.

Now a world at war threatened to disrupt his writing career. Very well, he would turn his back on that world, a world that had refused to heed him: some years earlier Henry had held on to a fantasy that if he could spend an hour talking to Hitler, make him laugh, the then-approaching conflict could be avoided. Miller had stayed at the Villa Seurat, talking, and never pressed for his audience with Der Führer. While at Delphi Miller, his passport stamped "Invalidated" a few days earlier, was awaiting passage on the next boat to leave Piraeus for New York.

Henry and his party visit the museum: the colossal Theban *kouros* statues, "which have never ceased to haunt me," and especially significant for Henry, the beautiful youth Antinous, "last of the gods," evocative of "the eternal duality of man." He continues, "Nothing could better convey the transition from light to darkness, from the pagan to the Christian conception of life, than this enigmatic figure of the last god on earth who flung himself into the Nile. By emphasizing the soulful quality of man Christianity succeeded only in disembodying man; as angel the sexes fuse into the sublime spiritual being which man essentially is. The Greeks, on the other hand, gave body to everything, thereby incarnating the spirit and eternalizing it."

Then, suddenly, impulsively, as if in panic, Henry wants to return to Athens. He had been in Delphi only two nights and one full day, and was expected to stay several days in all. After Katsimbalis and Ghika return with him to Athens, Henry decides that it was a premonition of the arrival of funds, and the presence of a ship that would take him to America in ten days, that had led to his desire to return, but these were quite clearly just excuses made up to cover his "imperious desire" to leave Delphi, and his rudeness to Byzantis. No, he did not wish to give time for disillusionment to set in. Delphi must be perfect *in his imagination.* Then he can preserve its idealized image intact.

Like the final situation of the travelers in E. M. Forster's masterful short story, "The Road from Colonus" — the aged protagonist is dragged away, disappointed, from the caravansary, missing the revelation that he is sure would have been vouchsafed him had he stayed — everything that happens to Henry in Greece after Delphi partakes of anticlimax. He makes a final brief circuit with the Durrells, this time getting halfway down to the Mycenean cistern before panic sends him once again back to the surface. He might have been called the Orpheus of Brooklyn, but Henry was no Orpheus: the Underworld was not for him. He was a man of light. He and the Durrells spend a miserable Christmas in Sparta: "To me at least," Henry writes, "it was really beginning to look like Christmas—that is to say, sour, moth-eaten, bilious, crapulous, worm-eaten, mildewed, imbecilic, pusillanimous and completely gaga." Unlike Forster's protagonist, however, Henry comes away rich in experience and realization.

"The Greek earth opens before me like the Book of Revelation," Miller would write in the concluding paragraph of *Colossus.* "I never knew that the earth contains so much; I had walked blindfolded, with faltering, hesitant steps; I was proud and arrogant, content to live the false, restricted life of the city man. The light of Greece opened my eyes, penetrated my pores, expanded my whole being. I came home to the world, having found the true center and the real meaning of revolution.... I refuse categorically to become anything less than the citizen of the world which I silently declared myself to be when I stood in Agamemnon's tomb. From that day forth my life was dedicated to the recovery of the divinity of man. Peace to all men, I say, and life more abundant!"

Miller leaves Greece for America on 28 December. With the world crashing into war, he drafts *The Colossus of Maroussi,* a paean to cross-national, multi-lingual friendship, to Greece, to peace. An idealized yet real portrait of Greece and the Greek character. Restlessly, still professing to believe that the war has nothing to do with him, Miller sets out on his year-long tour of the United States with the avowed intention of writing a parallel panegyric to his native land. He is appalled at what he sees, and he sets down his thoughts with blazing honesty. *The Air-Conditioned Nightmare* is a book so vitriolic toward American civilization that Miller withdraws it from publication, even though it was contracted for by New Directions. He does not wish to—or dare to—so criticize his country in the midst of a desperate war. He would write a sequel, *Remember to Remember,* two years later.

Long before *The Air-Conditioned Nightmare* finally appeared, Miller had found refuge on Partington Ridge in Big Sur, south of San Francisco, overlooking the Pacific Ocean. The man who had lived most of his life in cities, in Brooklyn and in the Fourteenth Arondissement in Paris, the confirmed urban dweller who liked to claim that the soul thrived on garbage cans, now found himself in wild isolation, living in an abandoned convict's cabin, without heating system, without running water, without close neighbors. It was Greece that enabled him to make this transition. Like the Greek women carrying water up the goat trails from the springs, Miller now had to carry or drag all his supplies up a sand-and-stone trail from the Pacific coastal highway. In hot weather he stripped bare to a thong to do this, like some ancient Hellenic athlete.

Daily from the thin walls of the cabin came the clatter of Miller's typewriter. Perhaps recalling Durrell's cry of "Rosicrucian!" on seeing the Pleiades through the powerful telescope in Athens, he launched into his long-promised vast trilogy, *The Rosy Crucifixion*, the *Sexus, Plexus,* and *Nexus* volumes. Literary criticism may not have dealt favorably with the trilogy—even Miller's great friend Durrell urged him to withdraw and revise *Sexus*—yet in it Miller finally finished writing the June saga, his life with and inspired by her. If she had indeed pointed him in the direction of Delphi and the Rosicrucians, that direction turned out to be nearly the whole of his creative life: after *The Rosy Crucifixion*, he had neither the energy nor the inspiration for further revelations. And his trip to Greece, climaxing at Delphi, inspired Henry's greatest non-fiction, *The Colossus of Maroussi*.